Klein in the Trenches

Contemporary Psychoanalytic Studies
17

Contemporary Psychoanalytic Studies (*CPS*) is an international scholarly book series devoted to all aspects of psychoanalytic inquiry in theoretical, philosophical, applied, and clinical psychoanalysis. Its aims are broadly academic, interdisciplinary, and pluralistic, emphasizing secularism and tolerance across the psychoanalytic domain. CPS aims to promote open and inclusive dialogue among the humanities and the social-behavioral sciences including such disciplines as philosophy, anthropology, history, literature, religion, cultural studies, sociology, feminism, gender studies, political thought, moral psychology, art, drama, and film, biography, law, economics, biology, and cognitive-neuroscience.

Klein in the Trenches

Working with Disturbed Patients

Robert Waska

Amsterdam - New York, NY 2012

Cover Photo: Robert Waska

Cover Design: Studio Pollmann

The paper on which this book is printed meets the requirements of "ISO 9706:1994, Information and documentation - Paper for documents - Requirements for permanence".

ISBN: 978-90-420-3574-4
E-Book ISBN: 978-94-012-0849-9

Printed in the Netherlands

Contents

Preface

This book allows the reader an intense participation in the day-to-day practice of psychoanalytic treatment with the most disturbed, most complex of patients. The great deal of "live" case material shows the actual moment-to-moment interaction and verbal exchange between patient and analyst, a rare opportunity for the reader.

The book covers the clinical and theoretical difficulties that all psychotherapists and psychoanalysts encounter when working with patients who rely on certain rigid and destructive defense systems. It provides a generous number of clinical reports that show what actually happens in the room and how to technically cope with these often quite vexing transference situations. The reader is provided a vivid look into the technical approach of modern Kleinian psychoanalytic treatment and effective ways of working with the confusing issues of projective identification, enactment, and acting out that are so common with the hard-to-reach patient. I provide many examples of careful and thoughtful interpretive working-through of these multifaceted clinical problems.

Throughout the book, the modern Kleinian approach is outlined as a vital contemporary method of psychoanalytic treatment in which analytic contact can be established with even the most difficult to reach patients, offering them a chance at psychological growth and transformation. A wealth of detailed verbatim case material is used to illustrate this slow but often profitable journey.

Important technical questions of how the modern psychoanalytic practitioner works within the transference, how to monitor the counter-transference, and how to make interpretations are fleshed out in each chapter in this user-friendly and experience-near text. A nuts-and-bolts approach to the analyst-patient dialogue creates a fascinating window into the actual clinical exchange and a clear conceptualization of such important concepts as enactment, interpretive acting out, projective identification, analytic observation, psychic retreats, use of the counter-transference, and the clinical meaning of therapeutic success or failure.

This volume shows the therapeutic power that the modern Kleinian approach can have with patients who are the most troubling to treat. By attending to the interpersonal, transactional, and intra-psychic levels of transference and phantasy with consistent here-and-now and in-the-moment interpretation, the Kleinian method can be therapeutically successful with borderline, narcissistic, or psychotic patients and at varied frequencies and duration. This book shows that a broader range of patients can be helped in private practice settings.

Section I examines the difficult task of bringing about psychic change or emotional movement in patients who feel psychologically broken, but who also fear the consequences of difference, growth, and transformation. These are the demanding borderline patients, the controlling and entitled narcissistic patients, and the difficult-to-contain psychotic patients who all struggle with painful and frightening paranoid-schizoid phantasies of loss, abandonment, persecution, and intense grievance. They often are unable to commit to the process of analytic treatment and barely start before leaving. Other times, they continue for a while but often become quickly mired in complex impasse states and gradually or suddenly withdraw from treatment. Some of these individuals are able to stay in analytic treatment for quite some time and manage to establish analytic contact long enough to start a process of inner transformation. Projective identification–based transference states in which there is a great deal of acting out and repetition of archaic trauma are common, testing the analyst's counter-transference stability.

In Chapter One, the summary of one patient's successful journey in psychoanalytic treatment is used to examine the ways change occurs. Extensive case material highlights this particular patient's path from more paranoid-schizoid functioning to a more integrated whole-object capacity. In discussing the work with this patient (C), I show how counter-transference can help or hinder the working-through process. Projective identification is outlined as a significant factor.

The dangers of separation, individuation, and peaceful differences were central factors in why this patient stayed in a rigid psychic retreat. However, once this patient's narcissistic and sadomasochistic styles of organizing his object relations were addressed, his intense sense of loss and emotional trauma were more accessible. By the end of his treatment, these issues no longer felt as dangerous or unreachable. Rather than being an unbearable memory the patient had to evade, this patient's childhood history became more of a clinical resource in understanding and resolving how and why how he acted out. As a result, much of internal emptiness, loss, and collapsing connection he felt between self and other was no longer a threat. He could live with a new experience of hope, calm, and inner freedom.

In Chapter Two, case material is used to investigate patients (Tom, Gill) who either passively or directly and aggressively demand the analyst "do" something for them. They want the analyst to take some type of action, give some sort of advice, or fix them in some particular way as soon as possible. There is no apparent desire to be curious, to learn about themselves, or to work out whatever conflicts are at hand. Instead, there is a searching, waiting, craving, demanding, and entitlement that colors the transference.

These are patients who sit in front of us waiting for their ship to come in delivering the love, attention, and answers they have been waiting for. They resist facing the emotional fact that this special ship, this idealized object, has in fact sunk long ago leaving them alone and lost. But, in order to avoid this terrible inner loss and painful mourning, these patients protest and demand to be fed, healed, and filled with reassurance and love. The analyst is viewed as a way station to getting this deserved reward, treated as a frustrating detour away from reaching their entitlements, or felt to be someone who is withholding their just rewards. Theoretical issues and clinical problems are examined from a Kleinian perspective.

In Chapter Three, case material is used to explore the difficulties in working analytically with psychotic patients (in this case, Y and Z) who are prone to excessive splitting, manic idealization, and projective identification. Clinical issues of transference acting out are addressed, and the importance of utilizing counter-transference information (Segal, 1977a, 1977b) is explored. The conflicts between life and death instincts are quite common with the more disturbed patient, and the way these dynamics play out in the transference and create intense impasse states are illustrated in the material. Specifically, the pathological distortion of the good object is identified as the core conflict in work with certain more primitive patients. The Kleinian approach is demonstrated, and case material illustrates the need for clinical patience, faith in the analyst process, and the ability to accept slow progress or even no progress at all.

In Section II, I provide detailed case notes to offer a rare glimpse into one patient's childhood memories. From his adult perspective of fifty years, this patient (John) reflects back across his upbringing as a way to recover, organize, understand, and profit from the meaning of his past and its impact on his adult life. John has suffered from borderline conflicts surrounding internal experiences of idealization, abandonment, loss, and angry demand that leave him on an eternal quest for a version of self or other that never appears.

Chapters Four through Seven show how John's resultant acting out with drugs, alcohol, sex, and suicide attempts, as well as a pattern of chronic depression and crippling anxiety, left him very confused, disabled, and disturbed. Only through years of various types of psychological treatment, medications, and multiple therapists did he manage to find success, happiness, and the ability to be a part of society. Part of his continued healing was to tell his story once again in my office setting. In doing so, he sifted through the blurry pages of his life one more time, making a bit more sense of it in the process and finding a bit more integration in his current life.

From a Kleinian perspective, I highlight points in John's development where the borderline or paranoid-schizoid experience seemed to have solidified. At the same time, there were critical moments of internalization and identification that either helped to balance the more persecutory perspective or added an element of idealization. In illustrating these points, I show how the Kleinian approach considers the ongoing relationship between external and internal and how the intra-psychic elements of attachment and phantasy are shaped by projective identification processes.

Section III consists of four chapters that examine a new Kleinian concept and technique. This technique is critical when working with the more destructive narcissistic or borderline patient. Chapter Eight presents the clinical tool and theoretical concept of analytic observation, and offers case material on three patients (M, W, and H). Analytic observation is a technical tool for moments of acting out and impasse with narcissistic or borderline patients seeking to control, deaden, or devalue their objects and in the process avoid any painful or anxiety-producing focus on themselves and their flaws, dependence, or uncertainty. While traditional interpretations aim at sharing a possible motive for certain transference situations, analytic observations are more descriptive of how the patient seems to be using his objects or needing to place themselves in the object relational world. This observation of what and how are part of a more direct, containing, and defining technique useful with more destructive narcissistic acting out. Once this interpretive limit, translation, and calling attention to the nature of the object relational maneuver takes place, the acting out often will dissipate enough for a more traditional interpretation to be helpful and to be taken in by the patient without so much attack or complete avoidance. "This is what you seem to be doing to me, to us, or to others" is the interpretive mode of analytic observations. This is important in more difficult moments with more disturbed patients who need an immediate containing observation of what is happening in their phantasy world. Later, hopefully, they will be more receptive to looking at the meaning of such action, internally and externally.

Chapter Nine uses an extensive case report of a volatile couple (Nick and Nancy) in early phase psychoanalytic treatment to examine the way certain narcissistic or borderline patients, operating in the realm of paranoid-schizoid functioning, act out in the transference in ways that must be firmly interpreted. These communications to the patient must be defined, confrontational, and direct. As such, these are defined as analytic observations that therapeutically inform the patient about the nature of how he is treating his objects or himself and the narcissistic intent of the phantasy.

I focus on the narcissistic nature of manipulation or devaluation of the other and often the elevation of the self. These analytic observations pave the way to more traditional interpretations that detail the link between the acting out and the unconscious motivation, conflict, and defensive reactions. However, the acting out in the transference must first be contained with these more disturbed patients. Confrontational yet therapeutic and supportive observations of unconscious phantasies being acted out can create movement in negative impasses and provide a transition from simple limit setting and containment to more symbolic meaning and conflict resolution.

Chapter Ten follows a more disturbed patient (G) who made a narcissistic attack on life, genuine change, difference, or dependence. This suffocated the transference and left the treatment dying. This patient advocated false change, pseudo-growth that made him feel triumphant but resulted in no real internal shift. To learn or feel was to be vulnerable to emptiness and personal failure. This anti-life, narcissistic control shifted when I made analytic observations that were direct, containing, confrontational, and, at their core, life affirming.

These analytic observations were offered in combination with more traditional interpretations, but because of the patient's denial of vulnerability and his quest for fame and entitlement, the interpretive links to meaning were destroyed or ignored. Therefore, analytic observations provided a pre-interpretive technique that created a much needed focus and translation of his phantasy state and just exactly how he was trying to control his objects. Over time, these therapeutic observations helped the patient face the reality of his acting out and aided him in considering a new way of viewing himself and the world. In the process, he began to take on the grief and mourning necessary to advance into the depressive position where he could see himself as more capable and others as more reliable. He began to see himself as more loveable and the world as less cruel and loveless.

In Chapter Eleven, case material is used to show how, with a more neurotic patient (N) who existed within a deadening psychological retreat, the transference became a lifeless place where growth was aborted and disallowed. This became an impasse until the analyst used analytic observations to define and translate this deadening onslaught and then followed up with more traditional interpretations that examined the underlying object relational conflicts that led to the complete withdrawal from feelings and desire.

Finally, I use a case of a very volatile couple (A and B) in crisis to show how analytic observations provide much needed limits, containment, and confrontation that may eventually enable more traditional interpretations of phantasy, defense, and conflict. The destructive aspects of the death instinct are seen as creating a neutralizing, controlling, or predatory retreat wherein the more loving, forgiving, libidinal aspects of the patient's narcissism are unreachable. Analytic observations help create an opening to this closed-off psychic system.

Acknowledgments

I want to thank all my patients for reluctantly, yet bravely, inviting me in for a challenging taste of the most private internal conflicts they experience between self and other. In doing my best to help them through their emotional impasses and frightening internal choices, I continue to learn about the human condition, about myself, and about how to provide better clinical care to those with whom I meet.

As always, not much is possible in life without someone you can depend on, love, and be loved by. My lovely wife of almost three decades continues to be my greatest coauthor, editor, and inspiration in life.

I wish to thank the *New Therapist* journal for permission to reprint material in Chapter Two that has been previously published, as well as some material in Chapters Four through Seven.

Chapter Two was previously published as: Waska, R. (2011). Working with the unconscious conflicts of entitled and demanding patients. *The New Therapist*, *72*, 10-24.

Some material in Chapters Four through Seven appeared as: Waska, R. (2011). Following the footsteps of a borderline: The "As Told to Me" series. *The New Therapist*, *75*, 21-23 and forward.

I also wish to thank *Psicanálise*, the journal of the Brazilian Psychoanalytical Society of Porto Alegre, for permission to reprint Chapter Three, which was originally published as: Waska, R. (2012). Psychotic distortions of the good object. *Psicanálise*, *14*:1.

SECTION I

Hard-To-Start Treatments, Strained Travels, and Unfinished Journeys

One

Understanding Psychic Shifts

In trying to understand a patient's progress, stagnation, or decline over time, many factors come into play from a psychoanalytic perspective. The nature of the patient's interaction with external objects is important and the impact of projection and identification is critical. How the patient uses or misuses his or her objects is helpful to explore as well in terms of whether phantasy objects are seen as helpful, loving, and forgiving, or unpredictable, unavailable, or simply a source of gratification. The nature of the patient's primary defensive systems, pathological organizations (Rosenfeld, 1987; Steiner, 1990), and psychic retreats (Steiner, 1993, 2011) are important to examine as the findings help explain how viable change can be embraced or to what degree change will be avoided and resisted.

All these factors can be investigated through an analysis of the genetic, historical experiences the patient has had and how the patient has organized and filtered these experiences. The clinically vital parallel to this is the psychological patterns that emerge within the transference situation. The analyst observes and interprets how patients own and present their past, how they play out that past experience with the analyst, and how they react to establishing analytic contact (Waska, 2007, 2010, 2011) and working through their conflicts. As patients emerge from their psychological conflicts and depart from the therapeutic relationship, first by an emotional separation and then a literal separation, they must be self-sustaining yet dependent on others as well. They must be able to function and relate in a healthy and reciprocal manner with others, internally and externally. How patients are able or unable to successfully claim their lives as their own, separate from the desperate object relational phantasy struggles they have been a prisoner to, defines when termination is near.

CASE MATERIAL: MY TIME WITH C

After two years of seeing me in once-a-week psychoanalytic treatment with occasional twice-a-week sessions, C came in and told me, "I have been doing a lot of thinking about our work together and I think this will be my last day. At least for a while. Today is the day I want to stop. I feel we have really accomplished a great deal. There have been many changes and I feel I have improved in so many important ways. I have grown and you have really helped me get there. I listen to what you say and it has really made a difference."

During the rest of the session, C summarized how he felt he had changed. I wasn't completely surprised by his announcement because there were indications over the previous few months of his wanting to try out his "own new wings" and "no longer feeling like [he was] living in a crisis state."

However, it was still somewhat sudden, and C looked somewhat nervous telling me about it, "hoping I agree with it." When I asked him about this aspect of it, he told me he "still worried about what I thought but also was able to have his own mindset and not give it up or hide it if he thought I was not in agreement." This was indeed a major change in C's internal experience of himself and his objects. He could trust in his own mind and risk expressing himself while trusting that his objects would not be hurt or retaliate if they felt differently.

C came to see me two years prior at the insistence of his third wife. She was convinced he was cheating on her and at the very least was sure he was "on the verge of straying" due to what she said was his "constant flirting with every woman who comes into our restaurant." C had left his first wife for his secretary, and after several years of marriage to her, he had an affair with his current wife. During the course of that now nine-year marriage, C had been caught by his wife downloading nude pictures of someone he met online. As a result, she demanded he "take his sick mind and find help or else." C came in and told me, "I need help with what my wife calls my perversions and my sexual addictions."

This formal sentencing by his wife was part of the transference theme for the first year at least. Indeed, I used this "formal sentencing" concept to make many interpretations of C's sadomasochistic stance with me, his wife, and throughout his life. While it sounded like his wife had ample reason to be angry and fearful of his actions, from what C told me she was prone to mood swings and angry attacks in which she would smash things around the house and throw him out for days at a time.

In the counter-transference, I noticed myself feeling like siding with C some of the time and with his wife at others. It did seem like C was aware of how destructive his past actions had been and how he had used women along the way for his own sadistic desires. He told me, "I have not made any inappropriate moves towards anyone for two years and I made a promise to myself to respect my wife." This seemed genuine although also based in a sadomasochistic attempt to keep the peace. On the other hand, I felt oddly uncomfortable with C during the first year and sometimes wondered if I was with a man far more disturbed and dangerous than I realized. The trigger to these feelings was often his seemingly ignorant and arrogant reaction to my recounting some of his deeds with his wife or prior marriages. He would respond in a very narcissistic way and minimize what he had done to the point where I had to confront him with his crime.

During most of the first year of analytic treatment, C related in these ways, very characteristic of a thin-skinned narcissist and at times more removed like a thick-skinned narcissist (Rosenfeld 1987; Bateman, 1998;

Britton 2004). This meant I had to take a rather strong and often confrontational approach with C during these moments, and in doing so I had to delicately thread the line between acting out a role in his sadomasochistic phantasies and asking him to take ownership of his own life instead of constantly sacrificing his mind and heart to avoid conflict and find love. I interpreted that his resulting resentment drove him to cheat and flirt for revenge.

I think this was a necessary confrontation that some thin- and thick-skinned narcissists may need (Rosenfeld, 1989; Waska, 2011) at some points in the treatment to help them access a more object relational sphere. However, I also think it was C's projective identification pull that created an enactment on my side of certain sadomasochistic ways of relating, similar to what was taking place in his marriage.

So, by noticing my counter-transference, I was alerted to what appeared to be a complex splitting and projective dynamic in which C both ignored and denied the hurtful nature of his prior behaviors but also was quick to say yes to any accusations made and brand himself "broken and bad, beyond repair." These powerful and aggressive phantasies required constant interpretation and represented both a pathological organization as well as a difficult-to-locate psychic retreat.

C's sadomasochistic pattern of feeling on the ropes at all times with all people was present in his work life as well. When meeting and negotiating with the suppliers for his restaurant, C always felt they were on the "edge of being furious" with him for imagined mistakes such as changing the times they were to meet. Of course, I noted to C that this was also alive in our relationship, as he almost without any apparent feelings cancelled one of our sessions to take care of some business at the restaurant but then seemed angry, lost, and desperate when I had to cancel one session a few weeks later.

When I asked about it, he responded, "I don't pay attention to anything about my feelings because I want to do what I want without feeling like someone is controlling me. Besides, this is a business transaction and I don't expect there to be any feelings involved." Of course, this was after a year of my bringing up many aspects of how he did have feelings about the treatment and about me, both positive and negative. However, when he felt I wasn't available when he wanted me, he truly seemed to go to pieces and was desperate, but didn't say anything about it and simply waited to see if I noticed how pained he sounded.

So, I interpreted that he was manipulating me while also feeling completely alone and lost. C was angry and wanted me to console him and be there when he wanted me but he wasn't about to admit to that vulnerability. Instead, C wanted to control me and punish me with his desperate voice on my voicemail but no mention of needing me unless I brought it up and offered my care and assistance.

At work, C worried all his suppliers would leave him for "not being an easy person to work with." In fact, when they did give him feedback, he was always touched to the point of tears when they said they "loved" to work with him because he was always "so professional and easy to get along with." As I mentioned, in the transference C said to me, "I dread the day you won't want to put up with my crap anymore and you tell me it's over." He continued, "I am so relieved and thankful when you seem to just go on week to week listening to me and not getting upset or impatient. But, I still worry about it."

So, with most people in his life, C created this phantasy in which someone would become furious or fed up with him and "leave him for good." He had a very difficult time considering that any of this might be his own aggression and conflict that was being projected onto the object. Instead, he told me, "I just lie awake at night wondering how long it will be until someone just goes off on me or tires of me and walks away for good." As we made our way through the difficult transference of this more arrogant and removed narcissistic organization, slowly C revealed the more masochistic and dependent side of himself. He was sure it was only a matter of time before his wife kicked him out for good, and "only a while before you get so sick and tired of me complaining and never changing that you will shove me out on the street for good." This more frightening phantasy of rejection and abandonment became more the focus during the latter part of the first year and way into the second year. Here, some of C's past came into bearing.

It wasn't until the second year of treatment that my confrontations of his projective identification mechanism helped him to start owning some of his aggression, grievance, and needy demand and realize that he could in fact stand up for himself with others or simply express his own unique and differing opinions without crippling or destroying the safety of the bond or connection.

This was a major shift and positive change. Before this change took place, I noticed myself in the counter-transference wanting to "make him" stand up to his wife and stop being such a victim to her domineering ways. Over time, I was able to see how, while I was making accurate and helpful interpretations about how he was purposely positioning himself under the thumb of his wife, I was in the process putting him under my domineering thumb. So, that became the more direct transference investigation in which we explored how and why he needed to be a victim with me and have me be angry or stern with him and demand him to grow up and be strong.

In the process, I interpreted that he was able to hide in this masochistic psychic retreat and stay passive, without having to risk being himself and possibly engage the object or possibly lose contact with the object. In other words, out of my awareness of the initial enactments, I was able to interpret his transference process of avoidance with intimate engagement and his pathological dependence on me as aggressive authority who might abandon him if he had an identity.

In the work with more disturbed and disturbing patients, the analyst's counter-transference becomes a fertile planting ground for the numerous and intense projections the patient tries to disown. In this process, the analyst can become colored by projective counter-identification (Grinberg, 1962) and begin to bend to the passive or not so passive pressures to act out certain roles, functions, or affects that the patient places within him. This is very similar to Betty Joseph's ideas of how the patient comes to use the analyst and pull the analyst into various unconscious and interpersonal states of mind (Joseph 1985, 1987, 1989). The patient, in an emotional and interpersonal manner manages to herd the analyst into certain ways of being that complement the roles, functions, and affects the patient is struggling with.

During the second year of psychoanalytic treatment, C began to talk about his childhood experiences and we explored how they shaped his feelings and thoughts as far as his view of self and others. C's parents had a very volatile and dysfunctional relationship that was very much affected by C's mother being a drug addict. Apparently, from what his father told him years later, C's mother was prone to violence, lying, and was often gone from the house to pursue drugs or home under the influence. After years of fighting, the father elected to divorce his wife and left to another state far away.

After a year, the father was contacted by his brother who told him he "better go get C because it has gotten really bad." The brother said that C was living "under horrible conditions and he needed to be removed right away." As a result of his mother's drug addictions, C was neglected and subjected to ongoing violence and abuse in his house from all the drug addict friends his mother brought over. There was some suspicion C's mother might have been prostituting herself as well. So, C's father came back and literally just took C away one day. He drove C hundreds of miles back to his home and C lived there until he was eighteen and left for college.

As an adult, C tried to contact his mother and learned that she was now off drugs, but now a frail and elderly woman barely able to take care of herself. C feels very sad for her. Over time, we have explored his strong sense of loss and abandonment that he still carries from childhood. One of the more haunting memories he has is of when he was seven years old. He took a road map and found out where his mother lived. Then, he tried to draw a line from her house to where he was with his father so he could, in his words, "make my way back to her." He tried to figure out on the map how he would have to travel if he rode his bicycle across the country to be reunited with her. C just couldn't figure it out and felt he was "forever stuck and unable to get back to her." He often broke down sobbing when telling me this. C said, "That day that I was taken away from her is the day I think I was broken inside. Something happened to me that feels like it can never be repaired. When I try and think about it, I realize I feel in a million pieces without any glue."

Over time, as we explored these feelings and ideas, it became clear that C felt he had lost his mother and was now left alone, a helpless child without his beloved mother. But, at the same time, C felt intensely responsible, now as an adult and probably as a child, for not returning to rescue and care for her. So, sometimes alternating and other times combined, C was the lost, broken, and forsaken child trying to find his way home and his mother was the broken, frail object without aid, left to suffer and fade away.

This terrible internal blend of suffering and loss created a particular emotional reaction in C as an adult. One of the more severe ways C held onto his phantasy of an abandoned child, motherless, out in the cold, and at the mercy of the cruel world, was a psychotic anxiety state he entered when hearing a crying child. If he was walking on the street, sitting on a bus or in the park and heard the cry of a child or a baby, he panicked. He was overwhelmed with anxiety and began to cry. Then, C often would make "an emergency check-in call" to his God-son's house to make sure his five-year-old God-child was safe and OK. In other words, C suddenly felt the crying child on the street was his God-child and he had to rescue him. He had some degree of recognition that this was odd or not real, "but couldn't help it."

Over time, we came to understand that the first feeling C had was of extreme panic not just for the child on the bus or street that he felt was completely helpless, at risk, and in danger. But, this was a sudden psychic shift in which C thought he was seeing his God-child in danger and internally felt all children were in danger. Gradually, he was able to take in my interpretation that this was him. C was reacting to the phantasy of himself as a lost, lonely, endangered child and reliving the panic he must have felt as a child. Even if the child in the street was simply crying over being hungry, not getting a toy, or mildly skinning their knee, C psychologically took the elevator straight to the basement and felt the child was subject to extreme neglect or abuse.

It was striking when one day C heard the patient in the office next to mine. Another analyst in the office next to me had been treating a very regressed woman for years. Every few weeks, she would begin shrieking and sobbing so loudly that I could hear it in my office. When this happened and C heard it, he leaped up and started to cry. He yelled, "Oh God! They are hitting him. They are hurting him. We have to do something. They are going to kill him! Why aren't you doing something?" After I was able to calm C down, we slowly were able to work with the idea that again, this was a projection of C's own fears, abandonment, and intense anxiety over feeling neglected and abused. Over time, he was much less susceptible to these sorts of alarming reactions, but they remained as a "scary feeling in the pit of [his] stomach."

C's intense fear of conflict and his anxiety over being rejected was often played out in the transference. Over the two years of treatment, I frequently was interpreting variations on these conflicts as they emerged in the transference and within the counter-transference. C talked about being bullied by his wife and interpersonally pushed and pulled me to be the bully, the leader, or the oracle of knowledge. This all made me feel irritated and at times angry with C. I noticed how, in the counter-transference, I might end up feeling like telling him off for being such a victim and never acting like a man or an equal with his wife or with me.

In other words, the nature of the total transference (Joseph, 1985) was such that C engaged with me as both the one who is bullied and needs to be bullied. Over time, I certainly did act out some of these role dynamics, but fortunately, they were strong enough transference tugs on me that I was aware of most of them and avoided enacting them directly. Therefore, I was able to gradually interpret these sadomasochistic object relational patterns to C, and he was slowly able to make use of those interpretations. At first, he felt a victim to my interpretations and also felt a victim to the idea that he was a victim. So, he felt persecuted or judged by me but then was angry with himself for "being so pathetic" and bullied himself to stop himself from being a victim. But, over time C acted out less when I interpreted and instead made important use of my comments, gradually reflecting on himself, and thinking things through instead of collapsing into familiar feelings and phantasies of masochistic despair and fragmenting loss. He eventually could integrate our work together enough to make new choices in life and find new ways of relating to himself and others.

C told me, "I feel ready to take it all on the road. I want to see how I do with what I have learned and I think I will do pretty well. There are many things in my life that were pretty horrible and now they have improved or I am in the middle of making changes. That is one big thing. I know I really was stuck in being a victim with you, at home, and at work. But, now I am doing something about the issues in my life. I still feel very worried about causing conflict and getting into trouble but I am now sticking my neck out there and seeing what is out there." This was a very vivid description of how when a patient exists within the protective cocoon of a psychic retreat he feels protected but blinded to the reality and the rewards of the real world (Steiner, 2011).

C continued, "Like I said, my basic default is still that there is something wrong with me and that there is something terrible around the corner. I still wonder if there will be someone in my face about what I have done wrong or someone about to leave me for good. I go to that place fairly easily still. But, now there is a big difference. I feel that old stuff but I keep going. It is not immobilizing me anymore. I keep moving forward and I keep walking ahead. I am not running backwards."

Here, C seemed to be describing his emergence from the more narcissistic, paranoid-schizoid (Klein, 1946) realm of sadomasochistic relating. Instead, he was experiencing a gradual entrance into more whole-object depressive (Klein, 1935; 1940) functioning where symbolism was available and forgiveness, understanding, and survival were possible.

C went on to say, "I definitely feel ready to go out on my own. But, I do want to be able to know that I have this to come back to if I want to or need to. What we have here is something that I want to know is still there if I need it. It might be something good to return to at some point if I want." In reply, I interpreted: "You picture how we have built an US that has been very important. It has been out of US that you found yourself and if you forget yourself or lose your way, you want to feel secure that WE still exist and are here for you." C said, "I do think of it that way. It took a while for it to be an

US but I see what you mean. I didn't have a self before. Now, I feel like I have something inside me instead of feeling empty all the time. But, I want to see this as a place I could return to in the future if I ever wanted."

I interpreted: "You want to be able to refuel if you notice your emotional gas tank is running on empty." C nodded and said, "I haven't thought of it like that but that is exactly right." Here, I was thinking in terms of a Kleinian version (Carstairs, 1992) of Margaret Mahler's work on the infant/mother dyad and the infant's need for refueling during the rapprochement phase of development.

To me, C was now testing the waters of the depressive positions and finding his way as a separate entity among other separate entities without feeling overwhelmed and in danger of persecution or abandonment. However, if he felt too anxious, he wanted to be sure he could return to the safety of our nest, a fused state of protection with the idealized parental breast. Of course, we had worked long and hard to define the limits of this desired fusion as it also carried with it the sadomasochistic state of emptiness, guilt, fear, and loneliness he had suffered with for years.

At the end of C's treatment, I could somewhat assess the degree of his internal shift and growth by my own counter-transference feelings. His shift from being such a victim to his wife, to me, and to others to now feeling more like an equal adult shifted my own feelings away from despising his wife or looking down on him as weak and wimpy. I now saw C and his wife as now operating as equal adults negotiating in a marriage instead of in a master/slave dynamic.

In fact, C told me in the last few months of the second year, and in this final session, "Now I just tell her like it is. I don't hide anything. That means we don't always agree, but somehow we make our way through it." I interpreted: "You don't see her as much of a bully or someone who caught you doing wrong and now will get rid of you. She sounds more forgiving or less volatile in your mind so you feel calmer and more confident to be yourself." Here, I was interpreting the nature of C's former pathological projective cycle and now the healthy results of a more mature projective system. He agreed and said, "She is just a person with opinions, just like me."

I asked, "I wonder if you are worried about the conflict with me, if I don't agree that you should stop now." C said, "No. It is the same thing. I wish you thought the same but it is OK that you don't. I don't think it is a big deal if you have different thoughts. I still worry about what you think and hope you are not angry with me. But, I feel I can go on anyway and it will be OK." I said, "We can be different and still survive and coexist." He nodded and gave me a "thumbs up." Here, I was interpreting C's transition to the depressive position where we were separate and different but still could coexist without one of us being injured or one of us wanting to run or retaliate. We could stay and play even if we were from two separate places.

SUMMARY

Grinberg (1968) notes how borderline, narcissistic, and other primitive patients are prone to acting out. This is often the search for the nourishing, protective, and guiding object to cling to and follow. But, the acting out is also an angry reaction to the felt lack of or failure of a containing object that can sustain their separation anxiety, grief, guilt, and loss. With C, he felt he had to hide or erase this feeling of angry retribution and revenge for his perceived abandonment and betrayal. By projecting these dangerous feelings, he was then surrounded by angry and rejecting objects. So, the containing object, the ideal good object, even if found, was never welcoming. This created a persecutory cycle of paranoid phantasies and unbearable guilt (Grinberg, 1964) in which the lost object was now purposely neglectful and absent. As a result, C was always hungry, lost, and worried that he was to blame for it all. This brought back the most fundamental and terrible infantile state of mind of when absence was intolerable and the missing object was no longer a good object temporarily absent, but a persecutory non-object cruelly missing and permanently gone, yet forever haunting the empty, hungry, and desperate child's mind and heart. This caused the psychotic reactions to crying children and the distressed patient next door.

Grinberg (1977) has described how many borderline patients have experienced, either in phantasy and/or with actual external caregivers, traumatic separation and loss. This has usually been based in the infantile experience of a mother who has not been able or willing to receive, contain, or modify the infant's unorganized inner conflicts. This idea of Grinberg's, based on Bion's container concept (Bion, 1962), has been elaborated upon by other Kleinians and examined as a fundamental psychic state of mind in which the infant feels helpless in the face of loss, abandonment, or rejection by the object. This leaves the infant in a blank emotional void and an internal sense of meaninglessness. This was certainly the case with C. His unfortunate trauma and tragedy early in life created certain mindsets that grew with time into unbearable and crippling states of object relational experience.

Steiner (1996) has noted that the theory of projective identification enables us to formulate the aim of psychoanalysis as a psychological integration in which the patient regains parts of himself that have become unavailable because they have been split off and projected. With C, he had split off and emptied himself so severely that he no longer had a self to operate from or rely on. To have a self felt dangerous, so he sacrificed himself for the hopes of being accepted and not rejected. But, in the process he "broke" himself. This was part of why he said he felt "broken beyond repair" as well as it being an identification with his broken vision of his unavailable mother.

According to this model, conflict is not something that analysis can solve for the patient, but what we can sometimes do is to help the patient to utilize his own mental assets more optimally, so that he can struggle to resolve his conflicts in his own personal way. Serious inner pathology results if projections are not gradually renowned and reworked as part of the self. This tests the capacity of the patient to face emotional reality and to bear the reality of loss and mourning.

Many patients such as C resist this because they do not want to have to relive the original trauma regarding separation, so they avoid or attack the separateness that is part of the working-through process in psychoanalytic treatment. Loss is denied as well as the denial of rage against the absent object. The internal situation often becomes highly structured and object relationships are bound into pathological organizations that are very resistant to change.

Steiner (1996) has outlined how there are two stages in the successful working-through process in which patients can emerge in full ownership of themselves, having given up on finding the ideal self or ideal object and having challenged the anxiety, guilt, and hopelessness of their prior state. Instead, they move towards the creation of a new vision of self and other as well as an acceptance of what the self and object have been, are, and will be.

In this two-stage process, Steiner (1996) outlines how first the object is used as a container to collect, integrate and give meaning to disorganized parts of the self. Containment relieves anxiety and provides a sense of being understood but does not in itself permit a true separateness to be achieved. There may be a new security and integration, but true autonomy and individuality is not achieved. In this first stage, the patient internalizes a containing object so relief from anxiety comes from a sense of being understood by the internal object and guilt is absolved with the permission or forgiveness granted from the internalized analyst's authority.

To understand oneself, contain oneself, and forgive oneself has to arise from within. This comes from a separate and different identity that is often in opposition to the object on which one was once so dependent. To think for oneself the authority of the analyst must be questioned and the authority of the self must be respected. This was the great accomplishment of C at the end of his treatment. Even though, by his own description of his emotional state, it was only partial, he still managed to develop his own thoughts and desires separate and even in opposition to the object and still felt reasonably sure of the survival of both parties. This was a move towards independence and towards facing the pain of the mourning process inherent in the psychological rewards of the depressive position.

Two

Entitled and Demanding

There are patients who unconsciously choose to remain in the realm of the paranoid-schizoid position (Klein, 1946) as a method to avoid certain conflicts, anxieties, and disappointments encountered in the depressive position (Klein, 1935, 1940). They have a meager and reluctant foothold in the depressive realm of functioning, but this is often a perverse or corrupted grasp into the yet to be reached, more mature ways of relating to self and other. These patients have become convinced of the immediate or future benefit of believing in the idealized state in which self and object are united or re-united in a special and blissful state. They believe they will be saved, fed, rewarded, or finally bestowed special blessings and love that are owed to them.

So, to give in to the whole-object world of the depressive position means to give up these visions of control, perfection, and fusion. The depressive position is not a world of "I love you because you are perfect and you love me because I am everything you wished for." It is a much more mixed bag of "I love you in spite of your flaws and you love me despite my problems." The patients investigated in this chapter instead want to continue on a childhood treasure hunt and are determined to find the pot of gold and the rainbow that leads to it. The nature of the psychoanalytic process is extremely difficult for these patients as it means they must give up this treasure hunt and realize that no matter how long they sit at the bus stop, there is no magic bus coming to pick them up. These patients dread the awful disappointment that comes with the reality of life, the often less than special status of life as life, without any magical cure or reward. The patients examined in this chapter use multiple and complex defensive strategies to force reality to bend to their wishes, be it an active or passive stance, a masochistic or sadistic move, a pleading and dependent cry, or a demanding and independent approach. As noted by Scharff and Scharff (1992), some patients who face the anxieties and loss of the depressive position attempt to jump over it into a manic state of control, thus eliminating concern, loss, difference, remorse, or sadness. Due to these kinds of radical attempts at self-preservation and competitive hunger, many of these individuals terminate treatment prematurely or create a variety of treatment impasses. They are in a psychic standoff that often is played out in the transference and can greatly affect the counter-transference. Strong demands, either explicitly or subtly, are made of the analyst to instantly fix and heal. The patient insists on retaining the illusion of being great, special, or deserving to avoid a sinister, primitive state of persecutory loss.

OVERVIEW OF TREATMENT AND APPROACH

In the moment-to-moment transference situation, the patient is either actively engaged or actively disengaged with the psychoanalyst on many levels. This aliveness or deadness within the total transference situation (Joseph, 1985) and the interpretation or non-interpretation of it is what can define a treatment as either analytic or non-analytic. The interpretation of the current state of the transference as well as the patient's phantasy experience of the object world (rather than interpretation of the past or external matters) is critical in general (Joseph, 1989), but even more so when the patient's phantasies, transference stance, and defenses have begun to shift the treatment into something less than analytic. Certainly, the analyst's own counter-transference enactment of projective identification dynamics or personal conflict can escalate this problem. Overall, the resulting loss of analytic contact (Waska, 2007) often occurs within the more interpersonal realm of the analytic relationship.

The ways a patient tries to move the treatment away from analytic contact to something less object-related, less relational, less affect focused, and less self-reflective are numerous. Primitive fears of persecutory guilt, retaliatory objects, and phantasies of loss (Waska, 2002) are prominent in many patients. Defensive stances that prevent, erase, or attack analytic contact include psychic retreats (Steiner, 1993) and "no entry defenses" (Williams, 1997) in which the object is pushed away and avoided. Also, the defensive aspects of the death instinct, greed, paranoid phantasies, and internal self-destructive bargains are all part of the clinical picture with patients who experience change as dangerous (Waska, 2006). The conflicts around mourning and loss are frequently defended against by a retreat into pseudo-depressive states (Steiner, 2005). Rey (1994) has noted that any successful contact within the psychoanalytic situation involves not only psychic change and understanding, but also a corresponding sense of loss, neglect, and disappointment which is avoided and defended against. I would add that this sense of loss and neglect is always present if the transference and phantasies are being explored.

The patients examined in this chapter dread many things in themselves and in their objects, but the worst of those fears has to do with the loss of the ideal qualities or the ideal potentials in themselves and in their objects. The decline and descent into suffocating regularity, predictability, and the depressive position combination of good and bad is unbearable next to the quest for specialness with guarantee. Either be special or be nothing is the phantasy. These patients feel they must either find a special rewarding object or face the past, present, and future with no good object. This creates a suffocating anxiety and the need to immediately demand that something or somebody reassure them of their special destiny.

Since the psychoanalytic method is designed to help the patient make the transition from more paranoid functioning to more depressive integration, every moment of analytic contact is a moment of dread and despair for this more disturbed patient, as he or she struggles with change and a new way of being with his or her objects.

Therefore, successful analytic work always involves the patient's moment-to-moment retreat, attack, hiding, and attempt to shift the treatment into something less than analytic, something less painful. Thus, the analyst must include in his interpretations an understanding of this retreat and attack, while attempting to steer the treatment back to something more analytic, something that contains more patient↔patient and patient↔analyst contact. The support that we analysts should give our patients is a subtle and sometimes not so subtle belief that we will help them survive this painful contact and stay with them till they get to the other side of this frightening process of change. This contact that they dread is the contact with the reality of life on life's terms and as such we are the representative of this whole-object place of difference, loss, and disappointment as well as the rewards of integration, forgiveness, and hope. Since we are the vehicle of transition from the alleged security of paranoid phantasy to the seemingly dreadful changes of depressive functioning, these patients fear making emotional contact with us.

As mentioned, projective identification is often the leading mental mechanism patients employ within the transference setting. Therefore, the interpretation of projective identification is essential and figures prominently in any discussion of technique. Patients in the depressive position relate to whole objects that have a certain lasting quality to them. The ego's aggression is balanced and the object can tolerate it and bounce back. The stabilized ego projects its own remorse and guilt into the object and finds a forgiving and trusting object in return. Love and trust are projected and introjected. Disputes occur and relationships have pain, but things can be counted on and wounds heal.

In the paranoid-schizoid position, internal experiences are more frightening and fragmented. Splitting protects the fragile nature of the early ego and its part objects. Good is separated from bad until the ego is stable enough to withstand its own ambivalence and stormy relations to itself and other objects. Oral aggression, envy, and the intense desires to unite with and own the mother's body place stress on the splitting process. These instinctual forces can drive the ego to use excessive and destructive forms of projective identification. This type of projective identification, aimed at achieving union with the idealized object, can break down the process of splitting and lead to destruction of the ideal object. The ego is left with the bad aspects of the object and self-fragmentation. The internal experience is one of deep and psychologically fatal loss. The ego loses the ideal object, which is replaced by a bad, persecutory object. Within the paranoid-schizoid position, this leads to ego de-stabilization and feelings of annihilation. Therefore, this experience of loss in the paranoid-schizoid position is quite different than the type of partial loss and restoration encountered in the depressive position.

Paranoid-schizoid loss is complete and leaves no hope. The threat is to the ego, not to the object. Not only is restitution unavailable, but the loss is automatically followed by the arrival of an angry or rejecting persecutory object. A two-fold sequence of loss and attack bring the ego to a state of fragmentation and implosion. Since these patients avoid the disappointments of the depressive position, they also forfeit the rewards of its built-in forgiveness, understanding, and acceptance of what is and what can never be, rather than the constant craving for what should be but never has been that constantly brings out the rage, despair, demand, and disappointment that haunts these patients.

In analytic treatment, patients experiencing these states of loss and persecution can develop nearly intractable transference conflicts. The work is slow and the patient often has difficulty staying in treatment. Hope is absent and the analyst is felt to be a constant threat. Analytic contact is difficult to maintain in these settings, but crucial to consistently reach for. In the successful cases, this involves a slow process of exploring these frightening phantasies, via examination of projective identification and splitting within the transference. Acting out is frequent.

Interpretation is helpful in two specific ways. First, it serves as an ongoing detoxifier of projective materials, and second, it represents a potential new object for the patient's ego to introject. This of course entails a working through of the particular ways that the new object will be experienced as lost and then returning as bad. This is the essence of the working-through process and is a lengthy task. Once in the depressive position, mourning may present a significant threat, enough so that regression to paranoid-schizoid defenses is evoked. This is one of the core conflicts for the patients described. We can help by containing their chaotic states of anxiety and grief until we can find a way to interpret them therapeutically, but as Steiner (1996) has noted, containment is not ultimately healing unless the patient is willing to both take over the process and also accept the state of mourning that will follow.

During treatment with these types of patients, the analyst is frequently called on to struggle with, detoxify, and translate the patients' projections into something less anxiety producing or disorganizing. This is often the most difficult aspect of the treatment, as patients do not want to take the projected parts of self or object back. They feel threatened by re-internalizing them. Analytic contact involves consistent interpretations regarding this refusal of new knowledge and self-reflection. These patients fight off the ownership of these unwanted aspects of their personality. Therefore, they often react to these interpretations with acting out and other defensive maneuvers.

In this way, the transference quickly shapes the character of the analytic treatment. Specifically, the patient's particular defenses, conflicts, phantasies, and method of relating to the object can end up defining the treatment, either limiting it or allowing it to be a path of change and growth. Steiner (1996) has reviewed the aims of psychoanalytic treatment and how the theories of conflict and later of projective identification have influenced the goals of psychoanalysis. While in agreement with his ideas, I wish to expand them to include the fact that the clinical dynamics of conflict and projective identification can in themselves end up defining the nature of the treatment.

In other words, if a patient is overusing projective identification as his or her primary mode of relating to the object, not only will the goal of analytic treatment be the exploration and modification of that pathological method of object relations, but in some cases, that dynamic could end up corrupting the treatment. Some transference dynamics are such that the analyst is unaware of the pathological shifts and the analyst becomes part of an enactment that actually fosters a pathological shift. In some other cases, the patient's unconscious efforts to strip the treatment of any analytic contact are simply too intense to prevent.

So, the patient's phantasies, transference, and defenses all work together to shape, distort, enhance, or influence the therapeutic encounter into being a particular form of therapy. Likewise, the analyst's counter-transference can create various states of acting out, collusive enactments, and role responses that further distort the treatment into something less than analytic.

If the analyst is flexible to the needs of the patient but still clear about offering the opportunity for an analytic encounter by using interpretation, transference work, and exploration of defenses and phantasies, then the patient has the opportunity for psychic change and psychic growth, be it face-to-face, once a week, or multiple visits on the couch. However, the patient's intra-psychic and interpersonal interaction with the analyst will determine what the treatment ultimately becomes. If the transference is not recognized or properly analyzed, it can shape, refine, or corrupt the treatment in terms of its analytic quality and potential.

CASE MATERIAL: BUILD ME A BOAT AND HURRY UP! MORE DISTURBED AND MORE DEMANDING PATIENTS

Tom was thirty years old and shuffled into my office carrying a check his mother had given him for me. He was an intelligent man but had never completed college classes because of what sounded like a complete mental collapse. He had been in several day hospital programs and was put into the inpatient unit twice before. Over the last ten years, he had attempted suicide by cutting his wrists, drinking bleach, and taking pills. Currently, he felt his life "was useless and a waste" and he "thought of jumping off the bridge or a building." Tom insisted his only problem was "social anxiety" and "only wanted to find out how to be more social." When I noted that he was on anti-psychotic medication as well as antidepressants and anti-anxiety medications, he yelled, "That is for social anxiety!" He had seen numerous therapists over the years but never stayed with any because, "I didn't like them and they never helped me." Tom lived with his parents and had no friends. He had worked a few part-time jobs over the years but none of them had ever worked out. His two older brothers lived out of state.

Working with Tom was immediately a challenge. When Tom sits down at the start of a session, he usually appears agitated, irritated, and impatient. He looks at the floor and then at me and back at the floor. After a few seconds, he yells at me, "What? What the fuck!!?? What do you want?" In trying to engage him in exploring his internal experiences, I have found him stubborn, anxious, frightened, and aggressive.

Overall, Tom is extremely demanding and feels anxious for and entitled to "the answers" and he wants them "right now." If I don't deliver the goods, he becomes furious and, in the counter-transference, I fear he will discard me. I take this to be an important piece of information about how he regards his objects and the way he views himself. When Tom tells me about his extreme anxiety, I interpret that his constant projection of hatred, anger, and demand makes others seem either totally useless, so his world is lonely and empty, or intimidating and scary, which makes his world persecutory and vile. So, to facilitate analytic contact, I immediately began confronting his transference of anger, anxiety, and demand.

Tom seemed to always be very angry when I asked questions and would always yell, "I don't know!" or "I don't know the answer!" or "I don't know what to say!" followed by grunting and cursing. In the counter-transference, I felt such a withholding, withdrawal, and angry dismissal that I wanted to pester him with questions and really put him on the spot. Noting this emotionally and also observing myself acting this out to some degree by the amount of questions I asked, I interpreted this transference and counter-transference dynamic by stating, "You seem to have brought us to a place where I am the constantly questioning father and you are the one-word withholding teenager. We are in a total standoff." Tom responded, "Just like my fucking father." (I asked for details and over the next few sessions learned of a quite abusive and rocky relationship between him and his father while he was growing up.)

In noticing this standoff, I was then able to see that the pressure I felt might be the pressure he felt, and I especially thought of how he sounded when he said, "I don't know what to say!" I pictured a torture victim yelling out that they didn't have any information to give, no secrets to provide. So, I interpreted, "I wonder if you feel pressured to perform, to give me the goods and you don't know what the goods are. You look like you are being tested and feel very anxious and worried that you are failing my test." Tom immediately relaxed a bit and said, "Yes. I do feel like that. I have no feelings or thoughts and I don't know what to tell you." I interpreted this hollowed out, empty-core result of his projective identification process by saying, "Maybe by always having to focus on me and what you think I am demanding, you lose sight of everything inside of you." Tom nodded and was silent for a moment.

Later on, Tom talked about feeling very isolated, bored, and lonely. He told me that he had no friends and he always felt extremely anxious when around other people. I suggested it might be that he saw others as he saw me, demanding that he perform immediately, which left him feeling empty and not knowing what to say. He said, "That could be." I asked him if there was anyone he liked to hang out with, or wished he could hang out with, like perhaps his father, thinking of the probable ambivalence he would have with his father. Tom said, "No. I don't get along with him at all. But, I like to do things with my mother." I asked him about that. He said, "I really like to hang out with her and do things with her. We have fun. But, when I look around and see other thirty-year-old men, they are not hanging out with their mothers. They are with their friends, girlfriends, or wives." He was quiet and looked sad. I asked him what made him feel sad. He said, "I feel like I've wasted my life and have nothing." Then, Tom fell silent and gradually grew agitated and finally said, "What! Shit! What do you want! I know all this shit! How does that help? I need to know what to do!" I said, "You are upset telling me about these painful things and feeling like you have wasted your life. Maybe it is easier to get angry at me than to have to join me in investigating these painful issues." Tom yelled, "What the fuck? It is the same crap I have told all the other therapists!" I said, "I wasn't there then. This is me and this is you and me. I want to know the details. I need more from you." Tom rolled his eyes and grunted and threw his hands up in the air and said, "Fine!" Here, I was using my counter-transference experience of him being the one that holds the power and has everyone come to him. I was reduced to always pleading and wondering and waiting for him to come to me. I realized this was an important aspect of the transference and his phantasy state so in my interpretation, I was taking back my rights to be taken care of, to be listened to, and to be given to. I was also demonstrating my boundaries and exerting my belief that it is OK to have a give-and-take relationship that is formed around help and care instead of a violent back and forth or a deadened one way street. The result of this interpretation was a sudden reduction in his anxiety and a momentary acknowledgment of "Fine!" which indicated his allowing us to be together for that moment instead of separate in his normally harsh and adversarial manner.

Another session found us discussing Tom's job. He felt "stuck in it and unhappy with it." He had been fired from his last job for not showing up on time. He told me he was bored and fed up with this current one. I said, "You are telling me you feel unhappy and stuck, but you are not telling me if you do anything to change that." Here, I was interpreting the transference dynamic in which he was presenting himself as this passive victim and looking to me to "do something" and give him the answers. Tom said he had looked online for "a while" for better jobs but after not finding anything he had given up and now his mother continued the search for him. He said this in a way that seemed dismissive, arrogant, and entitled. I interpreted that he was demanding immediate answers from me and wanted immediate results from his job search and when he became fed up with having to make his own efforts he looked to me and his mother to be his personal fix-it crew. I interpreted that if he pressured himself so savagely to know what to say to me, he probably was savage in the way he looked for a job as well or even in how he wanted a girlfriend and a social life. He wanted it all NOW. When it wasn't immediately delivered on a silver platter, he became angry with himself, very anxious and lost, and then lashed out at others for failing to fix him, rescue him, and make his life the one he wanted.

Technically, I also noticed that the way he demanded so much right away from me left me as the powerless object needing to feed him on demand out of intimidation. I was only the delivery boy and he had all the rights to request, demand, and own. So, I noticed that it was helpful to point this out in my interpretations when he refused to answer questions or acted smug and devalued my inquiries. I told him, "I want more. You want something from me and from being here, so do I." This was a step towards positioning myself as a whole object that deserved attention and had the ability and right to gain something in life. This was the opposite of what Tom thought of himself and what he imposed on himself and his objects.

At the same time, this was a tricky process in the total transference situation (Joseph, 1985) and the complete counter-transference (Waska, 2010). I had to be watchful about the repeat of a sadomasochistic dynamic that Tom seemed so familiar with and comfortable in. So, when he was withholding and angry about my questions and inquiry, I also interpreted that, in being so silent and withholding, I was now the demanding one insisting he provide what I wanted immediately and therefore he was the one who was failing, the one who was bullied. But, he also got to be the withdrawn silent bully who refused to give and be in control through not giving and only demanding a fix.

The analytic treatment with Tom continues at this time much in the same manner. We continue to struggle with his sense of entitlement, detachment, distance, and devaluation of anything but a master/servant relationship in the transference. However, it appears that with my consistent interpretation of his fear of facing the lonely devastation of having no one and being nothing to anyone, he is slowly relaxing his grip on having to be special and entitled at all times, constantly projecting all his anger, hate, and demand into others, leaving him alone and without. Bit by bit, he seems more willing to interact and sometimes allows himself to emotionally and mentally consider what could be possible if he mourned what was never possible. He is less anxious and psychologically combative but still extremely cautious and challenging.

As Kernberg (1992) notes, it is always important to look at all developments in a patient's life, including those outside of the treatment setting and the patient's experiences in the past as well as the present. This was part of my stance with Tom as I sought out his feelings and thoughts about his life in totality and day to day, including our relationship. The Kleinian approach embraces this constant examination of external reality but also sees it as important to always put these findings in the context of Klein's (1952) discoveries regarding how the transference always derives from a combination of real and phantasized aspects of the past and present as well as defenses against both the real and the imagined. This makes it vital to stay close to the immediate nature of the patient's here-and-now transference state and the nature of the analytic contact (Waska, 2007) that is being fostered, cultivated, or fought off.

CASE MATERIAL: PASSIVELY WAITING FOR MY SHIP TO COME IN. MEANWHILE, I AM SINKING

Gill was like a broken down superhero. He had been told by his mother growing up that he was destined for greatness. She told him the world would be amazed at his talent and intelligence. This constant cheerleading for Gill's greatness was routinely interrupted by his mother's angry and violent mood swings in which she would tell him he was stupid and useless. She would beat him and bully him.

As a young child, she brought Gill to various specialists who tested him for I.Q. and she would tell him how spectacularly he scored. Indeed, Gill was always at the top of his class as a child and then into high school. On one hand, he believed what his mother said and felt very smart and special. He remembers thinking of how great he would become as an adult and "all the good things that would happen in his life." This sense of having superpowers and being above others followed him into his teens and into young adulthood. Gill told me, "I always figured I would be rich, important, have an incredible job, and have sexy movie stars pawing their way to my door." He told me the world seemed ready to welcome him as the next superstar up until he began his first job out of college and until he got married. Gill told me he felt the ceiling had come down on him at that point and all his specialness was taken away. He said, "I always pictured I would end up with a Playboy bunny or something like that. I really believed I would be with someone sexy and famous. But, after I got married I felt like I had to give up all my dreams and accept something more mundane and ordinary."

Here, I felt he was looking down on his wife and seeing himself as a superhero who was now chained to a mere mortal and unable to enjoy his super status anymore. Also, the more I learned about his job, the more this same type of conflict emerged. From his description, he worked at a company that provided no training, no stimulation, and no future per se. It was a place where he could almost do nothing and get paid a very high salary. He exerted hardly any mental effort but was able to complete a great deal of work. So, he felt "high on the money." Gill told me that this constant flow of money also prevented him from leaving what he felt to be a "horrible waste of my brain and a daily dose of humiliation." Apparently, most of the male workers were the "redneck macho good old boys type" who loved to curse, be insulting to anyone that provided a target, and bully." Gill said that he was never that type of person so he stuck out like a sore thumb and they made him the emotional punching bag of the office. They picked on him and made fun of him at every turn.

Over time, I interpreted that Gill never fought back and never asked them to respect him, and he seemed to look to me to step in like a father and tell him how to set boundaries and push back. But, I also interpreted that he could certainly have found a much better job a long time ago, but he would have had to give up all the money, the tie to greatness, and his "high" of having a piece of specialness regardless of the price. Also, I drew a parallel between the job and growing up with his mother, where he never felt he could fight back, received a great deal of special praise, but also paid a terrible price for the promise of greatness. I said that there, too, he probably wished his father would have stepped in and stopped the abuse somehow, but that would have meant the loss of his mother's promise of greatness.

Gill responded, "I think I understand what you mean and I agree. And, you are right that I could have easily left that shitty job and found a better one but no one would give me that huge amount of money for doing absolutely nothing. It is too good of a deal to give up. Also, I didn't want to sink to their level and I am not like them so I didn't know what to do." I interpreted that he both looked down on them, not wanting to sink to their level, but also wished to be rescued, to have someone, me or someone else, step in and set things straight. I added that he didn't want to give up the abuse because he felt the easy rewards of greatness were too good. Therefore, he was willingly playing a destructive but temporarily rewarding game. Gill said I "hit the nail on the head in a couple of ways" and told me he felt his father "really ignored what was happening" and that his mother gave him an "extremely mixed message."

Once again, I interpreted that Gill probably wanted me to step in and tell him what to do and save him, but to give me that power left him powerless and helpless in the meantime. Gill told me, "I have always wanted someone to magically appear and save the day. I feel like there are thousands of situations where I really need someone to just step in and take my hand and show me the way. But, it never happens, and I know from asking you so many times what to do that I won't be getting it here either. But, that is OK. I just wish I could figure it out before it is too late."

This "too late" was the reference to Gill's sense of his life looking so optimistic and promising at first and how he really felt he was going to be the next messiah as his mother told him, but now he felt he had missed that opportunity and was headed downhill fast. Practically speaking, he did not have any job prospects after this job ended and had lost all his savings on stock market investments that had gone bad. He couldn't go to his family as his mother was extremely poor and from his description was psychotic and barely taking care of herself. She had remarried a man who did not like Gill and ignored any of his requests for help over the years. So, internally and externally, Gill really felt on his own, without help and desperate to find the magic road to salvation. He still had the dim hope of "making it big and being famous and special" but now he simply hoped he "didn't wind up homeless and beat up."

There were ways that Gill showed me a more primitive or persecutory vision he held of the world. Regarding his job, Gill told me that he felt afraid of his coworkers and that if he did stand up for himself, he didn't know if he would be physically safe. He thought they were such a "bunch of frat boys" and were "so aggressive" that they might turn on him and beat him up. Gill went on to talk about how he was still very scared walking down the street, even though after talking about it over the last year with me he had begun to feel a bit better and more secure. He said, "I look down at the sidewalk and try to avoid eye contact so as to not end up in any conflict." I mentioned that he always tries to greet me with a big smile when I come out in the waiting room, but then he quickly looks down at the ground in a sheepish or humbled manner. Gill told me that he was surprised to see me pick up on that because he thinks of himself as "able to pull one over on most people, acting friendly and easy going." But, in fact, Gill said, he was extremely nervous and wanting to make sure I was in a good mood and to not have to make eye contact with me just like in the street.

I said he must be afraid that one of us is close to anger and that things could easily get out of hand. He replied, "I certainly don't picture it that way, but when you describe it, I must feel that way since I am acting like that. I think I do that so much of the time with everyone that it is just automatic." So, here was this man who was a member of the Mensa Intelligence Society, in which every member has to have a genius level of intelligence, stuck in a dead-end job almost literally hiding behind his desk.

Additionally, it was interesting how Gill felt intimidated by me, people on the street, and coworkers when I considered how he presented himself physically. When I first met him, I felt slightly intimidated and nervous. In fact, in much the way he felt about me, I almost didn't want to make eye contact with him. He was a champion body builder with enormous arms and his whole body was a mass of bulging muscles. Gill had won numerous prizes at the gym where he worked out and was a very striking sight. But, as I met with him over the next two years, using the analytic couch, I learned that Gill had always been physically intimidated by others. At work, his coworkers ridiculed him for being a sissy and "too stuck up." Indeed, the more I spent time with him, the more Gill did seem like a small child hiding in a muscle builder's body. He tried his best to be extremely polite to avoid conflict. He accepted his role as emotional punching bag at the office.

Gill told me he felt like there was a mysterious force that attracted conflict to him. There were countless situations where he was out at a nightclub or walking down the street and another man had "challenged him" or yelled at him and asked him if he was looking for a fight. He said, "I freaked out last week when this guy yelled at me and asked me what was my problem?!" I took a cue from my own counter-transference reaction to his physical presence: I often felt like a motorcycle gang member was lumbering into office, looking menacing and perhaps spoiling for a fight. So, I interpreted, "I wonder if with all your muscles and being on alert all the time about conflict, you might look like your spoiling for a fight to some people." Gill was surprised and said he thought it could be a possibility, but it also frightened him since he "definitely want[s] to avoid conflict." In this regard, we gradually made the link to his fear of his mother "coming down on him without warning." I interpreted Gill's transference as well, noting how he engaged me with both a passive, masochistic style and a more silent version of a muscle-bound superhero feeling entitled to be famous.

Specifically, Gill seemed to have all the ingredients of a superhero: the intelligence, the muscles, and the early childhood whisper in his ear of fame and fortune. But, he also seemed unwilling and frightened to pull the trigger and actually become someone in his own life. He waited for fame and fortune to come to him, a much safer strategy and one that also showed the underlying arrogance and idealization of self that went hand in hand with his devaluation of self and terror of others. In addition, I think he was scared that if he was more assertive, he might be an out-of-control superhero and become violent and mean like his mother often did. The core anxiety, however, seemed to be that if he gave up hope for this idealized future specialness, he would have to face the devastating reality of his past and present, with a sense of loss and helplessness that was unbearable.

I believe, as a result of close examination of his transference, his phantasies, and his associations to the past, present, and future, that Gill was unable to face the transition to the depressive position and felt unwilling to give up his vision of self as special, destined by his mother to be great, successful, and loved in wonderful ways. To give this up would be to mourn this special yet perverse relationship with his internal mother, this prophet mother who launched the great ship of Gill into the seas for the world to behold. Instead, he would have to face an ordinary at best, but more often disappointing and abusive, mother who ruled over a neglected, confused, and scared child. I think Gill needed to keep the hope alive. He mentally forced this vision of a magical mother who one day would bring him special love and praise. But, to avoid the persecutory fears of being attacked for being too assertive and having his own identity, he had to be silent and passive, waiting for his ship to come in.

Also, Gill liked the idea of being rescued and guided, taken by the hand by me, his mother, or someone. But, as I interpreted to him over time, the price for this and the bargain he had to strike was to be a helpless, formless, passive infant without direction or purpose, looking and waiting for someone to show him mercy, give him permission to grow up, or take control over him and parent him.

In this standoff place between the paranoid-schizoid position and the depressive position, there are contrary bargains Gill made with the object. With excessive reliance on projective identification resulting in a breakdown in normal splitting along with patterns of intense idealization, often opposing and destructive combinations of phantasies about the self and about the other are fostered and maintained. It is this pathological mix of object relational phantasies that patients like Gill resist exploring, unraveling, and giving up. Life and death instincts are pushed by primitive phantasies into corrupted collaborations. Even though the price paid is very high and the deal with the devil is always destructive in the long run, the short-term illusion of special power, safety, love, and control is so inviting that these patients make severe compromise solutions to obtain the temporary fix or feeling of being special and loved with a damaging price tag attached.

So, in his mind Gill always joined the easy money at his job with the nasty abusive workers who picked on him and to whom he never stood up. Internally, he joined his cheerleading mother with his abusive mother and the idea of being famous with not needing to do anything to get there. But, then he felt scared and anxious and he felt cheated and denied. This was a breakdown of splitting based on his hunger for continuous and special status. It was not a more neurotic struggle of ambivalence between one thing or another. It was more a refusal to mourn the fact that the ideal mother wore wolf's clothing and the wolf could sometimes turn into a magical mother providing forecasts of miracles. He did not want to mourn the loss of his mother as he felt he would be losing all of her, not just parts of her. It would be the end. So, he elected to create an endless phantasy of false hope and promise.

Gill joined the idea of marriage and love with the idea of being in jail and the ideas of being kept away from all the goodies he deserved, forced to have kids, and never being able to have sex with gorgeous movie stars. He joined the idea of being a body builder who has skill and strength with the idea of having to desperately protect himself from all the bullies that seemed to roam the streets challenging him to a fight. Gill never would allow one without the other. He always wanted this perfect combination in which he had it all. In doing so, he was unwilling to face the reality that he could have some and enjoy some, but not have it all or not have it be exactly as he chose. For him, this was too big of a risk, as it meant he could lose and be without anything or anyone forever.

When I made this interpretation, Gill said, "It sounds like I would be giving in to such a mediocre and boring life. I refuse. I have always been sure that I would end up being someone important and doing something unique. I hear what you say and feel like I am getting pulled down under the ground into something predictable, blue collar, and regular. It feels so plain and so boring, without meaning." I interpreted, "It seems you have been feeling empty and without meaning for most of your life because you have put yourself on hold, waiting for the magical day your mother's predictions come true." He nodded yes and said, "I always had this idea that I would be famous and special but I never put any effort into it because I thought it would just happen. Now, it has definitely not materialized and I feel I have nothing. If I don't find a new job soon, I will literally be homeless and broke."

During this time, Gill decided to try and find a position in the Green Beret forces, a special military fighting unit. He was very good with computers and he thought he could capitalize on that by applying for their technology division. It turned out that this had been a phantasy in the back of his mind for many years, picturing himself alongside the other fighting men, "making a difference and saving lives." Gill told me how he pictured the many places in the world where there was oppression and he wanted to be a part of stepping in and "stopping injustice." He also told me that he felt he would be proud to be a part of a team that "stood up to any outside intruder that tried to hurt America and do damage to the innocents."

Gill had talked with a local recruiter and was told there was a big need for experts in technology, as long as they could pass the rigorous physical requirements as well. After such a long time of really doing nothing for himself and not feeling motivated in any way to make external changes in his life, this was a marked shift. For several months, he began to investigate and research the various details about service in the Green Berets. He looked into the pay, the health benefits, the chances of staying in the States versus being sent overseas, the chances for advancement, and so forth. It was a big sign of progress that he dared to meet with all the different people and ask all of his questions directly, since this type of assertive behavior usually left him very scared and convinced there would be some type of fallout or punishment.

The sudden rush to be a part of the military was also a destructive compromise in which he pictured he could be the aggressor but on the side of good this time, instead of being like his mother—being mean for the sake of being mean. His ideas of fighting the good fight seemed idealistic and prone to some sort of backfire. I felt like a parent who doesn't want to crush the dreams of his child but cringes when he hears of the lofty and probably problematic, if not disastrous, plan being proposed.

For a few months, we discussed the extreme anxiety he had about passing the physical exams and rigorous boot camp challenges. When he actually ended up taking the initial physical tests of endurance they required to weed out the candidates, he did quite well, since he had spent years working out. When Gill prepared to take the various written tests and verbal interviews, he was terrified he would be found out to be a poor candidate and dreaded being accused of lying or covering up who he really was. He began plans to "immediately admit everything I ever did." I interpreted that he was so scared of being judged or punished for being himself that he felt he had to go to great odds to be a special super-honest and super-cooperative person to avoid conflict and hope for acceptance. He agreed but told me he felt he "couldn't help it. He was compelled to be super scrupulous in presenting himself in every detail."

So, Gill made sure to tell the truth about everything, including the two incidences in which he stole chewing gum when he was five years old. Of course, this made the interviewing officers see him as childish and odd which in turn made Gill scared of being rejected and judged. These types of situations kept happening with his interviews. After listening to my counter-transference in which I felt like I should dive in to rescue this anxious little boy making a fool of himself, I made the interpretation that Gill wanted me to step in and save him before he looked stupid, but he also felt compelled to push ahead no matter what with this "be honest about everything" stance. I also interpreted that he was seeing the situation as a terrible moment of exposure before the eyes of the court and he had better not lie about anything. He was repeating an early traumatic moment with his internal objects now with the interviews and with me. I interpreted this as his again being passive and feeling like, if he was a perfect little boy, he would be rewarded; and if he wasn't, he would be in big trouble.

In response, Gill told me how he felt much more intelligent and superior to all the other candidates but also was extremely scared they would yell at him and he would fail the tests at the boot camp. He pictured he would end up in the most horrible scene out of movies about boot camp where all the other men in his troop would turn on him, single him out as the unwanted problem, and beat him up. Noticing this ongoing internal struggle of wanting to be the perfect boot camp boy who was superior and won the attention and praise of those in charge, but how this demand for perfection came with the terrible price tag of persecution and rejection, I Interpreted that Gill was reluctant to accept that he might just be a average recruit and not really stand out either as extra good or extra bad. Of course, the rewards of this more balanced position were that it would make boot camp feel less scary and demanding. But, he would have to give up the goal of having this special destiny, fame, and acceptance.

In what seemed like a combination of self-preservation and self-sabotage, Gill told the Special Forces interviewer he was in therapy so they requested his medical records. When they received my paperwork indicating his ongoing anxiety problems, they immediately turned him down. So, Gill was left jobless, broke, and hopeless. He had to move into his aunt's home in another state. He immediately stopped treatment since at this point he now had no money, not even for food or gas.

Throughout the last few weeks I met with Gill, I noticed in the counter-transference how I felt scared, intimidated, guilty, and so on, but when I investigated if he was indeed the source, he always said no. I think that this was the part of Gill that he kept under wraps to avoid becoming like his angry, abusive mother. He was not able to find a way to have a healthy sense of assertion and desire, safely expressing his need, honoring his anger, voicing disapproval, or showing disappointment in something or somebody. He could not tell me he was angry that I signed the papers that prevented him from getting the job he wanted so much. He thought others were able to and allowed to speak up like that but not him. He feared turning into a violent, raging creature who was greedy, impolite, and pushy. So, instead of talking about his reaction to my letter and its consequences when I brought it up, he told me, "Life just has its ups and downs and no one is really to blame." I tried to interpret this cover-up and way of protecting me and himself from conflict but we ran out of time. Gill insisted, "We are good."

So, the treatment ended and Gill's special destiny looked like it was actually something quite ordinary, something tragic, and something out of his control. It was a sad and unfortunate way for us to end. I only hope that Gill finds a way to return to treatment to continue his work toward becoming less than perfect, less than famous, and less than special. Instead, hopefully he may realize he is one of many while still being quite unique and important.

SUMMARY

This chapter has explored the dynamics of patients who, while varying in degrees of intensity, have common psychological elements. The use of projective identification is extreme, which creates an inner void distinguished by emotional hunger, anxiety, and demand. This results in various unconscious phantasies such as, "If I am like you, if I sacrifice myself to you and think of you all the time, whether in a hateful or loving way, I may one day be rewarded with love and the cancellation of rejection and hate." This phantasy creates an angry, impatient longing and a violent resistance to mourning as it signifies unbearable loss, despair, and annihilation. These patients feel forgotten and lost, but it is by themselves. Even though they feel perpetually at the mercy of the object, they demand to be given to by this slippery unreachable withholder.

The Kleinian method is useful in the treatment of a wide variety of psychological problems, and when used as the technical vehicle in establishing analytic contact (Waska, 2007), it can be extremely useful in working with the more difficult to reach patient. While some clinicians (Carrese, 2010) recommend reduced frequency psychoanalysis for patients with so-called reduced ego capacity, I have found that the procedure of analytic contact allows for the standard psychoanalytic approach to be conducted at a variety of frequencies with or without the analytic couch for a variety of diagnostic profiles, but without the modification or reduction of analytic intent due to so-called ego deficit problems.

Rather, as illustrated by the case material, analytic contact is defined as the consistent focus on transference and counter-transference issues and how a working connection can be fostered in the moment-to-moment process of examining the patient's phantasy and internal conflicts. The pull or push towards or against a whole-object relationship between parts of the self or between self and object are all considered more important than frequency or use of couch. In this way, there is less focus on making a distinction between psychoanalysis and psychoanalytic psychotherapy and more emphasis on the working through of transference, counter-transference, phantasy, and unconscious conflict in the here-and-now process of the therapeutic work.

The patients examined in this chapter are all within the borderline and narcissistic range, and as a result they create a significant tension and ongoing disruption in the emotional seam between patient and analyst. It is this union or void that analytic contact is designed to follow, explore, interpret, and work through. Searles (1978) has described the importance of understanding the ongoing emotional climate of the analytic sessions, day in and day out. I think this is a similar recommendation to that of Joseph (1985) regarding the concept of the total transference situation, in which all elements of the session are regarded as part of the transference dynamic.

Searles (1978) notes that with the more difficult patient operating in either the paranoid mode or the depressive mode, the analyst may experience the counter-transference burden or dilemma of not being allowed to make helpful or complete interpretations for lengths of time, as a result of the patient's immediate transference state. Searles (1978) discusses how the analyst's struggle in these moments is to not force his or her reality, or at least what he or she believes to be reality, upon the patient. This difficulty in making interpretations can be very disruptive to the entire treatment since, as Kernberg (1978) notes, it is important to constantly be interpreting the defensive urges and actions of the more entrenched patient.

The type of individual examined in this chapter is a predominantly borderline and/or narcissistic personality, relying on primitive methods of organizing their internal experiences (Meissner, 1979; Bursten, 1973) and relying on pathological retreat (Steiner 1990, 1993) as a method of avoiding mourning. As Millon (1985) notes, these individuals show an adaptive inflexibility in coping with self and other, a tendency to foster vicious cycles of paranoid-schizoid phantasy and conflict, and a fragile grip on emotional stability. This brittle foothold in the depressive position, when if ever achieved, easily fragments and shifts to more destructive and immature systems of defense and acting out.

The patients presented in this chapter also have many of the characteristics described by Brown (1987). He describes how these patients demonstrate psychological conflicts and pathological conditions that are the result of a disturbance in the transition between the paranoid and depressive positions. Like Steiner (1979) has shown in his clinical write-ups, Brown examines the way these patients end up relying on pathological cycles of projective identification, idealization, devaluation, and splitting. These chronic patterns of relating seem to increase when the patient feels forced to face the difficult tasks of mourning, difference, disappointment, and lack of control inherent in the depressive mode. The shift from concrete action to symbolic thinking is resisted as it requires giving up control over omnipotent vision of self and object. Indeed, the core anxiety is that mourning is not about temporary injury to the object but a permanent and unbearable loss in which the self is banished to be without the desired object forever and without any sense of self for all time. Only pieces remain which are scattered in a chaotic and dangerous world. Better to demand for everything and everyone right away, to claim to be special now or at least eventually, and to calm one's self with false visions of loving rescue, power, and special status.

Three

Psychotic Distortions of the Good Object

Working with more disturbed patients in private practice involves clinical situations that challenge the analyst's abilities. However, the psychoanalytic method remains a vital, robust, and effective approach with the hard-to-reach, difficult-to-contain, and confusing-to-understand patients who make up so much of our day-to-day practice. These are the borderline, narcissistic, and psychotic individuals who want help but feel change to be dangerous (Waska, 2006) and rely on a variety of primitive defenses, pathological organizations (Rosenfeld, 1971; Steiner, 1987, 1990), and rigid psychic retreats (Steiner 1993) to protect themselves and to attack the envied or persecutory object. While these taxing and unstable patients exhibit some depressive capacity (Klein, 1935, 1940), for the most part they are suffering in a paranoid-schizoid realm (Klein, 1946) of mental experience and trying to escape into temporary emotional shelters or psychological foxholes to avoid what feels like a world of constant turmoil and distress.

MY APPROACH

I use a hybrid (Waska, 2010c, 2011b) of the classical Kleinian approach advocated by Hanna Segal (1974) combined with the more modern Kleinian views on technique expressed by Betty Joseph (1989), John Steiner (1993, 2011), Elizabeth Spillius (1983, 1993), and Michael Feldman (2009), as well as the object relational model of James Grotstein (1977, 1985, 2009a, 2009b), Otto Kernberg (1987), and many others who advocate the here-and-now exploration of the life and death instincts as they color the universal conflicts over love, hate, and knowledge (Waska, 2010b) and become evident in the transference.

In bringing this technical perspective to the real world of real patients whom we encounter in private practice (Waska, 2005), I focus on the core issues of loss (Waska, 2002), unbearable internal anxieties (2010a), and the complications inherent in transference and counter-transference (2011a). Effective interpretations (Waska, 2011a) that engage with the intense projective identification (Waska, 2004) process, so common with more difficult patients, are critical in the therapeutic efforts to find, maintain, and cultivate meaningful analytic contact (Waska, 2007).

CASE MATERIAL: PATIENT Y

Y struck me as a very intelligent young man with great curiosity about himself as well as the genuine desire to change and to find satisfaction in his life. At the same time, I felt cautious and suspicious about how he talked about his issues in a fuzzy, grandiose manner with excessive remarks about "spirituality and the essence of inner meaning, fulfillment of the heart, and true emotional resolution" that sounded like something he had read in a self-help book. Indeed, he had attended many such workshops and programs over the years but never had been involved in any psychotherapy or analysis.

The more we talked, the more I felt he was both articulate and insightful yet out of touch with reality. In other words, I thought that Y's grandiose, paranoid, and possibly delusional way of relating to me was buffered by a partial anchoring into a more intellectual, sincere, and eloquent manner of relating. As a result, I felt uneasy about who he was, what he was really all about, and how he was really going to use me or need me as an object in his internal world.

Y talked at great length about the "dynamic involvement" he found in the human potential workshops he had attended and the "interesting historical lineage of the New Age church he had recently converted to. According to Y, this church advocated strict or fundamentalist rules of behavior about routine confession, no sex before marriage, and regular prayer combined with a Buddhist mentality. Y seemed to be very drawn to the punitive aspects as well as the rigid structure. He talked at length about how he felt spiritually drawn to the church, how he had a spiritual awakening recently when he heard the choir singing. He fell to the ground crying and thought he could see the image of his dead mother at the altar. He told me he had met a member who had his mother's name and they introduced him to the head priest who had a sister with his mother's name, so Y felt it was "destiny" and that it must be "a special spiritual path that had brought him closer to being able to finally find his mother again." This was similar to his description of the time at a Zen retreat when he knew he "was Jesus and obviously had special mystical powers."

When I noted that he seemed to like the rules and structure of the church but that it was quite opposed to the way he had lived his life in the last three years, Y told me, "I love the structure. I need structure. When I picture the ultimate way of feeling at peace, I have the vision of being in my mother's arms." I said, "So, you feel the structure of the church is much like the security and structure of being loved and back in your mother's arms." He said, "Yes. Even better would be to be back in her womb. That would be the ultimate structure!"

Over the last three years, Y had traveled around the world in an aimless and desperate attempt to escape from his inner demons. At the same time, he felt it was a "wonderful quest in many ways, finding a spiritual path and many deep spiritual revelations along the way." Over the course of his first two sessions, I learned how Y had grown up in a family of four brothers, two younger than him. Y's mother died of cancer when Y was three years old and his father remarried a few years later. Y told me he realized about three years ago that his lifelong unhappiness and sense of fragmentation comes from the loss of his mother at this sensitive young age. This seems to have brought about his mental breakdown.

Y's older brother has some type of psychotic condition, possibly a bipolar state, and has been in and out of mental institutions. He has been given various anti-psychotic medications and mood stabilizers, which Y says he has tried in an effort to "find some calm and clarity during the rough times."

I interpreted that he identified with his brother and sought out the same kind of help with the medications. Here, I introduced an idea about his somehow seeing himself as his sick brother and needing the same treatment. I wasn't sure about anything else, but I felt it important to comment on that fragment. It was useful to see how concretely Y replied. He said, "I just thought his meds would help me with my moods and depression because my brother suffers with them as well." So, I simply kept my idea of him wanting to be the same and losing his identity in the process as a question mark. I knew he could be correct in diagnosing himself as suffering the same illness as his brother, but the way he described it had this more blurred "fitting into his brother" feel to it in which he seemed to desire fusion or sameness.

So, Y went on to explain: "The main and most devastating problem in my life is the death of my mother when I was three. She died of cancer, and I finally realized three years ago how much that has affected me and how that is the central core of all my issues. I must find her and reconnect that spiritual bond and find that missing part in me." He went on to tell me of his "mental breakdown" three years ago and his "voyage ever since to free myself." He told me he smokes pot every day to calm down and to find some peace of mind. Y also drinks heavily when he can't find enough pot. When we were discussing his long-time addiction to pot and how he uses it or alcohol to "self-medicate," Y casually mentioned an incident the prior week. Y told me that he had moved into the city about two months earlier and had quickly found a job in the small grocery store. His job was to stock the shelves. Y said he hated it because it was boring, and when he was done for the day, it was a long walk to the bus stop. But, he kept at it for about three weeks. Then, one day at work he decided to consume a "pot brownie," and when he started to feel really high, he went to his manager and told him that he was now too high to work and wanted to see if he could leave early. The manager promptly fired him.

I asked Y what he had expected would happen. Y said he wasn't too surprised but he "always hopes that people can maybe see the real truth and find a way to have a connection that transcends the weight of rules and convention." I said, "You seem to be hoping for a pure, honest, and all-accepting connection, perhaps the sort of thing you feel you lost out on with your mother dying." Y said, "Exactly!" I added, "It also seems to be a way that you sabotaged yourself and got fired. You could have hung in there and not told your boss or you could have elected to not get high. But, you took away something you had created in your life." Y said, "I do that over and over and over. I tend to achieve something and then give up on it or screw it up somehow. I did that with girlfriends and plenty of jobs." So, we discussed the elements of this pattern and how he seemed to be happy and proud of himself but then would turn away from himself and let go of that positive element and create a negative. Here, I was thinking about the clinical manifestations of the life and death instincts and the destructive conflicts that can occur in that phantasy realm (Steiner, 2004; Rosenfeld, 1971; Grotstein, 1985).

I noticed Y had a pen and pad on which he was taking periodic notes. When I made an interpretation, he wrote it down. He asked if we would be working psychoanalytically, and I said he probably knew I was an analyst. He said he did and wondered where I was trained. I paused and said I was trained in the city but wondered what exactly he wanted to know. He wrote something down again. I asked him what he was writing and what exactly he was trying to find out about me. Y said he had written down what I said about trying to search for the perfect bond and structure with his mother and how somehow it was always collapsing and he was unable to sustain it. He said he was also writing down where I was trained so he could look it up.

I said, "It seems you want to know me and own me in some way that also makes it hard for you to be here right now, knowing me this way." Y said, "I am just a curious person and I want to know what type of treatment I am having and a little about the person I am supposed to trust in that treatment." So, for now, Y kept us at that concrete distance but based on my counter-transference, it seemed that internally he was fishing around to know me, possess me, and get inside me. I thought this might be part of what I would term the extraction process of pathological projective identification in which the subject attempts to hijack or acquire certain aspects of the object to call their own. It becomes a mental robbery based in envy, intense anxiety over not knowing, and lack of control of the internal environment.

When I went to the waiting room to find Y for his second session, I found him standing there with his bicycle. He said he didn't want to leave it on the street and have it stolen so he wondered if he could leave it in the waiting room. I had several thoughts about this. While there was no one else out there, it is interesting that Y didn't think of how his bicycle would affect the next patient or how he might be affected by them. So, I think he felt it was *his* waiting room, and it felt safe to leave the bicycle there.

I was worried that someone would come into the waiting room and steal the bike so I suggested he leave it in the hallway by my office door. But, either way, I felt he was moving in. This sensation was confirmed when he entered my office and took out his cell phone and a charger and said, "Can I plug this in somewhere?" I had two feelings about this. I felt I had no choice. I had to either say yes or I would be telling him no in a very rejecting way, telling him that there was no room for him in my home.

The other feeling was that he was indeed moving in. So, I said, "Looks like you are moving in! I wonder if you have decided you can trust me. But, with such a fast move in, I wonder if you will be able to stay for a while?" I said this based on the feeling that this was an impulsive move into me and could easily be followed by an impulsive retreat. Y confirmed my interpretation when he said, "I have always had a hard time with commitment. I have a pattern of really getting into something and then it all falls apart. I give up on it."

I asked, "Do you give up or do you choose to retreat and pull out?" Here, I was seeing if Y was able to consider himself as an active player in his life or just a passive observer. I wondered if he was caught in a more persecutory vision of himself or knew he was participating in what happened around him. Y said, "It feels like I just give up. I go into the job or relationship with a lot of hope and excitement. It works out and I am happy for a while. I am very successful at most of the jobs I take on and I have been very connected with a number of women. But, at some point, I feel it is almost going too well and I give up and stop trying. I think I can't handle it and so I sort of fade away."

I said, "I wonder if something about being successful, happy, or close makes you anxious and then you have to fail. Almost punishing yourself or running away from something positive." Here, I was interpreting a possible fear of success, a dread of closeness, and a reaction to having dove too deep into the object or situation. Y said, "I think that could be. I tend to fail at commitment."

So, having only seen Y for two visits, it is unclear what his struggles are and how the treatment will unfold. However, by adhering to a modern Kleinian approach, I was able to make a few interpretations and help Y open up in certain ways that has begun a therapeutic process in which we have already established a degree of analytic contact and have started to explore and examine his internal world and the various unconscious phantasies and conflicts with which he is suffering.

In the counter-transference, I notice that my feelings and thoughts sometimes parallel his description of himself and his emotional patterns. Specifically, I notice myself liking him as a person, trusting him, and wanting to engage in a working relationship. However, at the same time, I have an uneasy feeling, a slight distrust, and see him as possibly more disturbed than he appears and possibly ready to terminate at any moment. So, I am keeping this counter-transference data in mind as we proceed. I think it may help me understand him more and find my way as we continue our analytic journey.

CASE MATERIAL: PATIENT Z

Z's brother Bill called me about eight months ago to see if I could see them together in weekly treatment. Bill said he was "very worried about Z's moods and his drinking and drug use." Bill said Z had a drinking problem and was getting "more depressed than ever and more and more out of control." When I asked if Z would call me on his own behalf, Bill said, "Never in a million years. He doesn't own a phone and doesn't like to use them because he thinks the government is eavesdropping. Plus, he doesn't think anything is wrong with him so he wouldn't want to call you. He is willing to come and see you if I go with him, but he wouldn't go on his own."

So, I began meeting with Z and Bill once a week. Z has alternated between "I am only showing up to make my brother happy," "Maybe there is something to learn but probably not," "Why the fuck would I want to do this bullshit," and "I will keep coming till the court is off my ass and then I am out of here." His reference to the court had to do with his being arrested for public drunkenness and destruction of property. While blacked out drunk, Z had gotten into a fight with a local street person and ended up breaking the door of a local business by kicking it until it broke in half.

The reason we met only once a week was not only because of Z's resistance to coming at all, but also because his brother could not afford more and Z had to take an hour-long bus ride just to get to my office.

Z was raised by parents who had lived in a sixties hippie commune where everyone followed the Indian guru and his teachings. While the guru's teachings were about being good to others and always finding a way to be charitable and giving, Z's parents took this to mean giving to almost everyone but their own family. So, the parents moved to India for a while to work and the children were simply taken along for the ride. They were home schooled and told to pray and to respect the guru. From Z's description, his mother is probably borderline or high-level psychotic with bouts of intense depression. He remembers how "she would shut the door to her bedroom and we wouldn't see her for days. She would get really depressed. Other times, she could be really weird and angry. Sometimes, I would ask her something and she would only answer by telling me about God and all the wonderful things the guru did. I think she got some kind of treatment at some point or some medications. I don't really know."

When Bill was eighteen, he moved out to "get away from that crazy crap and finally have my own life and my own choices." Z told me Bill "had always been my mother and father when I was growing up. He was the one that took care of me. So, when he moved out, I went with him." I asked if his parents cared, and he said they thought he was "in good hands" and they were "busy with the guru's work." So, to this day, Bill looks after Z and tries to help him out whenever he can, financially and emotionally.

When I first met Z, I was a bit put off by his appearance. He was homeless in that he had no home of his own. But, he had a fair number of friends from dealing drugs as well as the fellow street artists he knew. So, he took turns staying nights at their apartments and sleeping on their couches or floors. When Z began treatment with me, he had just finished a stint dealing drugs in a nearby city. After getting into a drunken fistfight one day and having someone pull a gun on him over some drug deal gone wrong, Z decided to move out of town to escape the danger. He was now back in his home town, where his parents lived. Z was told he could not live with them because he had torn up their home when he was drunk and on drugs. So, now he was staying with a friend who was a street artist and a heroin addict. Z managed to make enough money from selling drugs to buy food. He enjoyed cooking and liked to make elaborate dinners for his friends. This was one of the many aspects of his fragmented self that was healthy, positive, and creative but was constantly challenged by the side of him that was so self-destructive.

I was impressed by his interest in art and cooking as well as many other elements of his psychology that seemed to all hold promise if we could find a way through the more death instinct–driven behavior that overshadowed his life. It was Bill who brought him to me to see if we could find a way to work through this painful pattern of non-living. For his part, Z told me he "couldn't really give a shit and would not waste his time going to therapy. But, if Bill wants me to come, it is cool and I will do it." I interpreted, "maybe it is difficult to let yourself want something positive or to consider change for yourself. But, for now, we will take what we can get and see what we find."

Z looked like a drug-using homeless person. He wore disheveled clothing, had knotted hair that was past his shoulders, had a large beard, and slumped in the chair in a way that said, "I am here but don't expect anything from me." He had a psychotic look in his eye and spoke only when spoken to. His fingernails were dirty and broken, and he smelled of pot and cigarettes. His teeth were a mess and he was missing a few that had rotted out from never brushing. Z was well known by the local police because he was often hanging out on the street and getting drunk. They had been called to the scene many times when Z was drunk and yelling at people walking down the street, or when Z was trying to talk to store owners and they were intimidated by him.

During the first month of analytic treatment, I thought that Z's psychotic troubles were probably due to severe psychological conflicts and persecutory phantasies. But, I also thought that it could be helpful if Z took some medication so he could feel less anxious and fragmented. Specifically, he was up most nights, paranoid that someone was going to attack and kill him. So, he rarely slept more than a few hours. He had paranoid delusions about many things in his life and felt it difficult to trust anyone. So, I suggested he be evaluated for antipsychotic medication with the hopes that it would sedate him enough to be able to sleep more and feel less anxious while we began to explore his internal issues. When he asked me why and what for, I told him it appeared he had the symptoms of schizophrenia and that the medications would help him not feel terrified at night and would help him stop thinking about people coming to attack him and kill him. I said that it was important for him to feel less anxious in general and that it would help us have more of a chance to really focus on who he was and what was going on in his life. Z seemed to be fine with this. Bill took him to his psychiatrist appointments and Z began to take a low dose of antipsychotic medications in the third or fourth month of treatment. He took this on and off for about three months.

Unfortunately, in the seventh month of treatment, he ran out and did not go back for a refill. This was part of his dynamic of going along with the help of others passively for a while and then failing to follow through. And, he would never have made the appointment for himself or gone there by himself. His fears and reluctance to establish any structure for his life due to his resentment, judgment, and anxieties made him unable to provide himself with the most basic elements of daily living. I took my time in recommending that Z go for a medication evaluation, as I knew it could be a counter-transference reaction and acting out of my own anxiety or the patient's projection of either a sadomasochistic relationship or a rejecting object. Therefore, I thought about it, considered it, and discussed it with Z a great deal (Charlen, Yeoman, and Kernberg, 1999).

Z's internal world seemed to embody the clinical manifestations of the death instinct. His transference and phantasies were dominated by his anti-life efforts to keep himself separate from others. He kept himself psychologically distant from others. Also he was literally distant from others in that he often was wandering in the woods or sleeping in the forest for days at a time. On one hand, he was very popular with all the other street people and was seen as a very generous, likeable fellow by all the artists he met and all the people he drank with. On the other hand, Z made sure he never took part in regular social norms, didn't have a regular job, didn't try to have an apartment, didn't have a girlfriend, didn't drive a car, didn't brush his teeth, and didn't care about the laws and regulations we all have to live by. He tried to be above it all and separate from it all. In this case, it seemed he used the death instinct in a defensive manner, appearing to be a libidinal narcissist (Rosenfeld, 1987) in many of his ways of living.

If I inquired about his feelings towards himself or the world, or about the chance of change by seeing me, he was very quick to advise me on "the dark and shitty condition of our planet," the "vulgar and horrible nature of people in general," and the "extremely remote if not non-existent chance that [he] would ever want to be different, be a part of the so-called normal society, or have a desire to stop drinking and getting high."

Indeed, I noticed that this death instinct–colored transference was so intense, predictable, and quick to emerge in most of our sessions that it forced a pathological pattern between us. Any time I said something about Z possibly wanting or needing to change, or if Bill brought up the need for Z to drink less, maybe get a job, find a place to live, or even just brush his teeth, it was met with Z's humorous yet dark and attacking stance of no life, no growth, and no change.

This stance was what initially shaped Z's artistic direction as well. For years, Z had painted colorful yet very dark images on pieces of cardboard and tried to sell them on the street or at local flea markets and farmers' markets. The images were usually of scary monster faces, hands with claws, and bloodshot eyes. Z signed them FHD. He told me it "says it all." He explained the letters stand for Fly High and Die. I said, "You only get one bright moment and then it's over?" Z said, "If you are lucky. But, you can have a hell of a party trying!" I asked him why his art was always so dark. He said, "I am just aware of the reality of the world. People are awful, and why would I want to be a part of all that crap? I just like my life the way it is. You don't get it. Life is awful and people are awful. I don't want to do anything different. I like painting and getting high. What is wrong with that?"

I said, "When you say life is awful and people are awful, I wonder if you are talking about your early years with your family. That sounds like it might have been fairly awful at times." Z laughed and said, "Oh, God. Not the family shit! Do we really have to go there? That is so lame!" Here, Z was comical and easy to get along with but also very resistant and clear in his message of not wanting change and always seeing the world so darkly. He showed me some small pictures he had done and he obviously had talent, but it was restricted by this "fly high and die" stance. I asked him why he only painted these scary and gloomy images and he again assured me that he only "paints what he sees." I wondered if he ever tried to paint something else, something with a different message. He told me he "hates himself and hates the world so there is never any other energy to tap into."

I asked Z what was so terrible about himself, and he said, "I am useless and stupid just like everyone else. I let people down and I am not a good friend." Bill said this was far from the case and that many people regard Z as very trustworthy, loyal, and kind. Z said, "Well, if they are another artist or someone that I have known through drug dealing and can vouch for them, then yes. Otherwise, no fucking way!"

Regarding the discussion about Z's artwork, I noticed myself falling into a regular way of relating to him about it. Over time, I noticed that this was similar to other examples in our discussions, where I would find myself trying to balance out his extreme negative view of himself and the world. Clinically, I viewed it as a way that Z, through projective identification, always took on the stance of the death instinct, and I countered with the life instinct. Every patient has a unique mode of transference and a special way of communicating verbally and interpersonally. Z's style was very laid back, casual, humorous, and passive. At the same time, he would slip into more paranoid and combative moments where he wanted to stop treatment and saw no point in exploring his life. But, when he was in this more light and sarcastic mode, I would match him in that style with interpretations that were framed from that perspective.

So, for example, one time I said, "I think you are selling yourself short. You could be selling many more paintings if you branched out to include more positive ones, maybe a *relax and live* series instead of the *live hard and die quick* series." Z laughed and said, "I don't have that in me. There is no goodness or life in me. The world is a bad place and I have to warn people." I replied, "It seems so uncomfortable for you to show me the more alive, happy side of you that has hope and wants more in life." He said, "I don't want anything. I have it all. The world is bad and I am going to show everyone!"

I replied, "You want someone to realize how they are treating you and that you maybe deserve better? It sounds like you want someone to take responsibility for their bad actions and then maybe it can be put right?" Here, I was interpreting his internal family-of-origin conflicts in which he seemed to still be dealing with a profound sense of abandonment and the resulting rage and hurt. Z responded, "Whatever dude! I don't think anyone cares. I know I don't." I replied, "Well, here we go again. I have to stand up for you and say that you do care and others care about you. You have some good in you but you want me to find it. It looks like you make it a point to not admit any goodness to me or Bill or anyone. What makes it so uncomfortable for us to see you as a good guy who is lovable?"

Z replied, "What the fuck? You are weird dude!" So, here I was working with him in the projective identification–based transference and pointing out in a roundabout way that he seemed to be angry with his objects and wanting to say he was unlovable until his objects rescued him and assured him he was lovable.

At other times in the analytic treatment, Z talked more directly about how disappointed he was with his family and how "lame and shitty they are and were." When I replied, "Maybe you are still upset and wish they would recognize what a good son they still have," he said, "Oh hell no! I am just glad to be as far away from them as possible." I replied, "I wonder about that. It seems you maybe miss them but are very angry about never having them care for you like they should have. Maybe the way you don't take care of yourself now is a reaction to those feelings."

Z said, "No way! I don't care about them anymore. I just want to be far away from their crazy bullshit. Having them be caring is weird and creepy!" I said, "Weird because you never had it before and maybe your mad because it is too little too late?" Z replied, "They don't know how to care. They are too busy figuring out what the guru says and what prayers they should be saying." I said, "And you feel forgotten in the shuffle." Here, I was pursuing what seemed to be a fairly obvious link between Z's childhood feelings that are still alive today and his way of reacting to them, defending against them, and finding a way to remedy them by saying he was entirely self-sufficient and projecting his need and desire into me. His paintings also seemed to be an angry reaction to his family's failures. Now, all these negative feelings had captured Z and left him with a very restricted and destructive lifestyle.

Much of my way of relating to Z and how I talked with him was a deliberate counter-transference matching. By this, I mean that I think the analyst often has many subtle and important clues that are both evident in the room from how the patient speaks and acts but also through the patient's method of projective identification communication.

Rosenfeld (1987) has noted that projective identification can serve several purposes, and communication is one of them. I think Y, the first case I presented, was using it in a manipulative and appropriating manner, as well as communicatively. Z was using it in an expelling, omnipotent manner, and as a communicative gesture.

So, guided by this counter-transference matching with Z, I found it helpful to speak with him in a down home, casual, and often sarcastic and humorous fashion. In other words, I tried to speak to him in his own language. At the same time, I kept my own identity intact and spoke to him of what I thought were important psychological matters, and I would confront him on issues if necessary. While I was flexible and willing to be shaped by his transference, I still made very traditional interpretations. Thus, by maintaining my own identity but still reaching out to him, I think I was demonstrating how it was safe to have a unique personality and manner of being while still safely giving in and joining with the object.

When Z was literally tearing his hair at one point in a session because of how knotted it had become without proper hygiene, I interpreted that it was right after he had been talking rather tersely around our discussion of his family and his recent failed attempt to find a job. He was also telling me how he was "sick of this therapy crap" and would be "moving on as soon as the courts let me."

I said, "I think that you have problems with your hair but also have some emotional knots that we have to work out." He rolled his eyes and said, "Holy shit, Doc! Can't you do better than that? I can't believe it." I think my comment was accurate and put in a way that helped him stop his acting out and consider things for just a moment. He became less anxious, if just for a bit.

Next, I said, "I think you are upset and disappointed about not getting that job. It was very hard for you to put yourself out there for the interview, not something you normally risk or allow yourself to do. And, I think you are fed up with your family and feel they have really forgotten you right now. You were telling me how they said you will have to pay them back the money they gave you last week as soon as you can. But, you don't have a job, can't really afford food or clothes, and yet your parents are only willing to give you fifty bucks as a loan. So, maybe you are angry and hurt and now are taking it out on me and on our work together."

Z seemed to calm down and said, "Whatever, dude. Yes. I thought it was pretty harsh for them to tell me I had to pay it back soon." Bill turned to Z and said, "I think part of it is that they are angry about how you broke up their furniture last week and got so drunk and high. They don't trust you sometimes. But, I also see what you mean and have experienced them as harsh like that myself, with no sense of ever understanding what we are going through. They were like that when we were kids and still are, even though our father seems to be trying to be better."

Z replied, "I think you are right. I felt bad about going crazy that night, and I made sure to clean everything up and fix everything the next day."

This was all a reference to how Z had taken some heroin and gotten drunk and then "trashed" his parents' home while they were away for the weekend. When I brought it up, Z was quick to say, "I only took a little heroin and just a few beers but things got out of hand. I replied, "There is no such thing as a little bit of heroin. You have a problem with drugs and drinking that we need to continue to work on. But, when you trashed your parents place, I think there was another issue. You seem very angry with your parents for not being parents when you were young and needed them. You have told me how they were more into helping the guru than noticing their own children's needs. So, maybe that deep anger comes out when you are high, and then you take it out on them by trashing their home."

Z said, "I don't care about them anymore. I have moved on. I am living my own life and I don't think about any of that ever!" I said, "You protest too loud. I think there is something there but maybe it is uncomfortable to admit." Z said, "Whatever, Dr. Phil," a sarcastic reference to a television therapist seen by many as ridiculous and prone to corny, amateurish comments about people's dysfunctional childhoods.

Over the eight months I have been seeing Z, there have been many indications of his enormous psychological conflict with his now internalized family that has been projected and then fought against as an external enemy. He spends many days and nights at his parents' home but as a visitor, sleeping on the sofa while his parents allow some of the guru followers and recent converts to stay in the spare bedroom. His parents, particularly his mother, seem to completely deny the severity of his mental problems and his substance abuse. They simply suggest Z pray more and devote himself to the guru. I have interpreted that he must wish they had been more engaged with him emotionally when he was growing up and also now, but that instead he feels ignored and placated. I have interpreted his sorrow, rage, confusion, emotional hunger, and loss many times over, with Z taking in my comments some of the time and thinking about them, while other times refusing to consider them and quickly expelling them as useless.

Since his painting—both creating the paintings and selling them on the street—was such a big part of Z's life, we discussed it quite often. He had occasional success selling his work but also got into drunken fights with other artists and had used the art selling as a front to sell drugs on many occasions. I often talk with Z about his art to explore how he is limited by his death instinct–fueled phantasies and feelings regarding his family and his lack of value in their eyes. I interpret that he has so many conflicts and difficult feelings about them that his art is restricted and censored by them. As a result, he can only produce angry, scary, revenge art. This is in line with Hanna Segal's ideas about the breakdown of healthy symbolization in psychotic conditions (Segal, 1975, 1997).

Z is unable and unwilling to risk, admit, and accept that there could be something else inside of him, inside of his parents, and in the world at large besides the ugly, murderous, shocking, and aggressive energy he puts into the art at present. His art shows how much of an outsider he feels he is as well as how much he makes himself an outsider by producing something that pushes most people away with fear, disgust, or confusion. I have interpreted his art as a creative way in which he hopes to share and connect, as well as grow and feel proud about himself. But, this more life-instinct movement is curtailed by the death-instinct movement of his grievances and hurt, as well as his fear of separating from his family and finding his own successful path in life as an independent adult. He hates that when he was dependent on his family as a child they let him down, so he wants to prove he needs no one at all, ever. But, in reality, he is unable to care for himself and is still incredibly dependent on his brother and his family for the most basic care. Part of that is how he refuses to do anything for himself. So, when I asked him why he doesn't make his own appointments with the dentist, psychiatrist, or other people he needs to see, and instead waits for others to do it for him and take him there, he said, almost literally holding his hand, "Because I don't give a shit!" I replied, "I think you have the capacity to do these things for yourself but you are seeking some revenge and making sure somebody finally holds your hand and takes care of you. Unfortunately, you pay a great price for that. Maybe that is because you have turned some of your anger onto yourself." Predictably, Z snorted and rolled his eyes at me in response.

Indeed, I have interpreted that he could easily be doing more to help his brother help him, such as making phone calls for food stamps, putting together a resume for job interviews, or taking his medications on his own. There is no give and take, only take. Z refuses to give to himself in terms of self-love and the basics of daily care. And, he does not do much to give to others even when they are giving much to him. This includes his participation in the analytic treatment. He holds back and doesn't say much and doesn't participate much, even when I am paying attention to him, providing my understanding, and trying to be useful to him.

So, rather than have a mutually beneficial back and forth, Z passively pulls in his brother, me, and others to care for him, make his calls for him, drive him to his appointments, remind him to get refills for his medications, and put together resumes for his job interviews. I have interpreted his angry art and his identity as an angry rebel artist as a fear and angry refusal to mix the good with the bad. In other words, I am interpreting his combative stance against depressive position integration of both good and bad aspects of the self and the object. He strongly defends his splitting perspective of the world. I have also interpreted Z's stance as a "fringe artist who speaks for the darkness" as his way of rebelling and not fitting in, yet it is also a defense against his intense sense of loss, fear of fitting in, and conviction that he can't fit in.

Overall, Z often listens to my interpretations and seems to consider them. But, he often expels them, devalues them, or simply ignores them by not responding; however, over the eight months that I have worked with him analytically, there have been many shifts and signs of progress. This is the fragile and easily voided and corrupted progress so common in the work with difficult patients who exist in the borderline, narcissistic, or psychotic realm of experience.

As a result of our analytic work together, Z's internal world has become less chaotic, fragmented, and persecutory. He is less omnipotent, judgmental, and entitled, which results in his being less self-destructive and more open-minded. As we have worked with his persecutory and narcissistic phantasies and object relational conflicts, there have been significant external changes.

Z has gone from being drunk several times a week, often resulting in physical fights and police arrests, to only drinking a few beers a night and only getting drunk a few times a month. When he does get drunk, he tries "to stay indoors and lay low, so as to not get into trouble." Z still smokes pot every day but less of it, and he has gone from taking other heavier drugs on a very frequent basis to only a few times per month. Also, he has reported selling drugs less. I think he probably lied about some of these activities when we first started, but after a few months he told me he was "just going to tell the truth because he didn't care anyway and you can't do anything to stop me."

Z seems to dress better with cleaner clothes that are not as torn, and he seems to be bathing more often. He reports eating better and thinking about his health a bit more. As I mentioned, he wanted to be told, shown, or guided in many of these changes, but when Bill talked with him and I made interpretations regarding his lack of oral hygiene, Z did end up going to the dentist with Bill and having some initial work done on his significant oral problems. He said, "I was thinking about maybe brushing more often, but it is hard when you don't live in one place and don't own a toothbrush. Plus I just don't give a shit!"

During the sixth month of his analytic treatment, Z applied for a job and started working at a local cannery. It was a job that only lasted for one month but was still major shift in Z's outlook at society. While he had wanted a job for the last few years, he had never actually gone out and looked for one. He was convinced that "no one would ever want him since he looked like shit and people are shitty and nasty and love to judge." I interpreted this as part of his conviction that he was unwanted and forgotten, but that he wanted to be accepted and to fit in yet felt a great deal of conflict about that desire. At the same time, Z fought back at this rejecting object of society in his mind by not looking for a job—an "I will show you" attitude and a "why would I want to work with the likes of you" reaction to his phantasy of being judged. Instead, he relied on selling drugs or doing odd jobs like collecting cans or landscaping in which he felt righteously free and not a "part of the system."

Z began taking medications, on and off for about four months until he ran out and never got them refilled. This was also a sign of his letting in a bit of the world without automatically turning away from help and seeing it as a persecutory intrusion. Also, the fact that he has stayed in treatment with me for about eight months is a major achievement psychologically. Granted, he would never have come in at all or stayed if Bill were not with him.

Z's art has changed as well. He often argued and laughed at me when I brought up how he was putting his positive, life-affirming side into me and having me come up with various creative and more loving than hateful ways for him to express himself creatively. Nevertheless, he actually did begin to make some of those types of changes on his own, very gradually. So, while he still concentrated on perfecting his skull-and-crossbones image, his dagger-in-a-clawed-hand picture, and his bloodshot-eyes series, he also began to paint more welcoming and mainstream images, such as Hollywood actresses from the sixties, close-ups of leaves, hot air balloons, and a series on tools. Also, Z tried volunteering at a local school and taught the kids how to use different paints on a variety of surfaces. He was quite nervous about it and practiced his teaching plan many times before his first day. But, he followed through and was successful at it. Of course, when I brought it up as a new way of being or a sign of his letting himself live life a bit more fully and feeling like others were OK to give to and receive from, Z quickly reacted and told me it was an anomaly that would probably never happen again and that I was too corny and full of fluff. So, again, I was left to represent the life instinct, and he clung on to the death instinct through his excessive use of projective identification. However, it was not as emotionally violent.

In the transference, Z showed me respect from the beginning, but kept his emotional distance. Over time, he seemed to trust me more and we shared a few laughs as we slowly sorted out his complicated life. In the last few months, he shared his interest in my life. He wanted to know my interests, where I lived, and what I had done before becoming an analyst. I said, "You are more trusting of me and want to get to know me. Maybe we can get along and learn something together?" He replied, "Maybe. I just want to know who you are." So, it seemed he was allowing himself to be interested in me, which was new. Normally, he never wanted to know anyone and refused to let others know him.

I asked Z what he imagined about me. He said he thought I was probably "an old hippie who has had some experience with smoking weed and probably enjoys art. You probably live in the country or out of the city and are pretty mellow overall. I bet you are into gardening and have a good time on the weekends. But, you seem to also be a bit reserved and shy."

I said, "I think you are seeing yourself in me and that may be a sign that you are feeling more comfortable. You think I might be like you and enjoy the things you enjoy. So, maybe you are feeling less anxious and see more good around you. That might mean there is more good inside you too." Z smiled and said, "Oh, Doc! You really like to lay it on thick. Whatever, dude!"

I said, "It looks like you picture me as a grown-up version of yourself, someone who has made it past the hard times you are facing and now has an enjoyable life and a way to feel good about the world. If you think we ride on the same road and enjoy life in the same way, perhaps you are starting to let me in and feel like there is something good out there instead of always having to look over your shoulder." He said, "Maybe. But, you have to be careful. Those bastards out there can turn on you!" He said this with a smile and a laugh, so I said, "Yes, but I can tell you are not as trapped by that idea anymore. It doesn't feel as serious." He didn't protest my remark.

At this point, Z is more willing to accept the goodness or concern of others and to consider what I say without rejecting it outright. However, he still maintains a careful and protected distance and can quickly turn back to seeing me and others as persecutory and useless. In fact, he can still easily shift to a very paranoid stance, curse at me, and tell me he doesn't "need any of this bullshit anymore. I don't need you to be telling me what to do and I will be waving goodbye to you and this worthless crap very soon!"

And, while he will allow in the assistance or love of others in these new and limited ways, he still will not do much on his own behalf unless prompted and assisted. I have interpreted this as his continued feeling of being a child who longs for guidance and help with things, so now he will rebel and show his hurt and grievance by not being active or autonomous. He waits for his parents to become parents.

In the transference, we are more able to talk openly about how, through projective identification, he pulls me and invites me to be the one who stands for life, love, and longing while he stands for death, despair, and apathy. We go back and forth about what would be fun, useful, or important for him in his life, and then we talk about how he is so strongly opposed to any change, growth, or non-destructive pleasure. Instead, he gets me to be the one who thinks of it, is creative about it, and desires it. This element of the analytic treatment has been very important in his progress. The degree of change or reduction in emotional rigidity has been due to the continuous analysis of his projective identification–based transference and working with the intensity of his life- and death-instinct conflicts.

Over time, Z has relinquished some of his rigid adherence to the "fly high and die" approach to life and has stopped projecting so much into me. Instead, he has allowed in more of life and allowed himself to desire some degree of change. Z sees others with life-affirming feelings and thoughts and love for him as less of a threat or a hurtful reminder of something he wanted long ago and never got. So, the envy and grievance are not as much of a block to taking it in. While it is uncertain what the future holds for Z's treatment and his therapeutic journey, instead of flying high and dying, we have moments of taking flight and coming alive. Hopefully, this will continue.

SUMMARY

The goal of psychoanalytic treatment, whether short-term or long-term, frequent or infrequent, remains the same. The transformation of repetitive and maladaptive patterns of behavior, cognitive perspective, and relating is gradually resolved by working on the deeper internal and unconscious object relational dynamics that promote excessive reliance on such defenses as projective identification, splitting, idealization, and denial. The gradual exploration of transference, phantasy, and the interpersonal acting out of internal self and object roles is accomplished by analytic observation (Waska, unpublished) and interpretation. This creates a potential for integration, change, and a new way of experiencing the self and other.

Research (Vaughan and Roose, 1995) shows that the process of free association, resistance analysis, and interpretations that leads to a successful working-through of internal conflicts only occurs in 40 percent of analytic patients. This may be due to the high number of disturbed patients who come into private practice settings looking for help. These are the borderline (Kernberg, 1967), narcissistic, and psychotic patients who want relief from their anxiety and depressive states but also do not want to shift the psychic equilibrium they reside within (Joseph, 1989). My patient Z was certainly in this category, and I suspect, based on my counter-transference, that Y was also in this realm of psychic functioning.

When working with the uncontained, controlling, yet out-of-control nature of these more primitive patients, the analyst must accept a sense of confusion, helplessness, and lack of progress. Indeed, the analyst must find a way to have a fundamental faith in the therapeutic process, to believe that if we make the ongoing effort to establish analytic contact (Waska, 2007, 2011a, 2011b) there may be enough cumulative moments of insight, subtle change, or even a brief glimpse of life from a different vantage to allow our patients to have a chance to evolve and create new experiences of self and other at some point. We may be lucky enough to see that slight or sometimes radical shift, but we may have to be content in believing it may happen at some time down the road as a result of our assistance.

Galatariotou (2000) summarized the three elements of modern psychoanalytic approaches as transference analysis, working with pathological organizations, and the here-and-now interpretive process (Joseph, 1989). These are essential ways of working with all patients, but the more disturbed patients make these technical tasks more challenging by their acting out and rigid defensive systems that often take over the transference and lead to various enactments on the analyst's part (Steiner, 2000).

My clinical impression of Z has been that he desires the maternal love and union that could have been but never was, and now he is crippled by the longing for it, the envy of it, the denial of his hunger for it, and the rage and resentment over not having it. Yet, he fears this aggression will not only kill off his needed object but that it will also lead to a murderous revenge and retaliation from the object (Kavaler-Adler, 1993).

I think this is part of the horrible paranoia that keeps Z awake at night and is thinly and primitively symbolized by his "fly high and die" artwork. So, shifting from a world view of hate and loss to hope and love is the goal for Z, and probably the goal for Y as well. However, the mourning process can feel unbearable, especially for the more fragile patient. For both Y and Z, they were still splitting their objects into ideal, all good, but unobtainable pieces as well as into omnipotent, all bad, and hateful pieces. Y seemed to be lost in the quest and search for this mythical perfect object as a way to avoid facing the grief and rage he felt over the aspects of his object he resented. Z seemed lost in devaluing and attacking his object through projecting hatred into the world and into his art, unable to consider the more painful or vulnerable aspects of the positive side of himself and others. Indeed, while Y, in his delusional phantasies, seemed determined to search out, find, and possess his ideal object, Z seemed to have given up on ever finding any nurturing, soothing, or loving experience in himself or in others. He took that stand with pride, stubbornness, anger, and paranoia.

Much of my work with Z involved first making what I term analytic observations (Waska, unpublished). These are direct, containing, and firm translations of the patient's phantasies as acted out in the transference and extra-transference situations. These therapeutic observations are then followed with more traditional interpretations. Specifically, this involves making an informed analytic comment about *how*, in phantasy, patients are using their objects, where they are locating them in the dynamic object relational field, what value they bestow or steal away from those objects, and the type of conflict or harmony they equate with those objects.

Then, if possible, an interpretation is made as to the *why* of those matters, integrating the motivation and emotional reasoning of why patients color their internal relational world that way. This is in line with Hanna Segal's (Hunter, 1993) advice to try to understand patients' projections and then show them how they are doing that and gradually why they are doing that. This helps to find or locate, gather, and integrate the pieces of patients' minds that have been scattered about and lost due to the massive projective identification process so common with more disturbed patients.

Segal (1993) notes that more primitive patients rely so heavily on projective mechanisms that they are psychologically emptied, ending up with no real sense of self. Segal states that the object becomes the self and there is no difference between self and others. This is why I wondered about Y seeming to move into my office and into my life as if it were now his office and his power plug or his blurring phantasy of becoming one with his dead mother and back in the womb. Also, I noted how Z felt as hateful towards himself as he did towards others and as he imagined others felt towards him. It was all the same, a desperate persecutory blur.

Steiner (2011) notes how some patients hold on to their defensive systems in rigid and unyielding patterns that form organized and coordinated psychic contractions against the analytic goals of emotional expansion and vulnerability. They withdraw instead of risking or allowing any new emerging individuality that allows for the combination of dependence and autonomy. These pathological organizations give rise to psychic retreats (Steiner, 1993) that create difficult impasse states and moments of great uncertainty in the counter-transference.

One aspect of these pathological way stations or emotional foxholes is the enormous reliance on projective identification to ward off certain persecutory anxieties and depressive agonies. During the analytic process, the analyst must be willing and able to function as a temporary container (Bion, 1962) and help patients translate, modify, and metabolize their unbearable thoughts and feelings. This was a principle function I had to take on with Z and in the two sessions so far with Y. However, as Steiner (2000, 2011) notes, this has to be a temporary function since the goal of analysis with these more challenging patients includes the successful integration of the container function as their own. Rather than internalizing the containing analyst as an external helper that they must look to forever, we hope to help patients gradually mourn that analyst object and take that function over for themselves, becoming their own container objects.

Diagnostically, most patients like Y and Z can be understood as somewhere in the realm of borderline, narcissistic, or psychotic. Rosenfeld states,

> [A]nother essential aspect characteristic of all borderline conditions is the failure to internalize good objects which are necessary to strengthen the ego—the tendency of the borderline patient is to develop a transference psychosis or may lead to long lasting, repetitive acting out. This is often a desperate attempt by the patient to repair the disturbed link of mother and infant. However, the strong reparative drives are often covered by the chronic rage or despair. So, the traumatic situation is repeated in the analysis. (Rosenfeld, 1979, p. 204)

This lack of good objects is a major factor in the constant rage and despair which corrupts the reparative urges of the depressive position and leads to a pathological recycling of self-object dysfunction in place of genuine working-through. Effective analytic progress involves consistently targeting this pattern within the transference.

So, these patients suffer with a fragile, impoverished hold on or meager temporary taste of the depressive position as well as major and primary unresolved conflicts of the paranoid-schizoid world. This leads to overwhelming anxieties and a standoff with the good object.

Change and progress are deeply connected to the good object. In normal development, the good object is not only necessary for optimal growth, but the ego envisions the good object as encouraging and supporting growth. This is the life instinct in action. For Y, Z, and other patients who struggle against the good object, they are convinced it is a matter of time before the good object turns into a persecutory object (Waska, 2003). Often, change and progress are seen as the trigger to that catastrophe. This shift into a bad object is believed to happen by the changing, autonomous self-hurting and betraying the good object. Then, via projective identification, the good object becomes retaliatory and abandoning (Waska, 2004).

Part of why these patients are so difficult to work with is that they feel it is safer to keep the bad-object–bad-self relationship intact because it is under their control. The ego feels independent and fortified this way, compared to feeling dependent and vulnerable by making contact with the good object. To move toward the more whole-object status of the depressive position proper, is to accept that one is both dependent on the good object and at risk for hurting it or losing it. This threat is particularly harsh for these patients as it also means the collapse of the good and the return of evil and despair without shelter or hope. In other words, the hope and stability of the depressive position is lacking. Normally, there is faith that trouble can be rectified, the hurt object healed, and the loss tolerated and worked through. The good still exists side by side with the bad. I am highlighting patients who get halfway into the depressive mode of experiencing life, but fail to achieve, maintain, or regain the restorative aspects of it. The death instinct derails the healthy shift into depressive functioning, leaving the ego in a fight-or-flight mentality.

As Steiner (1987) notes, when these types of patients do make a move into the depressive position, it is very important to comment on and interpret these progressive moments. Doing so allows the patient a chance to reflect on and explore the anxieties that come with that change as well as the urge to start fighting off the good self–good object experience. This was the bulk of my interpretive efforts with Z.

Unresolved toxic paranoid-schizoid dynamics contaminate the ego's premature depressive venture. This creates the worst of both developmental experiences, pushing the ego to escape both, refusing to engage the very thing needed for healing and rescue: the good object. This dynamic is frequently punctuated by a brakes-on, psychological standoff, in which the patient refuses to allow contact with the good-object analyst or bypasses the good object and tries to construct an ideal, all-perfect being to become fused with. With patients such as Z, the individual is convinced it is better to hole up, stall out, and seal himself off from contact with the good object. The death instinct takes over as the primary method of experiencing the world and of coping with the frightening objects created by that perspective. Even though this creates paranoia, despair, and grievance, this inner agony is experienced as better than the dangerous movement toward the good object, whom they have no sense of control or trust. If you feel stuck in a minefield, it may be a terrible place to live, but it seems better to stay there than to try and venture out to the safer areas where no mines exist, because that journey to the better land could be fatal.

Psychoanalytic treatment, conducted from a Kleinian framework, links the patient's current psychological experience to early infantile and childhood interactions with the internal and external world (Steiner, 2004). As a result of greed, envy, frustration, and desire, the immature ego feels hatred toward the object, resulting in phantasies of an injured or dying object. As a result of identification, to ward off loss and guilt, the entire world seems to collapse and annihilation seems eminent. At that point, the history of contact with good objects is crucial to bring balance to this internal catastrophe. With ample good object experiences, the ego is able to approach and transition to the depressive position. There, mitigating factors such as guilt, integration of love and hate, reparation, restoration and forgiveness, compassion, and acceptance make it possible to make it through those overwhelming anxieties. There is a happy ending to the story. The self and the object are whole, good, and able to tolerate the inconsistencies, disappointments, and flaws that life, self, and others bring.

However, if there has been a lack of good-object experience, or if the good object has been tainted with abusive and painful experiences, the ego may not be able to tolerate the natural pain, despair, fear, and rage of living. This causes a breakdown of the internal world in which the very qualities that were potentially growth enhancing become disabling. Guilt feels very persecutory, reparation seems impossible, hate overcomes love, and compassion seems like a lie. Mutuality or dependence is deadly. The regressive qualities of the paranoid-schizoid position take over, making it feel worse, more ominous. So, the ego tries to block off both methods of relating and simply hides out or sets up a last-ditch standoff against the good object.

SECTION II

A Borderline Account of Disintegration and Eventual Integration

Four

John's Story

The life story of one of my patients in psychoanalytic treatment provides valuable insight into how actual life experiences shape a person's psychological viewpoint and how an individual organizes his or her object relational history unconsciously. Internal themes emerge based on a combination of unconscious conflicts regarding loving and hateful feelings and the desire for knowledge or answers along with the parallel conflict states of wanting to be loved, feeling attacked or unwanted, and hoping to be understood. Defensive systems and pathological organizations (Rosenfeld, 1987; Steiner, 1990, 1993) are built up and relied on but also become the limiting roadblocks our patients expect and find over and over again regardless of what else is in them or around them.

Melanie Klein and her contemporary followers have found there is always an important mix of actual external reality and vivid internal phantasy that combines to make up what the infant experiences and what the adult remembers. The Kleinian approach takes into account the actual external difficulties the infant has encountered with the environment and the failures of a parenting object to properly or successfully contain, modify, and translate the infant's internal emotional storms and mental confusions. These failures can be a result of parental dysfunction, infantile aggression or innate imbalances, external circumstances that extend past the coping abilities of both infant and caretaker, or a combination of all these factors.

This particular patient is a truly remarkable individual who has experienced years of disastrous external events and intense emotional reactions to his distorted view of life only to gradually emerge from his emotional rumble to become someone he is proud of and someone who contributes to life in an astounding way.

John told me his life story over the course of several years and in bits and pieces. I have condensed the initial portion of it for study in this chapter. By the time I started to treat John, he was fifty years old and a prominent figure in the field of social work, specializing in the field of child and adolescent research. He was celebrating over twenty years of a successful marriage, had a thriving career, and enjoyed many creative pursuits. However, it was not always such a bright picture.

John reports feeling extremely anxious and depressed from a very young age. From age thirteen to twenty-six, John lived an extremely destructive and disordered lifestyle. He has demonstrated intense borderline conflicts and acting out patterns based around loss, anger, and persecutory guilt (Grinberg, 1964) for most of his life. Drug addiction, alcoholism, suicide attempts, and self-mutilation were a regular aspect of his life for many years. Being sent to an inpatient facility for a year when he was sixteen, and to several psychiatric hospitals before that, was necessary. Many therapists over a span of thirty-five years slowly provided a sense of stability, but there were many painful and stormy times in between. Through most of these troubled times, John either avoided relationships with others altogether or found himself in very troubled and chaotic ones. Characteristic of early childhood trauma and more primitive ego functioning, John felt a constant flux of desperate need and idealization mixed with dread, suffocation, and distance seeking. It was only by the gradual process of change in his pathological reliance on projective identification from something very aggressive and needy to a more healthy process of internalization that he was able to modify his internal confusion and conflict.

This transition from a more destructive paranoid-schizoid (Klein, 1946) position to a more adaptive depressive position (Klein, 1935; 1940) has taken John a lifetime of hard work and struggle with many moments of disorganization along the way.

In an interview (Hunter, 1993), Hanna Segal notes that in the more narcissistic or borderline state of mind, destructive cycles of projective identification eliminate any symbolic function and create problems in thinking and relating. Perception is distorted by phantasy. This leaves the subject emotionally lost and unable to organize his or her experience of the world, except through very basic and primitive methods such as massive splitting, idealization, and devaluation. As a result, the patient is without an object that can translate beta into alpha (Bion, 1962) and without the internalization of that vital modifying ability.

However, bit by bit, John found a way to internalize more helpful objects and in turn had more phantasies of becoming a helpful object to those in need. This is still a work in progress, as he still sometimes courts an ideal object and still sometimes wants to become an ideal object for some helpless other. So, this naturally brings about feelings of failure and disappointment that are difficult to bear. However, over time, this has become more manageable. These are current and remaining issues John struggles with, but the real focus of this chapter will be the narrative he shared with me and the object relational plot that emerged, which still finds its way into his life.

When John came into treatment, he clearly stated both his desire to understand himself combined with his reluctance to look into the mirror. He said, "I don't want to be here. I am sick of dragging around these memories and these reactions to life. I just want to forget it all and be a blank slate. But, I know that is impossible. I spent many years trying to bury my feelings and thoughts and that only made it a whole lot worse. So, I think I want to finally take the time to just tell my story. I want to lay it out from start to finish. Well, at least from start to now. I have a lot of hopes for the finish but I just get so unsure, so mistrusting, so lost. Actually, I was lost. Now, I feel like I have more of a map but my GPS gets screwed up sometimes. By telling you my story and maybe learning something from it along the way, I want to end up with a better map, one I can count on even if I have to take a detour sometimes. I will do my best to start at point A and go to point Z, but I will probably zigzag along the way."

So, we began a psychoanalytic journey in which John did go from point A to Z and faced the totality of his life by sharing his life story with me. He challenged the traumatic and unresolved aspects of his life while recounting and cherishing the sweet and fortifying memories as well. In telling his story, John undid some of the more pathological projective identification cycles he was used to using and instead continued to build upon some of the more positive identifications with internalized objects that he could go to in times of need. He still would slip into periods of darkness in which he felt lost and close to giving up, but he was now more and more able to find himself when necessary and slowly refuel using his own inner resources.

In trying to trace John's early life and its impact on his way of experiencing life, one is struck by the sense of unpredictable change, loss, and consequential withdrawal. An insecure emotional foundation seems to be at the core of John's personality.

John was born to parents who worked for the government and moved around the world every three or four years. This constant transition and instability seemed to be part of what formed severe cracks in John's psychological foundation. His relationship with his family was problematic and the way he viewed himself and others was brittle, fragile, and prone to collapse.

John was born with medical issues that kept him in hospital for the first few months after his birth. His parents were frantic they would lose their only child. He made it through a painful and traumatic entrance to the world but it was the start to a lifetime pattern of separation and trouble with attachment. In John's recounting of his early life, he told me the details of his parents' own difficult and dysfunctional backgrounds with divorce, alcoholism, and violence. This left them to be anxious, controlling, and insecure individuals as well as caring but awkward and parents who avoided encounters with deeper feeling states. The combination of John's forced hospital separation from his mother and his mother's anxious and distant nature seemed to create an emotional divide between infant and caretaker.

From a Kleinian perspective, there was an unfortunate mismatch in early attachment that led to vicious and complicated unconscious phantasy states. These, in turn, created inner conflict that emerged interpersonally.

John's parents employed a local woman who was their maid and nanny. John developed an intense attachment to her. In this relationship, he formed an internal psychological image of an all-good nanny and ideal mother. Over time, we came to understand how this internal phantasy was pitted against John's unconscious view of his actual mother as a bad or unreachable mother. He looked to this nanny as the mother he could emotionally run to for understanding and love, a respite from the confusing and conflicted feelings he had with his real mother, whose own fearful view of the world made her seem overbearing, overwhelming, and threatening to John. This important but distorted bond with the nanny was shattered when John's family moved when he was three years old. This experience of loss seems to have followed and haunted John for decades to come.

When John's parents moved to Italy, they were one year into their marriage, and John was born. Relaying various conversations with his mother over the years, John told me, "My mother was extremely nervous about having a child. In some really awkward conversations, I learned she was overwhelmed with worry about her ability to care for me. For example, she worried about having enough breast milk because she was thin and believed this was somehow correlated to milk production. This kind of irrational fear is her trademark. I can only guess that my father had his hands full trying to calm her down. Why does she have such a scary view of the world? Maybe it was her own crazy upbringing. Her parents divorced when she was an infant and her stepfather was an alcoholic and a member of the Ku Klux Klan. Maybe some of my mother's obsessive, anxious, negative ways are the result of her early experiences. I guess the demons just keep on chasing you down, one generation to the next." Here was evidence of John trying to understand his mother instead of being overwhelmed with hatred, fear, or anxiety. This more positive use of projective identification is a hallmark of individuals more able to function in the depressive realm (Klein, 1935, 1940).

John told me his mother's stepfather later sobered up and seemed like a nice guy when John knew him as his grandfather. John told me, "For some reason, I was impressed and even proud to find out that he kept not one but two loaded shotguns in the house. One was for white intruders and the other, a more lethal caliber, for any black trespassers. He grew up in Texas, drove a pickup truck, and wore a cowboy hat. He told tough stories about working on oil rigs and making moonshine. I looked up to him but never felt I knew how to relate to him. I remember feeling intimidated but grateful when he took me in his pickup truck down to the hardware store to buy me some pellets for the BB gun he let me use when visiting. He was in his usual cowboy hat and two-day-old whiskers, looking gruff and weathered. We didn't talk on the drive and I felt nervous the whole time, but I could tell he was doing something nice for me and that felt good."

Here, John seemed to struggle with trying to identify with an image that didn't quit fit his own self but nevertheless he was drawn to the kindness and attention this man showed him. In some ways, it seemed John was able to see, on a deeper level, that this man was very defended and distant on the outside but still kind and good on the inside, much like John was and still is.

John remembers his grandmother on his mother's side as a very giving and forgiving woman who "treated me like we were in a Hallmark greeting card. She would sit me down in a cushy recliner with milk and cookies on a tray in front of my favorite television show. How much better could it get? She fussed over me and always seemed interested in what I was up to." I interpreted that John's view of her and his feelings towards her were reminiscent of his vision of the Italian nanny. He had found another good, yet idealized, object to cling to in his mind.

In a touching moment, John recalled "difficult times in my early twenties when I was depressed and overcome with drugs and drinking. My grandmother wrote me a letter that basically said, 'I know you are having a hard time. Just hang in there and keep trying. I love you no matter what.' Years later, I tried to return the favor when I called her at the convalescent home shortly before she died and had the nurse put the phone to her ear so I could tell her, 'I know you are having a hard time. Just hang in there. I love you.'" Here, John clearly benefited from the internalization and identification with a good loving object that he felt understood and accepted by. Unfortunately, the understanding and love had to emerge as part of a terrible loss and farewell.

In telling me about the other side of his family, I learned that John's father grew up in a chaotic and violent environment. He lost two siblings to illness before he was ten, and both his parents were alcoholics. John's father told him about times when "my parents chased each other around the house with knifes, yelling and screaming." From John's description, John's father found it very difficult to relate to John without being very awkward or judgmental at the same time. It was clear to John that there was some sort of great guilt and sadness his father always had towards him, as if he felt he had really failed John or made some misstep along the way in parenting. But, because there was rarely any open communication between John and his father, it remained an awkward and strained relationship.

John's grandfather on his father's side died of a heart attack at a fairly young age, and John's uncle died from alcoholism. John told me, "I remember spending time with my father's mother. She was always drinking way too much beer and crying about how her kids were not taking care of her. We would spend the afternoon in her cramped apartment with her collection of Don Ho "Live from Hawaii" records from her one big vacation she took ten years prior. We had to sit on her fuzzy furniture from the sixties, which smelled from her Pall Mall cigarettes. I felt sad for her but also turned off by those big hair curlers, the ugly bathrobe, and the slippers that she wore way too long into the afternoon. When she approached me with a Pabst Blue Ribbon beer in one hand and a Pall Mall in the other and said, 'Give ME a hug,' I felt she was taking instead of giving."

Here, we see John's inner skill at sizing up people and having an understanding of their psychological underpinnings. This was a skill he would later refine when he became an important figure in the social work field. However, we can also see his sensitivity to the cold mother who takes instead of gives and the black and white vision of his other "Hallmark greeting card" grandmother versus this "drunken loser" grandmother with a beer and cigarette in her hand instead of a plate of cookies and a hug. While this might have been the harsh reality of his two grandmothers, it also seemed to be a part of his splitting of emotional perspectives.

When John was a newborn infant in Italy, there were external conditions that shaped his internal experiences. In his first days of life, he developed pneumonia and a staph infection, so he was isolated in the hospital for a month. His mother was beside herself. She was sure she would lose her first and only child. John's parents have told him how pained they were to visit their sickly newborn and hear him shriek in pain and discomfort.

Over the years, John has asked his mother about her memories of his early years. Starting with her pregnancy, his mother told him, "I felt terrific the whole nine months. I felt very smug, looking at other women and thinking to myself, 'Ha! I am pregnant and you are not!' It was awful to have you so sick and in the hospital for so long after you were born. We finally took you home, but you kept coming down with bronchitis which kept turning into pneumonia. After one or two years, you got over it."

John told me, "Although my parents never came out and said it, it seems clear they feared losing me in that first year or two. It was only decades later that I could trace my aversion to hospitals and my dreams of dying in a hospital bed to this early trauma. But, I think that anxiety is also the result of my mother's constant worries and her worst-case scenario way of thinking. When she asks me if my cold is better or if I am eating right, there is something ominous, always some kind of life or death meaning to it."

John shared a recent interaction with his mother that gave some insight into his own struggle with feeling safe and stable in the world. He said, "My mother is seventy-eight years old and she told me last week that 'the joys of motherhood are about constantly worrying and making sure to always remember that the worst can easily happen. It is foolish to think positively.' Something that bleak has probably affected me. 'Something is always around the corner' is the message. I don't want to have that be my motto!"

Regarding his feelings about his nanny in Italy, John said, "In my heart, I think of her as my first mother, the one who showed me love in a way that mattered, a type of mothering that matched what I really needed so much at that point." Italian became John's first language, and he played with the nanny and followed her around as she cooked and cleaned.

John described what he felt to be an extreme difference in his relationship to these first two women in his life. He told me the nanny was someone who "gave me unconditional love and stability. On the other hand, my mother was and is a very anxious woman. She alternates from barely concealed rage and bitterness to a charming, kind person who obsessively chatters without ever stopping. I think she just didn't really know how to be a mother." These two extremes seem to have contributed to John's way of sometimes seeing his adult world as very black or white.

Continuing to describe his memory of this Italian nanny, John said "My image of her is of a chubby, smiling, middle-aged woman with an apron on and her arms outstretched, ready to catch me if I fell." Unfortunately, much of John's internal life has been an experience of feeling as though he is indeed falling and no one is there to ever catch him. So, he has the ideal object as an unobtainable entity, always out of reach while he struggles and suffers to find it. Peace of mind is impossible when in that state, only chilling emptiness and deprivation.

After three years in Italy, John's parents were reassigned to Jamaica. With deep difficulty, he shared: "I believe that leaving this woman who cared for me was something that truly left me feeling lost for most of my life. My mother's description of it is telling. She said, 'As we got on the train and said goodbye to your nanny, you started screaming. You were completely inconsolable.'" John added, "To this day, that feels like too much to endure. I want to turn away."

John said that his mother has told him, "When we packed up to leave, you didn't think you would see your toys again, especially the tricycle. You sat under the dining room table holding on to your tricycle and some favorite toys as the packers slowly put everything away in boxes and then took the boxes away."

Perhaps because of such experiences, John finds himself overly sensitive to anything associated with grief. Any story of tragic loss, a heroic tale of the underdog, the play about a hard-luck orphan, or television shows about the separations of wartime all grab him in the most unsettling way. The haunting melody from a sad movie, the news story of a mother searching for her lost infant at the mall, or even a cartoon about the ant family trying to find its way back to the colony all leave him troubled. In his words, "That stuff all makes me overly sentimental, and too sensitive. It grabs me by the throat." The "by the throat" phrase also shows the intense and violent aggression John projects and then feels threatened and attacked by. This rage, when projected, makes the world seem dangerous and John then isolates himself from that threat. But, this retreat only increases his sense of exclusion and internal hunger.

Now away from his beloved nanny, John faced both a crippling sense of loss and the new challenge of integrating with other children as he entered school for the first time in Jamaica. This proved to be an intimidating, foreign experience that left him lonely and quite detached from others, only promoting his already growing role as isolated outsider looking through the window and watching everyone go about their business. He wanted to be a part of it at times, but mostly shunned it and felt scared of it. This way of being separate and watching the world from afar left John safe in one way but quite alienated and rejected in another.

During his time in psychoanalytic treatment, John has worked hard to understand his past and its impact on his adult life. He was frustrated that there were almost no memories of his time in Italy and not much from his time in Jamaica. In corresponding with his parents, his mother offered to tell him what she could remember. This was a mixed bag. He said, "My mother has some interesting memories of what those times must have been like for me. It is an odd feeling when someone else holds your memories for you. Can you trust them? How have they filtered them, censored them, or added to them? And, how come my father never says anything about his memories? That makes me feel weird too."

John told me his parents were often gone, out at parties. They left him at home with a babysitter. Since he was the only child, he felt on his own many nights. John said, "I think my parents tried to make up for it by buying me whatever I wanted. My parents tell me that when I was four and five years old, I developed a habit of having temper tantrums and would frequently smash my best toys. Also, I would try and kick my father. My parents thought this was simply the result of me being too spoiled. I think I might have been angry at being left alone all the time. I was lashing out at them. Maybe, I was trying to tell them that I didn't want their gifts, I wanted their company."

John told me one memory from his time in Jamaica involving a bicycle ride. It was the big day of finally riding without training wheels. His father helped him to push off but with a look of intense apprehension. John recalls a mix of fear and excitement for himself and the idea that this "was more about his father than about me. I may be putting my own feelings on him though so I am not sure how to see it."

Here, John was insightful in wondering if he tried to place his anxiety into his father or if his father was unable to control his own anxiety and John felt overwhelmed by it in some way. This is the type of dilemma Bion and other Kleinians have explored in terms of the normal or pathological aspects of projective identification as well as the emotional dynamic of container and contained (Bion, 1962; Cartwright, 2010).

Another window into John early feelings and view of the world came through his descriptions of his first pet, a dog. He told me, "I grew quite attached to him. I think I used him to deal with my loneliness. I recall sitting on the driveway next to him. Like the image at school, I felt there was the world out there and then there was me and the safety of the dog. It was an attachment to the dog, but more of a bond based on survival, like the image of the two soldiers back-to-back firing at the advancing enemy. It was us against the world. And, it is only a matter of time before they get us." So, an important attachment was quickly shaped into a bond with something special that was then in contrast to all the rest, the dangerous "enemy."

In these ways, John's early psychic conflicts colored much of his outlook on life, and his view on life contaminated his internal world. This is a fundamental dynamic in projective identification and the way the inner world constantly influences the outer world and then in reverse. So, internalization and identification can be an enriching and satisfying experience or a constant frightening reassurance of how terrible the world and oneself are.

In Jamaica, John made friends with the five-year-old girl next door, had a new puppy, and learned how to ride his bicycle. But, he felt he had to ride well to please his father, never felt able to be an equal with the girl, and felt the dog to be his sole protector against the unpredictable world "out there."

So, the ordinary or even joyful events of childhood often took on this precarious nature.

Another memory revealed something more troubled about his early years. John told me that while playing at home, he accidentally broke a window and cut his arm from elbow to armpit. He said, "It should have been stitched up, but I felt I had done something wrong. I held my arm close to my side for hours, trying to hide it. Luckily, the pressure stopped the bleeding so I didn't need to get stitches." Here, there was evidence of some deep feelings of guilt, shame, or the lack of trust in his caregivers.

This incident was somewhat like another in which his parents were having a dinner party and John was in the back yard playing. He disturbed a hornet's nest by swinging too high on the swing and knocking it off a limb. He was stung repeatedly and was obviously in great pain, but went quietly through the party and retreated into his room to hide. "I thought I had been bad. Of course, when my parents realized what was going on, they rushed me to the hospital to be sure I was OK. So, they were kind and caring, but I thought they would be angry."

Here, there was evidence of how John may have internalized, over time, a distorted image of objects to identify with who were kind, caring, and giving but also judgmental, cruel, and not to be trusted. Perhaps this might be one factor in explaining John's lifelong blend of trying to help others and doing a great deal of good work to provide support to the underdog but also acting out in disturbing and destructive ways that left him hating himself and others.

This sort of separateness, isolation, and dark view of what others were thinking of him as a small child in Jamaica came out in another of John's early memories. He told me about his first days of school when he moved there. He said, "I remember standing on the playground and feeling very alone. I recall staring past the playground and parking lot over to a great expanse of open land, lush with trees and bushes. To me, it was nearly a forest. I felt very lonely and scared so I wanted to be over hiding in the forest. On one hand, this felt even more lonely, me and the forest far away from all the other kids. But, there was some sense of safety and calm in that. I felt different from my classmates and imagined them from my imaginary perch in the forest. I pictured them in their own group very separate from me. I didn't fit in and I didn't want to fit in."

This insight into his feelings and his own active role in those feelings was a hallmark of John's reflective and curious nature. His ability to consider his own psychology often brought about pain and fear but ultimately was his salvation. The healthy quest for knowledge is a cornerstone of mental health in the Kleinian model. To see knowledge as valuable and to want to know more about oneself and others is the way through so much of life's confusions and hardship. Of course, John's desire to be known was in direct conflict with his anxiety with and anger towards others, so there was often a psychological standoff in this area.

One problematic element in John's early development was his father's high expectations. John said, "I think he expected too much out of me. It felt like he was always criticizing what I accomplished for not being enough. In first and second grade, I would come home with a report card that had all A's and one B. He would focus on the B and ask me to explain what happened."

In exploring his feelings about this, John has looked at the possibility that he has taken on this strictness and made it his own. In our explorations, we have considered how John has identified in part with his father as a much needed but cruel guide to both please and dread. So, he has internalized this experience of pressure and demand and made it his own. John said, "Now I am the one who wants an A in whatever it is and if I don't get it I feel like a big F. If I do get the A, I just a check the box and move onto the next task. But, if the box isn't checked, something very bad must have happened."

John's family lived in Jamaica for three years and then they traveled to the United States by boat to stay in Washington, DC, for a period. Discussing the boat trip from Jamaica to America, John recalled being left in the childcare room while his parents went to dinner. He said, "I felt scared and lonely. The room had all the necessary toys, the laughing and crying kids, and the resident babysitter. Going over to the little mock-up kitchen, I just sat there mindlessly playing with something, but felt scattered and alone. Maybe, I was in this kids' toy kitchen to get away from the other kids in the room, but in my mind I was at the pretend dinner table with my parents instead of in this scary place without them. I also remember playing shuffle board on the ship. I must have been playing with one of my parents. I think it was my father. But, I keep the memory as a fun, satisfying moment with the shuffle board equipment, the view from the deck, the handsome wood on the boat deck, and so forth. I took the people out of it." So, his disconnection from people and the relational world grew and the conflicts John felt about the world expanded.

John's family moved into a small studio apartment in Washington while his father prepared for his next assignment. John went to an elementary school just down the block. John's memory of the apartment was of a very stark, almost confining room with his parents' bed in the middle and his little cot over in the corner. There was a small kitchen to eat meals in. He recalls, "Eating in that kitchen was a blunted, uncomfortable, and strange experience. I was detached, not really thinking much, but feeling like I was in a strange, awkward, and strained atmosphere, combined with bland, boring food. I felt trapped, zapped of energy and hope, and confined in a depressing tension-filled space that felt way too small. I felt like I was an alien, watching strangers sit in front of me, no connection, no aliveness, and no warmth."

Much later in his psychotherapy treatment, John told me of feeling exactly the same way when he ate meals with his parents as a teenager and as an adult when they came to visit. This sense of being an alien in a depressing, deadened place was the way John felt later in life when he embarked on a cycle of drugs, self-mutilation, and alcoholism. As with all pathological projective identification methods of coping, this acting out only created a deeper experience of despair, anger, and desolation.

The elementary school in Washington was a place where John also felt like the oddball. He told me, "I definitely did not go out of my way to make friends. I kept to myself. In the classroom, I recall always sitting in the back of the room, feeling isolated and unconnected to the other kids. Sort of like breakfast time with my parents. Most of these kids had been going to this school with each other for some time. I just dropped in for the semester in-between living in Jamaica and moving to Rumania. So, I wasn't part of the friendships that already existed."

John went on to say, "One method the school had for encouraging the learning of spelling was to have a word in big print on a piece of paper. Each student would be given a straight pin to prick the outline of the word, hopefully remembering the shape of each letter as well as the whole word. I was in the back of the class, struggling to properly prick my word, but not really knowing what I was supposed to be doing. I accidentally pricked my finger and it started to bleed. Similar to the time in Jamaica when I was injured, I thought I did something wrong and did not imagine it was OK to ask for help." Here, there seemed to be a deep psychological fusion between his feelings of suffering, masochism, guilt over wrongdoing, persecutory anxieties, and blood. This may have built up unconscious phantasies and conflicts that set the stage for the times John engaged in self-mutilation later in his life.

John went on to tell me he had a few good memories of his childhood days in Washington, "wedged in between all that other crap." He said, "The walk from school back to the apartment felt peaceful, quiet, calming, and even reassuring. The apartment had an old-fashioned elevator with a sliding accordion door which felt very safe and familiar to me. Its old, musty smell somehow calmed me." This was interesting, as he was describing how the transitional times in between feeling disconnected from others at school and feeling tense and alone in the presence of his parents were the most calming times. It was the transitional area between the uncomfortable school time and the confining, awkward home life that gave John a sense of respite and relief. This is part of his still-present pattern of always looking to the next project but not feeling calm or relaxed once he arrives at it. Instead, he thinks of the next project. Therefore, he seems only content in that in-between area, the in-motion and not-settled or not-connected space.

After this six-month stay in the United States, John and his family moved to Rumania where they would live for the next two years. On the way there, the family stopped in Italy to sightsee and visit before driving on to Rumania. This was a special time and a special memory for John because he spent one night with his Italian nanny at her home. At this point, neither one of them knew enough Italian or English to have much of a conversation. But, John told me, "That did not matter. We did not need spoken language to get along. We understood each other just fine." He was sad as he told me this bittersweet memory of returning to someone so important in his life but having to say goodbye again. Again, there was a sense of ideal unity stolen from him.

When John's family arrived in Rumania, they moved into a large flat on one floor of a tall building where one other American family and many locals lived. John recalls the drab, depressing concrete buildings around town, reflective of the oppressive communist regime. It was a horrible time for the country in which the average citizen was constantly scared of being imprisoned, the economy was in ruins, and people lived in poverty, fear, and despair.

John managed to make some friends in the neighborhood, but since he only spoke English, he felt, "like a lone explorer in a strange, foreign land." During his stay in Rumania, he completed third and fourth grade in an international school. John told me, "I felt more a part of the crowd on the playground than I did in Jamaica, but I recall still watching everyone from afar. This sense of me versus them was still there."

One day, John cut his hand rather deeply on a toy fire truck while his parents were out one day. Much like the incidents in Jamaica, he said, "I felt profoundly guilty, like I had done something very bad or wrong. I tried to close up the cut by pushing the flesh together and running water over it, but the bleeding would not let up. I went to our neighbor who was a nurse and she put a bandage on it. Forty years later, there is still a big scar on my hand from what I felt to be a crime, something my parents would be angry or unhappy about. In reality, they were not upset; they were only concerned for my health."

This seemed to show the deep psychological issues of anger, judgment, fear, and mistrust that John carried around inside himself that he projected outwards. In excessive or pathological projective identification, toxic or unwanted feelings and phantasies are jettisoned into the object. If the object cannot filter these and return it in a more integrated form, the ego is left fragmented. Also, if the person projecting these volatile feelings does not want to have them returned, they are left empty and fragmented. So, the anger inside John remained an overwhelming entity, and he felt enormous guilt over what he was doing to his object at times, and other times this seemed to be more of a persecutory guilt in which he dreaded whatever rule he felt he had broken and what punishment lay ahead. It is unclear how or if his parents tried to help him understand that they were not angry like he envisioned, but regardless of what actually took place, John was left with this intense internal conflicts that felt unbearable. Again, this early experience may on some level have influenced John's self-mutilation later in life, in which he cut on himself when feeling overwhelmed with anger, guilt, anxiety, and despair. He became the object that he acted out upon.

Living in a communist country such as Rumania was a strange experience for John, as it would be for most people. But, for a child it was particularly odd. He often overheard his parents "talking about listening devices planted in the house, how the mail was read before we got it, how they needed to shred any documents before disposing of them, how the maid was a planted spy, and how ordinary people walking down the street were sometimes dragged into the cars of the secret police."

In this sometimes scary and very different land, John constructed fantasy worlds of adventure where he would venture out into the neighborhood on a quest, riding his bicycle into the unknown streets. Also, he would explore what felt to be the vast, cavernous hallways and stairways in his apartment building. In the basement, there were elderly Rumanians living in cramped, ancient one-room apartments. He said, "Some would give me strange looks and others welcomed me with friendly smiles and handfuls of unshelled sunflower seeds they sold in the market from big burlap bags. To this day, those little nuts bring me back to those crusty, old people who without the benefit of a common language managed to impart a gesture of kindness that made an impact on me." Here, we can see the growth of good internal experiences alongside the other more paranoid or sad ways of experiencing the world. The fact that John was able on some level to internalize and identity with these kind strangers was remarkable but also extremely fortunate, since as a result he was not completely overrun with these more primitive and disturbing visions of others that he also internalized.

During his time in Rumania, John realized Santa Claus was something parents make up for their children. He said, "I didn't want to shatter my parent's joy of believing that I believed. I pictured them being disappointed and sad. I tried to protect my parents by faking it. On Christmas morning, as I walked down the stairs to the Christmas tree, I felt tense and nervous that my stage act would not work. What if they saw through my act? They would be crushed! I felt responsible for their emotional well-being, for their Christmas fantasy."

Here, John was describing more depressive anxieties of hurting the object and not being able to take proper care of his objects. While a healthy development in some ways, John seemed to be describing the overwhelming task of having to take care of those who are supposed to take care of you. To see his objects as that weak or fragile meant John could not rely on them to protect him or take care of his needs. This is a more dysfunctional or perverted level of depressive position (Klein, 1935, 1940) functioning.

Turning to another topic, John explained, "One day, my parents told me I needed to go somewhere with them. It seemed mysterious and they acted peculiar. We arrived at a big building surrounded by a big black iron fence. Years later, I know it was the U.S. Embassy, but at the time I was seized with fear and had no idea where we were. They told me everything was OK and led me inside and down a sterile, quiet stairway. A doctor came out and I panicked. My parents handed me over to him and he took me inside an office. I was very upset and became hysterical. My pants were forced off and I was given a shot. Terror and a sense of betrayal is what I remember. It was one more blow to my sense of trust. Traveling around the globe, injections and inoculations are routine. Probably, I was already very averse to getting them, so this might have been the strategy my parents came up with. But the way I experienced it was traumatic." In his recounting of this incident, John shows the more integrated insightful ability he has mastered through his years in various treatments with various therapists and his own hard work taming some of his internal demons. But, the sense of betrayal, abandonment, and the sense of emotional rape that is conveyed in this memory is at the core of what left John to slip into such a complicated and destructive borderline world and how he still struggles with remnants of such phantasies and feelings. Klein and her followers respect the impact of both the external and internal world on the personality. Clearly, John was subjected to many actual traumatic events without much mitigation or soothing from his primary objects. At the same time, we have to notice that these are the events he remembers the most and not any others. So, he has filtered out and selected certain aspects of his experience and cast them into emotional stone.

It has taken John a lifetime of personal work and therapeutic assistance to gradually uncast that stone. Also, life is never black or white when it comes to a person's life history and that person's caretakers' intentions. Life is usually a messy mix of good and bad. While John's parents seemed to try to spare their son any grief or worry by not telling him what was coming around the corner at the embassy, this strategy seemed to bring greater grief and fear into his life.

In 1965, John's family moved to Africa, where they were to live for the next three years. Here, John seemed to continue having a deep sense of isolation but also felt a greater freedom and fulfillment about the world. He told me, "I distinctly remember walking off the plane at the airport. It was remarkably hot and very humid. It was dawn and the sun was casting golden shadows on the palm trees, making everything look magical and enchanting. I felt I had landed in a strange land and I felt unsure, but curious and excited." John's family moved into a nice two-story home complete with gardener, cook, houseboy, and night watchman. The servants lived in a separate building in the back yard, and the huge yard was filled with exotic plants, banana trees, and colorful flowers. The neighbors had peacocks in their yards.

John told me, "To me, my house and the neighborhood were one big exciting jungle to explore. I climbed up on the roof of our house, I scaled every tree in the yard, and I climbed over the concrete wall that surrounded the whole property. I rode my bicycle as if on a special secret mission to explore this uncharted land. I found my way through the village a few blocks away where the locals lived in their meager one- or two-room shacks with thin tin roofs and open sewer gutters. I would borrow the gardener's machete and hack my way through dense areas that literally were a jungle, again fantasizing that I was on some exotic adventure. However, when I look back at how I was hacking at everything with such a vengeance, I think I was a pretty angry kid."

It is interesting that the same sense of betrayal and trauma that threaded through most of John's life appeared in an Africa memory so much like it had in the Rumania memory. John told me of a day when his mother drove him to an unknown location and when they got there he realized he was going to see a doctor, presumably for an inoculation. He refused to get out of the car and fought back with all his might. Eventually, the doctor came out and had to take John in physically. While no kids like to get shots, John's reactions to this and his memory of it point to a much darker or intense meaning for him that echoed his overall experience of life as a place without safety or trust.

It is a memory of betrayal. It is a memory of being taken from a place of comfort and safety with a primary object to being turned over to a foreign place of pain. This sense of being torn away from home and placed in peril is at the core of John's internal conflicts.

At this point, John must have been a difficult, confusing, and frightening child for his parents at times. Unfortunately, that is also how he felt about them. So, there was no longer a good emotional fit, a good enough attachment between them for emotional growth, soothing, or pleasure.

John's family moved to Africa in the middle of a local civil war. The nation was divided and the government's military was killing the opposing tribe. Therefore, there were armed gunman at checkpoints on the street, tanks rolling down the block, and an occasional killing in the neighborhood. It is interesting that from age six to ten, John lived in the very bleak, dangerous, and difficult political climates of Rumania and Africa but never much reacted to them as such. One could say he was just being blind as kids often are, but it was more that his internal struggles were so strong and easily matched the ominous and strange nature of his outside environment that he in fact remembered these experiences as often being interesting and exciting. Indeed, John found Nigeria to be the best place he had lived in up to then. He loved exploring the area on his bicycle, hiking in the nearby jungle, and essentially playing spy or explorer in an unknown land.

One example of John's inner struggles involved a memory of a Boy Scout meeting in which the Scouts were being instructed on how to tell the height of a tree by the length of its shadow. John said he had absolutely no idea what the instructor meant and was mystified by the whole discussion. He said, "I felt scared, stupid, and very anxious. So, I thought I should just act like I understood because it felt like it would be worse to admit my ignorance. Part of it was me not understanding the math concept. But, most of it was about me feeling alienated, strange, and nervous around these other people and desperately trying to blend in. It was this terrible sense of 'over there is them' and 'over here is me.' We are so separate and different. I wanted to escape but I had to stay and pretend."

Here, we see the phantasy of possible persecution or punishment for not knowing and needing help overshadowing the lesser intense reality of simply not getting the math problem and needing to ask for help. This type of severe anxiety and internal conflict can create learning difficulties for some individuals as well as relational problems, as it did for John. In other words, troubles in the internal world can block any external growth, and for borderline patients the external world often looks identical to the internal world without any hint of as-if quality and no ability to reflect on the differences.

On the other hand, John felt more positive and enjoyed things in ways he hadn't before. Building model airplanes became a passion, and he dabbled in developing a small neighborhood newspaper made with a toy printing kit. He loved swimming at the local country club where he bought British comic books whenever he could, ate fries with vinegar in the English tradition, and spent his allowance on strange candies from a local vendor. John said, "I loved the Smarties, the English equivalent of M&M's but much bigger. I loved the roll of Trebor Mints, the strongest mint you ever tasted!" All this made him feel happy and excited. However there were elements of rebellion and protest that crept in as well. John also began experimenting with smoking cigarettes, readily available to anyone at the roadside stands.

Despite some more positive experiences while living in Africa, John continued to feel like a stranger in a strange land. He didn't have any friends to speak of, although he did spend time with one boy in the neighborhood. They played with toy soldiers and rode bikes.

In general, however, John felt apart. He was beat up several times at school and started to feel different from the other kids. He said, "I felt like they were the enemy so I kept my distance."

When John looks back on his parents during this and other times, he feels they were not very involved with his emotional life, but certainly made sure he had all his material needs met. He told me, "My mother said my father felt so guilty about dragging me around the world that he would buy me anything I asked for. As a child, I had the feeling that when I tried to express myself honestly, my parents would either make fun of me in telling me I was cute, dismiss me, or just plain not understand me."

John expressed this experience of neglect with various angry and desperate reactions. Just like he did in Jamaica, he would destroy his favorite toys. Since the toys had come from his parents, it was a way to lash out at them but also punish himself. When bad objects or ambivalent objects are internalized, the ego will attack itself. Depression, self-mutilation, and suicide are some of the results in patients who seek revenge upon their internal objects with whom they have identified.

John ran away for much of one day, after leaving a letter outlining his grievances. When he came back at the end of the day, "My parents thought it was cute and teased me." John said, "I was showing them my feelings through my actions, but they didn't get the message."

It was during his time in Africa that John developed an interest in music. This started with his listening to some of his parents' records. But, he also found other records and seemed to cultivate a real hodgepodge of tastes that reflected the mixed and complicated feelings he had. So, John enjoyed the hipster sound of Bobby Darin, the basic rock and roll of the Beatles, the childish fun of "Snoopy vs. the Red Baron," the late sixties craze of short-lived bands like Paul Revere and the Raiders and the Monkees, and dark songs by bands singing about the Vietnam war and the massacres America was responsible for. Fifth and sixth grade was a time when all these angry, fun loving, immature, and sophisticated feelings began to fuse together.

One of the most idyllic memories John has of his time in Africa was of a safari trip the family took one year. They traveled to Kenya and began a two-week loop that took them through several enormous game reserves, across plains, and up Mount Kilimanjaro. They spent the days locating and observing every type of wild animal one can imagine: elephants, rhinos, hippos, antelopes, cheetahs, monkeys, giraffes, birds, and alligators. They took a canoe down the Nile River, slept in a tent near Dr. Leakey's famous excavation site, sat around a campfire listening to the nearby elephants moving about, laughed with local tribal members, bottle-fed an orphaned zebra, parked next to a pride of lions, and walked among thousands of bright flamingos feeding at a lake. For years, John fantasized about returning to Africa to become a park ranger, defending the animals from poachers and helping the underprivileged people. He said, "Mostly, I picture helping the animals. That is more comfortable than dealing with people." The idea of protecting and saving the endangered seemed to be a way of reaching out to help in the way he wished someone would have done for him.

As we follow John's narrative, over and over we find the same basic elements of loss, mistrust, idealization followed by emotional distress, and a jagged and distorted method of experiencing the world due to primitive projective identification dynamics. His reliance on splitting and projective identification left John feeling the world was populated by evil poachers and helpless baby animals, both camouflaged images of disturbed and disturbing aspects of himself and his internalized objects.

Grinberg (1968) notes how borderline and other primitive patients are prone to acting out in search of and in reaction to the perceived lack of a containing object that can sustain their separation anxiety, grief, guilt, and loss. I would add that this acting out is not just part of a searching out for the lost object but an angry retribution and revenge as well, for the perceived abandonment and betrayal. So, the containing object, the ideal good object, even if found, is never enough and always at fault. This creates a persecutory cycle of paranoid phantasies and unbearable guilt in which the lost object is now purposely neglectful and absent, and the patient is always hungry and always has blood on his hands. This brings back the most fundamental and terrible infantile state of mind of when absence was intolerable and the missing object was no longer a good object temporarily absent, but a persecutory non-object cruelly missing and permanently gone, yet forever haunting the empty, hungry, and desperate child's mind and heart.

The search for and the disappointment in the needed and desired object of nourishment created more and more anger, despair, and acting out as John was in his teens and older. In his younger years, most of these painful dynamics were internal but later in his life they became more external as well.

Steiner (1992) and other Kleinians have noted the early, more immature stage of the depressive position in which the patient has great difficulty tolerating and accepting the loss of the needed object. This was certainly the case with John. In order to cope, he relied on splitting, denial, manic defenses, or narcissistic (Rosenfeld, 1987) and pathological organizations (Steiner, 1990) that defended him against paranoid collapse. However, these were very fragile psychological retreats (Steiner, 1993) that easily broke down into more borderline states of mind with persecutory and primitive depressive conflicts taking over. This is similar to Quinodoz's (1996) concept of untamed solitude as well as Palacio Espasa's (2002) idea of the more para-psychotic and para-depressive phantasies of catastrophic, irreparable, and life-deadening or life-draining states of loss. Only when the patient is able and willing to face, tolerate, and integrate the actual and/or imagined betrayal, traumatic loss, and perceived rejection, can they move towards the more mature stage of the depressive position where forgiveness, hope, and a livable future exist.

Grinberg (1977) has described how many borderline patients have experienced, either in phantasy and/or with actual external caregivers, traumatic separation and loss. This has usually been based in the infantile experience of a mother who has not been able or willing to receive, contain, or modify the infant's unorganized inner conflicts. This idea of Grinberg's, based on Bion's container concept (Bion, 1962), has been elaborated upon by other Kleinians and examined as a fundamental psychic state of mind in which the infant feels helpless in the face of loss, abandonment, or rejection by the object, leaving the infant in a blank emotional void and an internal sense of meaninglessness. This Kleinian description of the complex dynamics that can evolve and rule a person's psychology seems to fit with the conscious and unconscious experiences John relayed to me over and over again.

One of the ways the infantile ego copes with this difficult psychological situation is the internalization of a harsh and rejecting object and an identification with that object. This results in a turning of the despair, demand, and anger towards the self and the formation of a primitive and sadistic superego state. Grinberg (1964) describes how the primitive and sadistic superego attacks any growth and learning as well as creates a state of unbearable persecutory guilt and consequent acting out (Grinberg, 1968).

So, it was very difficult for John to seek and find knowledge about the world, himself, or others that was different from the flawed state of mind he held in which separation, suffocation, control, loss, betrayal, rage, and severe guilt all ruled the land. John's current life is complex and, for the most part, a fulfilling experience. As we can see, it wasn't always that way. He still struggles with his inner demons, threatening to pull him back into the abyss. However, he has changed and evolved in ways that are truly miraculous. In his own words, "Some days, my life makes perfect sense. I can trace a line from the day I was born and see exactly how I got to where I am today. Other times, it feels like a strange, crazy puzzle that barely fits together."

Five

Memories and Timeless Trauma

Allowing the patient to tell his life story slowly can encourage a gradual self-organizing principle and a self-reflective function. This, in turn, is part of a self-containing ability that does not permanently rely on the analyst as container but fosters an eventual psychic individuation resulting in an independent personal container to rely on. While interpretation of the transference is critical in all analytic treatments to promote eventual psychological integration and working through of core conflicts, in this chapter I will focus on one borderline patient's (John's) actual narrative without going into the other aspects of his treatment. Following one patient's life story and how he views himself and others in it can help both analyst and patient to understand just how the patient came about to suffer as he does and how he may have contributed to that suffering. Also, listening to each piece of the puzzle can help both analyst and patient to understand how the patient has eventually, over a lifetime, managed to change certain pathological patterns and retain others. Analytic treatment provides patients with a rare opportunity to truly tell their stories without interruption and with as much time as they need. Doing so creates a unique and healing emotional clarity. Projective identification has played a significant role in both the destructive and restorative aspects of John's life. We will see evidence of this in how he feels both a coconspirator in his problems as well as simply a recipient of fate. Sometimes, this was from a curious and accepting viewpoint and sometimes from a much more dark and persecutory stance.

We left off with John's exciting but troubled stay in Africa. His parents were beginning to be deeply concerned about his behaviors and did not know how to deal with him. They saw him as "out of control" because he was not minding their advice or rules. While they certainly provided everything he would ever need materially, there was an increasing wall of silence and disconnection between them and their son. John didn't want to do his homework, he didn't want to stay in the house even when his parents said it was dangerous outside with the civil warfare close by, and increasingly he didn't want to conform to their norms. While all children begin to test their independence and tend to rebel in various ways, this was more extreme.

John began to act out by killing small animals, by taking unnecessary risks such as climbing and jumping from high places, and by smoking cigarettes. He remembers hoping to gain attention from his parents with some of this and hoping to anger them with the rest of it. But, in the end, he felt, once again, alone and apart.

John succeeded in making his parents angry and frustrated, but he never received the attention, understanding, or help he also wanted. He wanted his parents to look through his vandalism, disobedience, and odd withdrawal to see and aid the wounded animal inside him. But, this was a tall order so understandably they simply were anxious, angry, and put off. This is an example of how projective identification can be used for communication, attack, evacuation, and control all at the same time (Bion, 1963; Rosenfeld, 1987; Waska, 2004). Due to its excessive and intense use in John's internal dynamics, it simply created the exact same tensions and despair in his parents as he had in himself. So, it was a vicious boomerang effect instead of a healing psychological system, which occurs in optimal or normal development and daily living.

After spending three years in Africa, John's parents relocated to Virginia. They decided John needed some sort of discipline and control that they couldn't provide. Unfortunately, this translated to their sending him off to a private, all-boys, Catholic military school in rural Virginia. Here, again, what was needed was sadly unseen and the "help" given was felt as more of an attack or sentencing. John told me he recalls how walking onto the campus of his new school felt like arriving in a concentration camp. Within a few months, just as if he actually was in a concentration camp, John began to lose his hair, lose weight, and cry every night. He felt completely without friends and only wanted to be home or at least away from that school. His parents seemed to ignore his emotional collapse and encouraged him to continue, thinking he needed to toughen up and learn how to be around other kids.

While certainly well-meaning towards John, his parents' actions were experienced as if he was being cast out to sea, where only danger and isolation were available. Over several years, John's character began to develop more into the direction of something dark, more removed, more rebellious. He had already begun to listen to rock music in Africa and now became enamored with the war protests and political turmoil of that decade. He started to move towards the more drug-influenced music of the day and learned more about the counterculture of the sixties and seventies.

The way John told me about this period in his own words was striking. He said, "Life in Africa came to an abrupt end in 1969. My father was reassigned to the United States for several years. I was ready to start the seventh grade. One day, my father called me into his office. I came over to his desk and he told me we were moving. He asked me to choose between three Catholic military boarding schools in Virginia. I was scared and confused. Of course, there was no way for me to know the difference between these schools so I just picked one, a school run by an ex-marine and staffed by nuns, located in a rural town several hours away from where my parents would live.

"Years later, my father explained that he thought I needed discipline and structure in my life. He said I would be able to learn independence and obtain a better education at such a school. Boy, he was wrong. The next two years were a depressing blur to me, punctuated by painful, sad situations where I felt alone, intimidated, and lost. The new house we moved into in Virginia gave me a few new feelings of stability, but they were tainted and broken by my having to live at the military school. I was allowed to come home for the summer, Christmas, and Easter. Otherwise, I could have my parents pick me up or visit me on selected weekends. For the eleven- or twelve-year-old child I was, this was traumatic. I felt unwanted and on my own. I didn't really like being at home since it always felt so awkward and weird with my parents. But, I hated not being there compared to this hell hole of a school."

Here, we see the threads of John's lifelong dread of being alone and lost but also his constant dread of being around others and connecting with them. This is very common in borderline patients who split their psychological vision of the world in ways that make them feel claustrophobic and completely at sea at the same time. So, they end up running from one extreme to the next. Projective identification is usually the internal mechanism by which this becomes an endless and pathological cycle that feeds on itself (Spillius, 1992).

This military school experience was very traumatic for John. He told me about it in great detail, each word laden with anger and sadness. He said, "The school was for kids from grades three to eight. All the standards were strict and by the book. Each dormitory was grouped by age. My dorm was one huge room with three rows of metal cot beds. We had to have these made to regulation as soon as we woke, to the point of literally being able to bounce a coin off the sheets. If they were made incorrectly, the sheets would be ripped off and we started again. Between each cot was one metal folding chair. On this, we had to place our bag of grooming items like toothbrush and toothpaste, our perfectly folded clothes for the next day, and our spit-shined shoes underneath. Our shoes had to be kept highly polished at all times and punishments would be given out for scuffs or dirt.

"Lining one wall in the dorm were countless lockers. The rest of your daily belongings were kept in these. Again, there were rules about how your locker was kept. Everything else a student may have brought with him to school was secured in a footlocker under each bed. Once a week, there would be an official inspection of each dorm. While we stood at attention by our beds or locker, each area would be scrutinized for infractions and each dorm and company would be graded for efficiency and excellence.

"Just like the real military, we had to wear a uniform. For weekends, we wore green fatigue pants, black t-shirts, and polished army boots. There was a standard issue belt, rules for how to wear the pant leg in conformity to the top of the boot, and the crease of the pant had to be just so. And, this was supposed to be our relaxed wear! For weekdays, there was a much more official uniform with shined shoes, tie, military hat which had to be worn at a particular angle, and a belt with a brass buckle that needed regular shining. Our heads were shaved in marine style, an extreme crew cut. Finally, for special inspections, parades, holidays, or other events, we had a formal uniform that included any metals we had won, emblems showing platoon or company excellence, and sharp-shooting metals. The sharp shooting was actually something I did enjoy. It was fun and I won a medal at it. Sometimes, when I went home to visit, my father would take me to a gun range and let me shoot a gun at targets. I enjoyed that. In fact, when I was about thirty-five years old, I collected several handguns and a shotgun that my wife and I took out to an outdoor gun club. We had a fun time with skeet shooting and using an outdoor handgun range. But, this fun time down in the dirt of the school's basement firing range was a tiny sliver of joy surrounded by the hell of the rest of my life."

John continued to tell me about the military school. He said, "We were fed cafeteria-style meals served on metal trays. We had a certain amount of time to eat and then bus our trays. For weekly drill, we were issued rifles that were real except for the firing mechanisms. We were taught to march in formation while carrying the rifles. In the winter, we would go camping in weather that often dropped below freezing. If it was below thirty-two degrees out, we were given a special patch to sew onto our sweaters. I remember being on night watch during one camping trip and it was about two in the morning. I tried to get a drink out of my canteen but the water was frozen solid. It was pitch black dark, freezing cold, and everyone else was asleep in their tents. All I could think of was how miserable I was, how alone I felt, and how far away home seemed to be.

"I was so homesick that during the first year my hair fell out. When examined by a doctor, he said this was a severe reaction sometimes seen in people undergoing tremendous stress, anxiety, or grief. That was definitely the case for me. During the evening when we were given a bit of free time, I would lie in my cot and cry, feeling terribly trapped and helpless. I would wake up in the morning and find small clumps of hair on my pillow. My parents didn't seem to put two and two together and continued to send me away except for occasional weekends and holidays. It was around this time that I also became quite skinny. Looking back, I am sure it was a sign of depression and extreme anxiety. Doing their best to help me with the external symptoms that became so obvious, my parents began buying cases of Ensure, a foul-tasting, high-calorie drink made for the elderly or for cancer patients who need to keep weight on."

It was indeed a shocking fact of John's adolescence that he was given a special nutritional supplement meant for those who were wasting away physically while, in fact, John was wasting away emotionally from depression and despair. John went on to say, "For the problem of my hair falling out, my parents took me to a dermatologist who gave me monthly treatments with a strong ultraviolet light that was supposed to stimulate the hair follicles to grow back." So, again, John's severe physical symptoms were treated, but the core and underlying suffering was ignored. Part of this problem was that John kept all his feelings to himself and rarely said anything about how he felt or what he thought. So, the only things that were communicated or easily noticed were his acting out behaviors and these physical symptoms. He withheld his feelings and retreated within. On one hand, his parents seem oblivious to their son's psychological plight. On the other hand, their son offered no verbal clues to what he needed or the problems he faced. Thus, there was a tremendous collapse of potential connection and understanding that left John feeling rejected. However, part of that was his own rejection of his parents and the world as a place he could trust or share himself with. Thus, we see the early emergence of a lifelong pattern of anger, persecution, rejection, and loss cycling back and forth in phantasy between self and object, fueled by increasingly intense projective identification processes.

This sadomasochistic drama of need, withdrawal, withholding, expectation, and abandonment is common in the phantasy world of the borderline patient. Alienation amongst dangerous strangers is the way the world is experienced and, therefore, one naturally withholds, and trust or love becomes the victim.

John went on to tell me more about his experiences at this school. He said, "When students misbehaved, the punishments were very much military style. The offender would be forced to do pushups, made to stand in the corner of the cafeteria (while the rest of the school got to eat dessert), told to run laps around the football field, and made to scrub toilets or other difficult and degrading acts. The one punishment that left me thinking this school was a truly bad place was what everyone called the crucifixion. The name was appropriate, given this was a Catholic school run by nuns who would gladly slap your hands with a heavy wooden ruler if you spoke out in class. Anyway, this punishment consisted of making the student hold two rifles, which weighed a fair amount, one in each hand with arms extended from the side, while standing at attention. The unlucky student would be made to stand like this in front of the garrison, the building that held all the rifles, while the rest of the school played on the field surrounding it. Among other things, it made an example to all of what their fate could be too. If the punishment were to happen at night, the student had to stand in front of the dorm lockers, while everyone went about their chores. When the weight of the rifles made the student's arms sag, the monitoring officer would take the butt of another rifle and hit the student's elbows until he held his arms straight out again. This would lead to the kid's crying, trying desperately to hold the rifles up to avoid getting hit in the elbows. It was a crucifixion. When I look at a photo now of one of those dorms with its cold rows of lockers, metal chairs, and small cot beds, and remember this type of punishment, I can't help but make the comparison to some kind of concentration camp or prison."

The few days of holiday vacation that brought him back home left John in his room alone or watching television, feeling depressed, empty, and angry. More and more, John retreated inwards into a darker view of himself and a more twisted view of the world.

At one point, I asked John is there had been any positive experiences at this school or at that time in his life. Technically, I think this was both an acting out of my counter-transference anxiety over how miserable and traumatic his story was and my genuine clinical curiosity about whether he was able to find and integrate anything good into this all-bad picture, or if the splitting was so severe that nothing good could be found in this world of misery. To be able to allow some good to mix with the bad is a hallmark of the depressive position (Klein, 1935, 1940) and shows hope of psychological integration and growth as opposed to the more strict all-good or all-bad world of the borderline mind and the paranoid-schizoid experience (Klein, 1946).

In response, John told me that he tried to make friends but he "thinks he was pretty awkward and withdrawn, which probably turned people off." Here, he demonstrated the healthy ability to reflect on himself and to take ownership of his contribution to the pathological projective identification cycles mentioned earlier. In doing so, he is able to have more of a choice in how he treats himself and his objects and create a less confining or destructive way of relating. This is a major step in psychological healing for the borderline patient, and John demonstrated the internalized function to do so at a fairly high level. This reversal of former deadening or anti-life aspects of projective identification attacks provides a new chance for psychological integration and genuine participation in life.

John went on to explain how he had one friend in this school with whom he liked to listen to music and kid around, but "over time our interests grew apart and I also didn't really know how to relate very well. So, I think I came off weird or selfish and probably pushed him away." As far as making other friends, John remembers feeling "extremely anxious and embarrassed about not knowing how to fit in or how to function the way everyone else seemed to know." John was assigned to the band section of the school where every member of the platoon played either a horn or drums. While there was some minimal training, most of the students apparently already had some knowledge of the instruments. John had none and could not play his horn at all. He did his best to hide this by faking it. This worked most of the time, as twenty-some kids were playing together as they marched around or participated in parades. However, when each student had to take his turn in waking up the entire school by blowing his bugle, it was painfully obvious who had talent and who did not. Of course, the other students made fun of John about it. John said what was far worse was the time when he had to take his turn playing the song "Taps" as they took the American flag down. This procedure was done each day while the entire school was assembled. John remembers the giggles and snorts as he struggled to make his horn produce even one note. He conveyed the utter powerlessness and helpless despair he felt in that moment, but it was clearly a replay of a place in the world he had felt many times over, which was now being painfully repeated internally and externally.

Continuing to respond to my question about any positive memories, John told me he fondly remembered playing with the school dog, a mascot that he felt close to. This was part of a lifelong pattern in which John took solace in being with animals rather than people, feeling less pressure, less anxiety, and much more acceptance. Also, he remembered "really getting into music at that time." Every day there was a play period when all the students could be on a vast expanse of grass, basketball courts, and benches. John liked to sit by himself on a bench with a small transistor radio listening to the local rock station. It was a lonely time, and he tried to feel OK fortifying himself with the newest songs and the then famous "Top of the Pops" countdown. He became familiar with all the latest stars and the top hits of the day.

Also, on certain evenings, there was a period in the dorms when the school allowed students to gather and relax. John listened to what others played on their record players and added some of those songs to his playlists. He became familiar with the rock scene that was going on at the time, including Hendrix, the Allman Brothers, and the Rolling Stones. It was the early seventies, but everything still had a counter-revolution, late-sixties flavor to it, and John started to identify with that view of the world. His taste in clothes, haircut, politics, and love of nature were some of the aspects of the counterculture movement that he embraced. His increased internal withdrawal and sense of not being a part of the world was now externalized to this fringe cultural identity that was against or at least very separate from the mainstream.

After graduating from the military school, John was told by his parents that he would be going on to another private Catholic school for high school. This time, they picked one in Pennsylvania. It was outside of a small rural town, many miles from any major city. This was the beginning of a very long thirteen-year road of drugs, alcohol, and destructive acting out that was to consume John's life and bring him near to death many times over. Much worse was the internal death he felt occurring over and over as anxiety, paranoia, depression, and a sense of complete collapse grew to be a daily experience.

John, like many teens, began to identify with the rock stars of the day, and he began to admire a few of the older students who had formed a rock band. He saw these different individuals and their lifestyles as a wonderful and separate alternative to the lonely, painful place in which he emotionally existed. So, through splitting and projective identification, John saw drugs, music, and the alternative lifestyle as an idealized way to step out of and away from the prison of military school and the prison of his mental despair and confusion. Sadly, as happens so predictably with excessive or pathological projective identification, the very thing one tries to escape from is the very thing one is creating. This move towards identification with the counterculture would prove to be extremely destructive and ushered in much more isolation and anxiety.

Emotionally, this new high school brought a climax to John's feelings of alienation, depression, and anger. When John relays his history to me, he always speaks with a sense of humor, insight, and learning. This is part of his resilient spirit and his sense of hope for the present and the future. Also, it shows his shift from a primarily paranoid-schizoid realm of experience to a more integrated depressive realm. However, this growth and psychic shift is very fragile, and John is still prone to regression, fragmentation, and partial emotional collapse when facing certain external stresses or certain internal phantasies. This is common in borderline patients who have done much work on themselves and have changed significantly. They are vastly different but sometimes the same. So, sadly and insightfully, John is able to see that the good times he did have during high school were unfortunately dwarfed by his intense rebellion, depression, apathy, and growing addiction.

John was at this new high school for three years, but things went downhill very quickly and never really got better. When John returned home on holiday or in the summer, it was clear to his parents that his behavior was very different. He was now smoking pot every day, drinking whenever he could, and taking LSD, PCP, and any pill he could find. John grew his hair, dressed as a hippie, and cut on himself with a razor. John told me, "I am sure that my parents were shocked and scared when they saw I had used a razor to carve the word POT into my hand after they gave me a lecture for smoking it. But, it seems odd that they didn't see that as a giant red flag and try to get me some sort of help." Loud music, incense, posters, and cigarettes were part of his retreat in his bedroom. The couple of neighborhood friends he had were put off by his dedication to getting high above all else. Dating was also unimportant. John's goal was to be as out of touch with reality as he could be. Actually, he did try to become close with several girls at this point in his life, but he felt so unable to relate to others, so anxious, and so drawn to the isolation of drugs and drinking that he broke off those attempts rather quickly.

During one session, John told me, "Last week, I mentioned to my parents some of my resentment about being sent away to these shitty private schools. As usual, my father became silent. Guilt and sadness swept over his face. My mother took up her predictable defensive, offensive, and aggressive way of talking. She is always very dismissive of my feelings. She said, 'Well, if you hadn't been such a difficult child and hadn't been doing all those drugs, you might have had a better time at the schools. We wanted to protect you by sending you there. You were such a small child, not even five feet tall in high school. We thought things would be very rough for you in public schools and we heard they were not very good as far as offering a good education. Also, with your temper, your wild nature, and your drug problems, we thought a discipline of private, Catholic military schools would do you some good. After all, in Africa, when you were twelve years old, you were grounded to your room but then cut through the screen and jumped out the window to go exploring down the street in the middle of a war zone! I remember being so embarrassed when I had to offer to pay the embassy for the torn screen. And, in Virginia, when you were fourteen and pulled a knife on us, we had to call the police to help. So, what do you expect?'"

John told me, "So, on one hand, I could easily imagine how difficult it was from their side, but also I felt once again blamed, misunderstood, and totally abandoned. They seemed to have no clue what I was going through or am still going through emotionally. Or, they can sense it and can't or won't get near it out of guilt and anxiety." Here, John seemed to be illustrating the Kleinian idea of the infant or adult wanting containment, detoxification, and translation for his or her projections. But, if the individual feels the object does not want to or is unable to do so, a sense of inner dread, collapse, and fragmentation occurs.

For John, and many other borderline patients, the resulting anxiety, anger, and emotional hunger becomes overwhelming, and the patient increases his acting out as a way to gain access to the object, to seek revenge, and/or to plead for help. However, this usually backfires and, as the object closes down even more, the patient feels that much more rejected and lost.

John went on, "Anyway, it is just another example of how I feel they don't get me and never will. The difference is I am trying to accept that, instead of threatening to kill them, trying to kill myself, or just sinking into some kind of alcohol and drug haze." Here he was demonstrating a great deal of growth and progress from that more primitive state of seeking revenge on himself and others and feeling so out of control. He was trying to forgive, accept, and understand. For a borderline patient, this is a very significant development.

Regarding his new high school, John told me, "My father's thinking was that I would receive a much better education there than in the public schools, and that I would not find as many things to get into trouble with. To his credit, I believe I did end up with a better education, but at a high price. Once again, I felt shipped off to somewhere scary and new, without a choice."

So, at the beginning of the next school year, John's parents drove for several hours through farmlands and rural towns to this new boarding school. They helped him unpack and move into to the dorm. John told me, "Except for holidays and summertime, I lived there for three years. Leaving home to go there for the first time, I felt worried, helpless, nervous, and resigned to being put somewhere that I didn't really want to go to in the first place."

So, John felt the same at the military school in terms of having no choice, being alone, and being overwhelmed by anxiety and helplessness. These are certainly some of the core feelings of dread that populate the phantasies of our more difficult patients who experience life as being in the grip of a unpredictable current dragging them deeper and deeper into the abyss. As in the case of John, sometimes external reality serves as the template for these persecutory phantasies and feelings. Then, over the course of a lifetime, the patient cultivates them with unconscious reactions, both internal and external, which sets in motion a psychological evolution of distorted object relational patterns involving rigid visions of self and other.

John reflected on this in his own way by saying, "It is clear to me that the sadness, anger, and trauma of feeling abandoned in all these different schools and moving to different countries still lingers with me. I use the words *feeling abandoned* because that was obviously not my parent's intention. In fact, they were trying very hard to love me and provide me with the best. Unfortunately, they did not see what I was going through. I couldn't find a way to communicate my needs, and the circumstances of life were at times out of their hands. All this combined to leave me with a not-so-wonderful experience of life that only produced more and more convictions about the world as a bad place."

Here, John appeared able to be truly reflective and integrate his feelings. This was evidence of the successful work he had done in years of psychotherapy and psychoanalysis, as well as periods of time on medications and in drug and alcohol programs. As a cumulative result, he had found a way to combine forgiveness, understanding, and acceptance as a bridge over the flames of years of rage and internal chaos. This integration was evidence of a more mature, whole-object depressive level of functioning that gave John insight and the ability to keep moving forward because he was hopeful he might find something good as he proceeded in life. This sometimes was still fueled by a search or quest for an ideal, followed by awful disappointment, but much less than before.

Relaying these life memories to me often left John both relieved and overwhelmed. He had to relive the pain to gradually work past it. He told me, "After telling you about some of my experiences at the new boarding school, I had another nightmare. In this one, I had been sent away to a boarding school somewhere far from home. I and one other teenage boy were the newest students. We were both very depressed and wanted to leave. We were outside by the side of a very steep, rocky hill. We were by two pay phones, both of us waiting desperately for a call from our parents, hopefully telling us we could come home. The teachers and faculty were gathered in a small crowd looking on, seemingly uninterested and not about to do anything to help us. The students were in a separate group, looking on in a very resigned way as if to say, 'We have gone through that already and it is no use to think you can escape. We have given up trying.' At some point, the other boy was so anguished that he got on a bicycle and rode to the top of the hill and then deliberately drove down the steep area and off a small cliff, to come down landing head first onto some big sharp boulders. His head was split open and the bones were sticking out of his legs and arms. Blood was everywhere. He was wailing uncontrollably, his face contorted with pain and despair. Everyone gathered close to watch, but no one helped."

When I asked John to associate to the each element of the dream, as is done in psychoanalytic treatment, and tell me what came to mind about them, he said, "The two phones remind me of a small room in a building at the boarding school in Pennsylvania. It had two phones and they were often being used by students to call home. I often heard kids crying to their parents and asking to go home. I wanted to ask my parents that too but felt I would be letting them down and they might say no as well. So, I tried to keep it all to myself. I made many calls to my parents, always feeling sad, angry, and desperate, but never telling them that. I felt they didn't want to know my feelings or couldn't understand them. So, what was the use in sharing? I felt that they wanted me at the school. In order to please them I had to find a way to survive it. I didn't really want to share myself with them, so I closed my heart off and withdrew."

Here, John was revealing an important unconscious phantasy in which he felt a terrible obligation to suffer so that he could continue doing what he pictured his parents wanted. He wanted to please them. But, to do so meant continuing to suffer, and to tell them he was not happy would mean he was disappointing them.

So, John was describing a more masochistic way of experiencing the world but also was sharing his view of the container object (Bion, 1962, 1963) as unavailable in a deliberate sadistic manner, closed off and rejecting. This more paranoid phantasy is important to understand when working from a Kleinian perspective. If the object is perceived as a welcoming, functioning, wise, and loving container, the resulting internalization process leads to a valuable integration, internal security, and whole-object functioning. If the object is perceived as a malfunctioning, closed off, and untrustworthy container, the resulting internalization process leads to extreme borderline or psychotic reactions and a sense of internal insecurity, paranoia, and lack of trust in one's own autonomy and ability to navigate the world.

John continued to share what he thought the dream meant. He said, "There is the loss, the abandonment, the lack of help, and the separation. The attempted suicide by the boy on the bicycle certainly speaks to an extreme level of rage, turned inwards and a complete collapse of hope. That is me. Anything that is good is gone. It is all black, dark, and lonely." John was silent as he cried.

Clearly choked up after relaying these feelings, John switched back to telling me about the school in Pennsylvania. This was a way to gather himself and turn away from that pain and emotional collapse. Even though telling me the story of his life made him relive the agony, it was in a paced, somewhat controlled manner that allowed him to feel some degree of mastery over it instead of the sudden jolt of intense chaos and trauma. Of course, this is the same principle that underlies the idea of why it is healing to tell someone else your troubles, your grief, and your frustrations. However, it is also part of that complicated situation with more troubled patients who feel they can avoid what feels like the persecutory nature of treatment in which they see the analyst as "making them face pain" when they imagine they could just avoid it by not going to see the analyst. However, John realized the benefits of telling his story but still suffered from the short-term pain as he worked on the building long-term mental benefits. For the most part, he believed that out of that temporary trauma he could construct goodness and peace of mind.

John told me, "My father had the idea that I needed to be more into sports and learn how to socialize. So he contacted the coach of the school's football team and arranged for me to be the water boy for the football team. This involved my having to arrive to my freshman year at this private school a month early to go to spring training with the team. I was housed in a dorm with the team who mostly knew each other from the last year of playing together. I was about five feet tall and suddenly cast into this place in the middle of nowhere with a bunch of guys older than I was. They were all about a foot taller and about fifty or a hundred pounds bigger. It was weird and scary.

"I felt completely out of place and, also, being the water boy only reinforced my image of myself as a loser and the inferior one. I had to be in charge of cleaning up their dirty towels in the locker room, making them Gatorade for the training games, and generally playing servant to whatever they needed. I tried to fit in and make sense of my world by identifying with parts of what I saw. So, I quickly learned about the Grateful Dead, what brand of cigarettes was popular, and where to purchase LSD, beer, hard liquor, and pot. Then, I started making those things my world as often as possible.

"Instead of this becoming a bridge to making friends with the other students, it became a detour and total detachment. I spent the next three years at that school doing my best to smoke as much pot as I could, drink as often as I could, and try any and all drugs that came my way. I was alienated from everyone except if they were able to supply me with my ticket out of reality."

John reflected on the odd contrast of all this unhappiness compared with a few good moments he remembered. He said, "When I think of the three years I was there, it wasn't always terrible. But, the things I enjoyed or felt interested in were part of an experience I hadn't signed up for. It is sort of like being strapped in to a ride at the fair and going through the haunted house. What you see might be scary, funny, interesting, boring, or confusing, but, you don't have much of a choice about it. You are strapped in and have to go along with it until it is over. So, I enjoyed playing basketball by myself in the big indoor gym. The cafeteria was in that building and I used to love the ice cold milk that was available from the dispensers. But, I hated going to meals because I had to sit at a table with the three people that used to beat me up regularly. So, I would eat my meal and drink my milk while listening to them tell me about how I was going to be beat after dinner.

"The snack bar and pool tables were in this building too. I used to love spending my money on the submarine sandwiches and ice cream they sold. After a while, I became pretty good at pool but I didn't have any friends to play with. I smoked all the time and I looked forward to going into town to get cigarettes and candy. On the way into the town, there was an old gas station. They had this ancient pinball machine in the garage where they fixed cars, and I would spend hours eating the beef jerky they sold, drinking their sodas, and playing this old machine that, if you rocked just right, would give you free games. I remember being drunk one night in the cold Pennsylvania winter and, with two other drunken classmates, climbing the fence into the local paper factory. Then, we climbed onto a massive pile of wood chips that was steaming and warm. We sat in it feeling the warmth and being overwhelmed by the cedar smell. That was a good moment. But, as I said, it was surrounded by a larger context of dread and despair.

"I tried to be on the track team but that quickly went by the wayside. I was not very athletic and I hated the running. But, I initially liked the idea and I was at least brave enough to try. Also, I remember enjoying the unique campus architecture. The only new buildings were the classroom facility and the gym. All the other ones, including our dorms, were old gothic styled mansions that had originally been the giant housing compound for the family that owned the local paper mill. They had donated it all to the monks and they made it into a school. So, there were gargoyles on the sides of the buildings and wonderful woodwork on the inside. It felt like we lived in medieval castles and we practically did."

John continued, "The monks were an odd bunch. The headmaster always looked angry and ready to fly into a rage. He was definitely not someone you wanted to be sent to for any infraction. But, he had no record of actually losing it, unlike the monk in charge of athletics. He was an ex-boxer and had, in fact, punched several students in the face and broken their noses. He was always walking around cursing under his breath and literally looking for trouble. My stint as water boy for the football team was made all the more worse by my having to report to him on a daily basis. Then, there was the English teacher who we called Dopey. He would walk around the campus at night sneaking up on anyone drinking or smoking pot in the many hidden spots on the huge school campus. He seemed to make it his life's work to find all drug users and punish them to the full extent of the law.

"One of the monk's in my dormitory was about six-foot-six, super thin, and goofy as could be. He was a super-optimist and quite naïve, so we could talk him into anything. He seemed to be the only monk who truly was trying to practice a life of service and kindness. He was always really nice but had almost nothing in his room. He was poor and looked it. This was unlike the other monk who was in charge of my dorm during junior year. His father owned a football team and sent him every conceivable goodie. This monk had a color television set in his room with a plush leather recliner to watch it from. Every month his father sent him a huge package with every kind of candy and fancy food. He always had lots of liquor and nice clothes too. There were also several monks who were obviously gay and could barely hide it. There was also a monk who ran the snack shop and, to his credit, he confronted me more than once on my out-of-control behavior. I immediately denied anything was wrong. I was too far into my defiance, withdrawal, and confusion to be able to grab the rope he was throwing me."

Six

External Motion and Internal Deadness

After three years of emotional chaos at his boarding school in Pennsylvania, John decided to share his feelings with his parents. John told me, "I finally told my parents I couldn't handle attending another year at the private school in Pennsylvania. I was sick of being beat up by the school bullies and was completely depressed about my life. Initially, my parents were shocked and contacted the school to find out what was going on. Regarding my allegations, the head of the boarding school told my parents I was always drunk and high, my grades were suffering because of my behavior, and that I had alienated everyone in my class because of my drug use. They said I had stolen money and created trouble in my dorm. Most of that was true, but it didn't really address my depression or the group of guys in my class that liked to beat on me when they were bored. So, my parents tried to do what they thought was best and sent me off to a carbon copy of that school only in another remote location.

"This was a very small town in Colorado that ironically had a state prison on one end and a Catholic boy's school on the other. The moment I arrived, I found out who had the drugs and how to buy beer in the little town by the school. I had no idea what was going on in my classes on any given day, as I sat there feeling lonely, depressed, hung over, and confused. I was drunk on weekends, high on pot every day, and completely out of touch with the real world. The beauty of the countryside was something I remember well about that time. But, it is in the context of sitting on a beautiful hill overlooking a gray state prison while I guzzled Mickey's wide-mouth beers and smoked hash. Or, it was when I was walking in the massive creek bed that was like an exposed cave, full of naturally carved out stalagmites and rock formations all in the middle of a giant field that was miles from humanity under the crisp blue winter sky. This memory is also a bit blurry, as it happened on several tabs of acid and a six pack of beer.

"Two months into my disastrous tenure at this new school, I was asked to leave after I was arrested for buying a large amount of LSD in the next city over. I was going to be the school's new dealer for all things mind-bending, but that came to an abrupt halt."

John told me, in a reflective moment, "Even back then, clouded by my sad mental condition and way too much pot, I had some insight into the human condition. Hitchhiking back from one of my purchasing excursions for pot and LSD, I was picked up by a soldier from the nearby army base. I had been standing by the roadside, shivering in the cold Colorado fall evening, hoping for a ride back to school. He picked me up in his tricked-out Mustang and we spend the next hour ride driving fast, smoking a joint, drinking beer, and listening to the way out sounds of Yes and Pink Floyd on his top-of-the-line stereo. On one hand, I thought this was all very much the ideal. The car, the drugs, the music, the camaraderie, and the successful score in the big city all seem so hip and right. But, talking to him about his life in the army and my take on his general demeanor both lead me to think he was lonely and trying hard to justify or play off what was a miserable time in his life, perhaps even a bad choice he deeply regretted. Also, in thinking in this deeper way about him, I had to consider myself in the mix. For a moment, before I pushed it back with another hit of beer and pot, I had to reflect on my own situation. I was all alone on a cold night in the middle of nowhere trying to smuggle drugs into a private school I hated and was flunking out of, where I had no friends. And, if I was able to go home to my parents, there I felt equally lonely, without friends, and empty at the core. I was suddenly aware of a terrible void within myself and no place to surface from it. I asked the driver to turn the music up and pass the pipe." John fell silent for some time, clearly feeling upset.

After a bit, he continued, "Meanwhile, my parents had been assigned to Taiwan. We had moved around the world every two or three years until this five-year stint in the U.S. So, since I was kicked out of Colorado, I attended my first public school for three months before we left for Taiwan. To use the word *attend* is a little strong, as I rarely actually showed up for a class. Mostly, I hung out with other kids who were skipping school, and we spent our time smoking pot, drinking beer, and dropping acid. I found a source for PCP as well. This is one of those drugs that weeds out the casual user and even the more delinquent teen. One or two puffs of this stuff and you are unable to walk correctly and you sometimes hallucinate. Most of my get-high buddies didn't want anything to do with it, so I found myself taking lots of walks by myself in the woods where I would take a few puffs and feel my brain melt down.

"This drug use was my warm-up to my short tenure in Taiwan. By now, the few friends I had and most of my family were well aware there was a major problem going on. I was not able to function in any real capacity at all. I was extremely anxious, thoroughly depressed, and very confused. Add some anger and loneliness in there and it was not a pretty sight. I was sporting long hair and a dazed look in my eyes. I spent far too much time holed up in my room listening to loud Jimi Hendrix music while staring at my black-light posters and lighting yet another stick of incense to cover up the smell of pot and/or cigarettes. My poor parents had no clue what on earth to do with me or for me. They bought me what I wanted or needed and recommended I study more and smoke less. But, I was a million miles away in my head trying to make sense of my place on the planet or simply giving up and trying to find an escape hatch from the planet I felt so unattached to.

"In fact, getting high and the search for drugs was about the only thing that felt like a secure foundation. It was a place to go, a devotion, and an identity. Without it, I felt like a wisp of smoke about to disappear, a train racing off the tracks into nowhere.

"Oh wait. There was something else that helped me feel grounded besides drugs. I started to cut myself. It felt great because in that moment all the other shitty feelings and terrible mental unraveling stopped. I could focus and be whole in the moment. Also, it helped me channel some of my anger and rage. So, I didn't just cut my arms. Sometimes, I carved the word *pot* in my arm to piss off my parents. They just looked at it with dismay and had no clue how to respond. I found refuge in this flesh carving until I was twenty-five and I had to go to the emergency room to be stitched up after I cut my arm up so much in several places it wouldn't stop bleeding. I still remember the look on the face of the psychiatrist when he asked me if I had done that to myself. Knowing he would have kept me overnight for observation whether I liked it or not, I told him I had been hiking through some old farmland and ran into a fence with barbed wire and got caught in it. He shook his head and looked at me as if to say, 'I know you are lying, but I can't prove it.'

"I don't want to blame my parents, especially since I think I would be dead or in jail many times over if it were not for their constant faith, love, and financial backing. But, I can't help but wonder how and why they ignored a young teen who had to drink a nutritional supplement in order to keep weight on, whose hair was falling out, and who cut words into his arm with a steak knife. But, I may not have been ready for help even if they had tried to provide it. Who knows?

"So, when I arrived in Taiwan, it was simply a matter of time before I completely imploded. I was enrolled in the local private school for American kids that were there with their government or military families. Like a heat-seeking missile, I instantly found the other students who used drugs. For me, Taiwan was a new heaven on earth, a place where I could truly blot out my feelings and not be a part of anything. I could retreat far, far back into the blackness of my mind and away from the places and people I hated, feared, and avoided. Unfortunately, this also meant I had no relationships, no one to talk to, no one to hold, and no one to hold me.

"There was no drinking age, so I could buy beer anywhere I wanted and I found two drugs that exactly matched my emotional needs. It was possible to walk into almost any drugstore and purchase powerful tranquilizers as well as a cough medication that contained morphine. I began ingesting both of these drugs on a daily basis. In the evening, I would combine these with beer to create an almost lethal mixture that left me stupefied and numb. The group of kids I hung out with liked to gather at some bleachers by a baseball park before they went out to various places for the evening. By the time they were ready to take off, I was so out of it they would tie me by my belt to a post so I wouldn't fall over or wander away and then come back for me later that night. I sat there passed out, tied to the post.

"Back in Virginia there had been a girl I was interested in, and we hung out sometimes, but my anxiety, depression, and inner chaos prevented me from pursuing it. We kissed a few times, and I think she had a crush on me, but I was busy with my mistress of intoxication.

"So, my first sexual encounter was in Taiwan, and it wasn't exactly a warm and healthy introduction to intimacy. While high on tranquilizers and morphine, I wandered into a local bar and was quickly surrounded by three attractive prostitutes. Since I usually kept to myself, and being a confused, depressed, drug addict wasn't much of an aphrodisiac for girls my age, I was happy for their alleged interest. Because we couldn't speak each other's language, the exchange of desire and money broke all fluency barriers, and I went home with one of them. Losing my virginity to a Taiwanese hooker when I was fifteen and strung out on drugs wasn't a very uplifting moment. I looked around this gal's dingy little bedroom, poorly lit and a mirror of her impoverished life, and felt lonely for me and sad for her. I walked off into the night trying to find a taxi and make my way home.

"As a result of my overall mental splintering, in which I felt lost and broken in a thousand different ways, as well as my severe drug abuse, I was not only unable to function at school but I was a disaster at home. I fell asleep in my food at the dinner table, I passed out on the living room floor, I left my drugs out in my bedroom and my dog ate them and nearly died, I scared the cook and maid, and I was abusive to my parents. I would scream at them, and I tore up their belongings more than once. I stole their money and kept them up way into the night with my unpredictable behavior. I held a knife to their throats and demanded money so I could buy more drugs and threatened to kill myself if they didn't comply.

"At one point, they convinced me to go see a therapist. She was a beautiful young lady who listened to me rant and rave. I developed an instant crush and made her sloppy gifts in my shop class where I would occasionally be coherent enough to pay attention and not just pass out at my desk. But, she was smart and paid attention when I played Neil Young songs on my tape deck for her. She knew I was listening to a song about me when the lyrics were about emptiness and the futility of life, wondering if others knew or cared, and the hope for change, whether it be by death or rebirth. I was lost and lonely, crying out for help while I teetered at the edge. She recommended my parents put me in a medical detox unit followed by a residential program in California.

"I knew nothing of her talks with my parents, so when my parents asked me to go into treatment I immediately refused. Several weeks later, it was a complete surprise when I came home in my customary state of oblivion and was greeted by four armed military police. They wrestled me to the ground and carried me off to the hospital. It was at the Taiwan American Military Infirmary that I found out what it was like to immediately stop using heavy-duty tranquilizers and morphine. I had my own private room next to the nurse's station so they could check on me frequently. It was a small room with a bed and a table, no windows except for the one in the door that they kept looking at me through. Almost immediately, I had what felt like the worst case of flu possible, and I started seeing spiders, hundreds of them, crawling up and down my legs. I felt trapped, scared, and without any meaning or substance to my life. After two weeks I was put on a military plane to San Francisco where I went to the military hospital for a stay in their psychiatric ward. I recall the good times of being on a day pass with a couple of other lost souls as we scored beers and cigarettes and relaxed in the sun at Golden Gate Park. Then, I went back to the ward to watch people scream and get restrained. In the therapeutic art class, I thought it was pretty weird that I was watching people actually weaving baskets. Wow!

From the psych ward, I was put into a yearlong residential program in Marin County. That is how I wound up in one of most beautiful areas in America."

Sunshine Acres was a long-term residential facility north of San Francisco specifically for adolescents with chronic psychological problems. John was transferred there after spending several weeks in the psychiatric hospital. The program was coed, with two buildings for the boys and two for the girls. There was a high school on the property, and the average stay was one year. The treatment plan was modeled after Synanon, a very confrontational drug program for ex-cons and hard-core addicts, combined with some tenets of Gestalt therapy and Transactional Analysis therapy. John was detached and very withdrawn for a while but slowly became more integrated with the day-to-day functioning of the program, and he began to build a sense of himself. He took many of the more positive caricatures of his hippie drug-addict persona to heart and flourished as the guy in overalls and long hair who did yoga and studied massage therapy. John learned macramé and how to make stained glass planters. He had an aquarium in his room, and he figured out how to care for the fish. He began to write poetry and talked about nature and ecological concerns. He attended family therapy sessions where he discussed his feelings on cassette tape with a therapist who sent it to his family, and they would reply by tape. He spoke up a little in the daily group therapy sessions but didn't really like them because there was so much confrontation and yelling.

At one point, the program challenged John by placing him in an occupational training class at a local high school. John had to pick from among introductory classes on welding, carpentry, restaurant management, or child-care development. He chose childcare. He went to weekly classes and found himself very interested. The teacher talked a great deal about the ideas of Transactional Analysis, a type of therapy popular at the time in which the parent, adult, and child aspects of each person were explored, and the way the person related from each of these three parts of him- or herself to life was examined. This made a great deal of sense to John, and he had been exposed to a more radical version of that at his residential treatment program.

After the classes, John signed up to be a volunteer at a classroom for severely disabled and retarded children. He helped feed, diaper, teach, and play with ten young children who were mostly in wheelchairs, unable to speak or move. This was a profoundly disabled population. He also helped out with other classes in which there were older autistic and disabled teens. This was the first experience John ever had of being with children or helping other people in any capacity. He seemed to take to it immediately.

This positive direction in John's life was rewarded by a job offer to take care of five of the children who lived in a nearby foster home. John went there by bus and became the one-on-one teacher for an autistic teenager who was blind. He took him for walks and helped him master dressing, eating, hygiene skills, and many other daily living skills. Also, John tried to help him feel more comfortable about human contact, touch, and relaxation.

At the on-site high school, John finished his high school diploma and enrolled in the nearby junior college. He also was a teacher's aide at Sunny Acre's high school program, helping other students with homework. Finally, he took on a janitorial job through the county, which paid him to clean the restrooms in the program's main buildings. So, John became a model student at Sunshine Acres. At about the nine-month mark, he found out that the insurance company that was paying for the stay decided to stop funding his placement. Suddenly, John had to enter the real world of California and live on his own, at around the age of seventeen or eighteen. His parents were still in Taiwan and agreed to finance his new life. Unfortunately, John had just started getting settled, comfortable, and confident in his life at the residential program. This sudden change was reminiscent in some ways of his other experiences of having to move. In listening to this part of John's story, I felt like he was being relocated yet one more time, all on his own, to fend as best as he could.

John's parents were very supportive in that they wanted him to succeed. They provided him with an apartment, a monthly allowance, health insurance, and paid for him to go to the junior college. It all looked very promising as far as a new transition to a new phase in John's life. He was working at the foster home and going to college classes to complete his basic undergraduate degree. He was cooking, cleaning his apartment, and waking himself up for his appointments. But, emotionally, this was too much for John. He was desperately maintaining a façade of normalcy, while inside he was starting to crumble.

John said, "I felt so out of place and had no clue how to be. I wanted to be a part of the world and have friends, but I also was scared of everyone and avoided getting to know anyone." A sad and telling example of this was how John baked little loaves of banana bread and on holidays would leave one on the doorstep of his neighbor to whom he never spoke and whom he didn't know except for the occasional wave hello in the mornings as they both left for work or school. He said, "I wanted to be friends but I also didn't want to be close. I was lonely, scared, and extremely ambivalent. I wanted it but I didn't want it all at the same time. So, I put all that energy into the loaf, wrapped it up, but made sure to put it on the person's doorstep when they weren't there and then ran away. Sort of like leaving a message on someone's telephone machine when you know they won't be there to answer in person."

Here, John was describing the intense psychological ambivalence that makes up the hunger and fear of his borderline phantasies. He wanted a wonderful union with his object but felt a persecutory or claustrophobic dread. This is due to the excessive reliance on projective identification so common in the borderline state.

Looking back on his apartment, John said, "It was a real rat hole, when I think about it. There was a full-blown alcoholic living upstairs. When I started drinking again, I would hang out with him and some of his friends. He saved stale beer from other people's parties, and he usually ended up peeing his pants he was so drunk. I felt strange sitting there, but also I didn't have to interact too much and liked getting drunk. My furniture was all rented, thanks to my father, but it was sort of odd having rent-to-own possessions. It all seemed temporary or unreal. I bought a Boy Scout cookbook that explained very simple recipes and did my best to get by. But, often I would just have things that tasted good like French fries with lots of ketchup and hamburgers. On one hand, it felt exciting to cook up my own meal in my own kitchen and then sit down on my little rental table and eat it. But, sitting there all alone in my little studio apartment with no window, not having any friends, and having just left Sunny Acres to now be in the big world was very lonely and very scary."

During this time in his life, John was surrounded by opportunities to either stay clean and sober and start making friends or to begin to devolve back into a life of lonely withdrawal and destructive behaviors. His inner resources were meager, but he tried to break new ground in how he approached things. So, instead of completely isolating himself, he tried to stay in touch with a woman who graduated Sunshine Acres a few months before him. She had been sent to the program for using heroin and being out of control at home. John looked her up and began visiting with her. He developed a crush on her and tried his best to court her.

But, she was using heroin again and John was able to buy marijuana from her, so together they would hang out and get high. She was usually depressed and trying to figure out how to get more drugs. He talked her into sharing some of the heroin and having sex with him. John tried the drug a few times and was immediately captured by its allure. His friend, to her credit, kept the drug away from him most of the time. She could see how much he liked it and didn't want him to go down the same road as she.

After about a year, she started not returning John's phone calls. He told me, "I knew at one point she had started to prostitute herself and was getting involved in things she didn't want to talk about. I heard a few months later that she died of an overdose. I never had a really strong connection to her, but in my mind, she was a potential girlfriend and I liked her a great deal. She was one of the only people I knew, and now I felt very alone again. But, much of the relationship was bittersweet anyway. I would take an hour bus ride to her house hoping she was home. She had cancelled her phone because of the cost. I got there and stood in the cold, foggy San Francisco street knocking on her door, and most of the time she never answered. Finally, one day the upstairs landlord came down and told me to go away because I was drunk and loud. He also said she had moved away and he didn't know where to."

Another person John began to trust and look to for closeness was a former counselor from the residential program. John was excited when he was invited over. It turned out that two counselors lived in the same apartment complex. So, there he was sitting in the apartment talking with two of the counselors that had been so pivotal and helpful to him in the program. Trying to be friendly and nice, they offered to smoke a joint with John. He accepted and felt excited about this special time with them. Looking back on it, he said, "I know they were doing what they thought was OK. But, I think I needed an authority figure I could count on and feel guidance from. But, since what I got was reefer, I went with that."

John remembers feeling fond of an older woman, probably fifteen years older than him. She lived with her boyfriend. John and this woman had been in the same child development class, and now John tried to reach out to her. He was interested in her romantically and was also just lonely and wanting a friend. They had "good talks together in the child development class." Over the course of several months, they met a few times at John's apartment and had sex. This was a much more positive experience for John than the prostitutes in Taiwan. The woman was very enthusiastic about the experience as well. But, when John suggested they "hang out more," she told him she was busy. When Christmas came, John prepared some of his home-baked breads for her and called her to set up a time to meet. Sadly, she told him to meet her at the bottom of her driveway. When he arrived, he could hear the sounds of a Christmas party in her house. When she came out to greet him, it was obvious he was not welcome to the party and she was just saying hello in an obligatory way. John gave her some home-baked bread with a card and felt great affection for her in the moment. But, she simply gave him a hug and presented him with a joint of "really great stuff."

While John was excited to receive the drugs, he felt cheap, rejected, and embarrassed. He felt like he was her fun on the side and now he was being shooed away so she could get back to her boyfriend and their holiday party. John felt a great sadness as he drove away. He went home to smoke the joint by himself. There was a sudden return to the extreme isolation he knew so well.

Here, an external experience of excitement and idealization followed by disappointment and rejection mirrored his internal seesaw of ideal union and hurtful abandonment, something so common in the unconscious phantasy world of the borderline.

A similar situation occurred when a gay man, some fifteen years older, befriended John at the grocery store. Over the next few months, the man would show up at John's apartment with a case of beer, the implied bargaining tool in exchange for sex. After repeatedly having to carry over a case or more of beer and a bag of pot for the chance to make out with John but never actually having sex, he gave up and never returned.

Once, John went back to Sunny Acres to share his poetry in a group setting. The event went very well. John was praised for the poetry and how well he seemed to be doing in the community. When they asked how things were, he said everything was fine, and they were happy for him. John was unable to communicate the growing despair in his heart, and they didn't notice it. Unfortunately, this was just like the way his parents didn't notice his problems and the way he, in turn, didn't share his problems with his parents.

At this time, John was going to nursing classes at a local junior college. Looking back, this seems to have been an identification with the residential program's nurse who took a special interest in John's progress, as well as an identification with some of the counselors and teachers there. He seemed to internalize the healing connection that can be made when someone tries to help another. As a result, John gravitated towards being a nurse, helping the handicapped children, and wanting to share the benefits of yoga and meditation with his classmates at that treatment program. In addition, there may have been some aspect of John's realizing how, in spite of their destructive ways, his parents were always trying to help him financially and otherwise.

At the local college, John tried to make some friends, but his anxiety and social reluctance got in the way. In his classes, John wanted to meet people and make connections but was socially awkward, reluctant, and psychologically conflicted about it. He had a desperate need to relate but rigidly avoided contact at the same time. He invited others into his life to a certain degree but then rejected them at another level. For example, he would suggest to a classmate that they get together for lunch, and the classmate would be enthusiastic and they would exchange phone numbers, but then John's anxiety and conflicted feelings about getting close to someone would get in the way and he would never call. If the classmate called him, he would make an excuse about being too busy and eventually the person would never call again. So, John ended up in the same lonely place as before. In psychological terms, this was a complicated mix of intense dependency and intense avoidance and rejection that mirrored and replicated his early childhood experiences in the world and his internal reactions to those experiences. This was a pathological projective identification cycle that maintained and intensified the borderline object relational struggles that ruled John's life.

After a while, John felt so anxious, lonely, and depressed that he began drinking more and smoking more pot. He found a local dealer who also had LSD for sale and began taking that. He started consuming it on a regular basis to the point that he no longer hallucinated on it but simply felt extremely high. He said, "After a certain amount of time, it was more about being extremely numb and almost senseless. Instead of tripping, it was more of a massive body and mind freeze. It was an emotional mega-buzz that removed me from the planet and took away all my worry and nerves. But, after a while, I just felt so burnt out that the emptiness returned and grew bigger than ever."

So, at this point, John had returned to his addictions and fallen prey to his emotional demons as well. However, there had always been, perhaps from the start of his life, a split of good and bad perspectives and experiences, of clarity and confusion, of direction and despair. So, while his life was starting to unravel, he was still going to school to be a nurse and he was loyally showing up to be of service to the severely challenged kids. He said, "With the kids, I was their one-on-one helper, tutor, and aide. I was amazed at how much personality and character each kid had. I really enjoyed myself and liked relating to them." In his psychotherapy treatment, we explored how it was far easier to have relationships with these kids, who could not really demand much back from John, than to have more back-and-forth adult relationships.

John continued, "Despite their extreme physical limitations, each one had a real uniqueness and expressed themselves quite a bit. The five children I helped were between the ages of six and eleven. They were the victims of cerebral palsy, muscular dystrophy, epilepsy, and various birth-related brain damage problems. They were all strapped into custom-made wheelchairs, had diapers since they could not regulate themselves, had towels around them since they drooled most of the time, took strong medications for convulsions and other conditions, and needed to be spoon-fed all their meals."

John was also the full-time, one-on-one caretaker for a nineteen-year-old, blind, autistic boy with a history of violence towards women. This duty involved teaching, coaching, and negotiating with the boy to try to be more independent and do such things as bathe, brush his teeth, get dressed, tie his shoes, and locate his silverware in the kitchen before meals. He resisted much of this, but gradually John made progress and the boy took on more and more tasks by himself. There was also an hour a day devoted to teaching him how to sort different shapes out of a box of small items in the hopes of his one day being able to work in some type of factory setting. Being severely autistic, the last thing the boy wanted was to be touched. John instigated a gradual program of brief should rubs to get him used to the idea that touch was OK. After a year of this, the boy tolerated it and actually seemed to enjoy it some of the time. In a sense, John was offering very tender, patient care to someone who had the external symptoms that John struggled with so much internally.

Sadly, this devoted, warmhearted, and talented side of John was eclipsed by the depressed, anxious, and emotionally constricted side of him. In addition, John's overall psychological condition was now made much worse by his return to drinking and drugs. As a result, he started showing up at work hung over, and while he really enjoyed his work, he counted the time until he could leave for the day and get high again. Several incidents occurred that changed everything. During a picnic, he and another aide were supposed to be watching the kids and getting them ready for lunch. John and the other aide stepped away to smoke a joint. By the time they came back, the kids had been sitting helplessly in their wheelchairs in the sun. Both of the foster parents saw how the kids had started to be sunburned on their face, arms, and legs and realized John had left them alone. He said, "I felt so bad. I realized I had done something that I couldn't take back. They didn't really trust me from that point anymore."

Later that year, another incident happened. At this point, John's drinking was much worse. He often blacked out. The foster home took the kids out to the beach for the weekend and stayed in a rented house right on the water. The foster parents brought along a friend of theirs, and one night after the kids had been put to bed the foster parents relaxed with some wine. They offered some to John. He ended up getting extremely drunk and blacking out. The next morning, no one would make eye contact with John, and he knew straight away he must have acted very inappropriately. After they returned to the foster home, he was told they didn't want him back. This was a devastating and shameful moment for John that pushed him further into drinking and emotional isolation.

At the apartment complex where he lived, John was starting to earn a reputation as well. On several occasions, the apartment manager had to use the master key to come in and turn down John's stereo after he had passed out in the wee hours with the music on full blast. John moved into a bigger apartment with a woman he met at the complex. He said, "I recall feeling sad for her because she seemed to be a very nice, good-hearted girl, but she had a nasty drinking problem and ended up sleeping with all sorts of losers. Unfortunately, I didn't give much thought to the fact that I was getting drunk all the time and sleeping with numerous women I met at the complex. I would wake up and feel that dreaded remorse that all addicts live with, but then you find a way to shove it aside with denial and some more alcohol or drugs."

Things had progressed to the point that John took a leave of absence from school. His grades had slipped and some of his teachers were asking him if something was wrong. He was pursuing the classes towards a nursing career but ended up at one of the finals with a nose bleed from too much cocaine, still drunk from the night before, and clueless about what the test questions meant.

It had been less than a year since he had graduated from Sunny Acres. John was now eighteen years old and moved into a broken down old house in Mill Valley. It was here that he shifted to a lifestyle of heroin and speed with the use of needles.

John's roommates consisted of two tree trimmers in their twenties who hung out with a welder from the local refinery. They drank a great deal but mainly focused on obtaining the most potent heroin they could find. A third roommate was a man who worked in a local factory and was addicted to speed. This was the perfect storm for John. The roommates taught him how to use a syringe, and he was quickly obsessed with the entire destructive process.

Seven

The Descent, Decline, and Eventual Resurrection

Continuing to describe his dangerous lifestyle with his new roommates, John told me, "It is amazing I never died of an overdose from heroin or speed while living with those guys. Shooting up and drinking was the main activity of any given day. However, I was still able to pull off a few other things. I had dropped out of school at that point, unable to study from all the drugs and alcohol. In addition or as a result, I was too anxious to show up, walk around campus, or interact in class. I was usually still drunk and/or high from the night before or at least so hung over and burnt out that I couldn't think straight enough to be in a class. Plus, I looked like a wreck.

"However, I continued to live a strange dual life of self-destruction combined with an ongoing desire to be a part of something better. I needed money to supplement what my parents sent me as my drinking and drug bills were pretty steep. So, I found a job at a fruit and vegetable truck a few blocks from where I lived with my roommates. It was owned by two hardworking brothers who had been in the location for years. They went to the wholesale farmers' market early each morning in San Francisco and bought cases of fresh produce. Then, they would sell it from their truck in a dirt lot next to one of the main roads in Mill Valley. I was one of two workers who would keep the bins stocked, trim the corn and the artichokes, and weigh up the goods for customers. It was hard manual labor but that was OK for me since, as I said, I wasn't in the thinking mode too much of the time. Also, I didn't have to interact with people too much or for any length of time. However, I really enjoyed the fact that it was outdoors. It was part of a natural, healthy lifestyle of fresh produce and organic living that I idealized. I got paid cash at the end of each day and I was given positive feedback for my efforts. Even though I was living such a terrible life, I really put myself into the work and tried hard to make a difference.

"At the end of the day, I was able to take home as much of the bruised fruit, the wilted spinach, and general overflow of the day as I wanted. So, I would come home with a big bag of wonderful, fresh produce every night and proceed to steam or sauté it to provide a wonderful healthy meal for the whole house. There we were, sharing a nutritious meal together and feeling very organic, natural, and healthy about it. Only problem was that after dinner we would bring out the hash, pot, heroin, beer, whiskey, and cigarettes to guide us all into oblivion.

While the one roommate and his friends helped introduce me to needles and heroin, the other roommate showed me the wonders of speed. He usually snorted it and, therefore, I did too. But, one day I met a woman he knew from a mutual speed dealer. She was a burnt-out speed freak from the sixties. No doubt very pretty back then, now she was a bit haggard and emotionally unstable. We hit it off rather well, and pretty soon I was visiting her regularly. The sex was wonderful. But, she had a five-year-old son, and I noticed how upset, confused, and resigned he looked when he had to sleep on the couch so we could have sex in the bedroom they shared in the small apartment. When we drove to the dealer to get more speed, he came in with us. He seemed to know what was going on when we turned our backs to him to shoot up the speed. His mother told him we were 'taking some medicine.' I hung out with her for about a year or two and enjoyed the wild times but felt like I was out of place. She told me about the boy's father and how he had died in a shabby motel when he had passed out from heroin and the building burnt down. I also found it fascinating but strange when we traveled to the famous Haight-Ashbury area of San Francisco to score some speed and, while waiting, she explained how she preferred shooting the drugs into her neck, as the 'big veins push the stuff to my heart faster.' I was at a point in my life where I simultaneously thought, 'That is a great piece of advice, I will have to try that,' and 'Oh my God, what have I got myself into?' Also, I was fascinated by the psychology of such a way of living. But, I didn't look in the mirror and realize my psychology was also quite disturbed.

"The last time I saw her, we were at an outdoor Grateful Dead concert together. Her young child was wandering around unsupervised while we drank, smoked pot, and listened to the music. As all drug addicts do, we would hide drugs from each other. So, when she began to act very strange and started to pass out, I realized she must have had some drugs that she wasn't sharing. She slurred her words about some kind of pills she had 'scored' and then went unconscious. I went through her purse and found them and took off to get high on my own, leaving her unconscious and her son unattended. So is the tragic life of those on the edge."

John fell silent and then told me he was very regretful and felt sorry for that little boy he left behind. John went on to say, "About ten or fifteen years later, when I was clean and sober, I drove past a bus stop and saw her and her son sitting there. They were having an argument while waiting for the bus. It was sad and disturbing. He was now a teenager, still hanging out with mom but looking very angry and rebellious, and she was looking much more haggard and even more crazy and odd. I thought, 'I was there and they still are!' I felt a shudder of anxious relief along with an intense inner stress that must be some form of post-traumatic reaction.

"This intense feeling is similar to the anxiety and emotional pain I feel when I am driving to my office in San Francisco with my stereo blaring the sounds of Jimi Hendrix or perhaps Neil Young. I am feeling really good, enjoying the music I like, going to my office decorated with the art I created and have won awards for, and I am driving a wonderful sports car I bought with money I earned doing a job I really love. All is good. I feel I am *that guy*.

I used to look at certain people and think how *that guy* has the nice wife, the nice car, a great job, is talented, and has fun hobbies, and in general has a great life. Now, I often can think of myself and realize I am *that guy!*

"But, then, I see the dirty old Shell gas station on the corner and I look to the left where the bathrooms are. Suddenly, I am back in time, thirty years ago. I had just left the drug dealer's house where I and my speed freak girlfriend had shared a needle. I still had some left from our drug buy and couldn't stand to wait till I drove back home to do the rest. I pulled in and went into the dirty, smelly bathroom. I still recall the look of fear and disgust when a man opened the door to come in and use the bathroom. I was sitting on the toilet with my belt around my arm as a tourniquet and a needle in my hand. He left and I struggled to hurry up and use the drug before I ran off in shame and fear. So, I often have these then-versus-now moments as I go about my day. Then, I try and shake it off and go forward into my current life.

With my heavy drinking, heroin and speed use, and emotional disorganization, I was not able to attend school. However, I still felt a need to be of service and was still interested in the human condition as a helping career. So, I found an ad in the newspaper for a volunteer job. Twice a week, I would drive my beat-up car to a local family with a ten-year-old daughter. She had almost drowned in a pool accident a year prior. Having been without oxygen from being under water so long, she was declared a vegetable with irreversible brain damage. After being in a coma for many months, she was now motionless, simply staring off into space. She no longer had any motor control, had to wear diapers, was spoon-fed, and had around-the-clock care. The family had begun a controversial new treatment called 'patterning.' The idea was that when an infant first learns to crawl, the motor actions stimulate basic brain development. So, this technique involved four volunteers working together to move her limbs in a crawling motion for ten minutes at a time followed by other special exercises. There were four shifts a day. I helped with the patterning exercises and also helped feed her. While she only occasionally grunted, I encouraged her to speak. Finally, I conducted stimulation sessions in which a variety of sensory objects, such as soft fur, scratchy cloth, sandpaper, a rock, water, putty, and so forth, were put into her hand and rubbed gently on her skin. I would tell her what the object was and how it might feel. I would say, 'That is soft' or 'This is hard,' and help her gradually make links and differentiations in her environment and with her body's sensory system. While I was often hung over from drugs and alcohol, I was always very focused. The family appreciated my work and could tell I was sincerely interested and dedicated to the work. I continued this volunteer work until I had to move.

"So, I would do my good deeds and then return to the den of iniquities where I lived. There, I found myself involved in the heroin drama in which one of us would have bought some but claimed to have none so they didn't have to share. But, someone would find out and say something nasty to the one with the drugs. It was a constant lack of trust but then a strange shift into brotherly bonding when we all ended up high, sharing needles and passing around the pipe. It is a miracle that we all didn't come down with AIDS from that. There were horrible fights between the two tree trimmers and the welder. Once, one of them stuck a small explosive device in the sink of another one's bathroom and blew the entire sink right off the wall. After the yelling and the cleaning up, we all had a great laugh. The sink was never replaced.

"In the end, there was so much dysfunction in the house and trouble paying the bills that we all went our separate ways. I found another roommate situation in the next town and moved in with four other individuals who liked to party but were a bit more responsible. So, I ended up being the strange one, the one who 'couldn't keep it together.' I had a small room in the back of the house, and I moved in my king-sized water bed. It was so big compared to the size of the room that there was literally no room to walk around. So, there was no furniture, just one big water bed, and I put all my clothes and stuff in the closet. One day, while driving in the country, I saw a sign indicating a sale on chickens. I ended up bringing home three chickens with the idealistic idea that they could live in the back yard of my new housing situation. This was probably a drug-induced fantasy based on the pet chickens I had as a child. Of course, my roommates thought it was bizarre. After three days, the chickens were torn up in pieces all over the yard from either wild animals or local dogs, and my roommates demanded I clean up the horrible mess. About this time, my former roommate and heroin connection contacted me and said he was out of work and wanted to 'do some traveling.' Since I was doing nothing except drinking all day and trying to find drugs, I thought it was an excellent idea. Sticking with my usual impulsive lack of common sense, I immediately sold my car for a few hundred dollars and packed my backpack for a hitchhiking trip up the coast.

So, with a good supply of weed to smoke and several bottles of whiskey, my old roommate and I took off hitchhiking up the California coast. We waited around forever for each ride, but we slowly made our way north. When we were dropped off each day, we tried to find state camping grounds by the ocean to unroll our sleeping bags for the night. It was beautiful country and truly amazing to see. But the bigger reality was that it was freezing cold, we were dirty and full of sand, and we were drinking our way through the little money we had. We had no goal or destination except to get high and hitchhike north. We talked about idealistic visions of reaching Alaska and finding a job in the fishing industry, where we heard there was 'good money to be made.' About as close to that as we got was the day we finally made it to a small town in Oregon. It was right by the ocean and was primarily a fishing town. We were smelly, dirty, hung-over, and aimless. There was a fish processing plant fairly close to the campsite we had staked out. So, we decided to sneak in there, hoping to use their onsite showers. We managed to make our way through the place and take a shower before getting caught, and we had to run out of there while still wet but at least clean. That town was about as far as we made it on our epic trip, since we had run out of money. The trip back felt awkward and unsettling. Without any drugs or alcohol in our systems, we felt the reality of things. We were going back to nothing. We had no jobs, no money, and no plan.

"Once back at home, I realized I had no car and that taking the bus was very inconvenient. The roommates I had were splitting up and moving, so I had to find a new place as well. I begged my parents for help with a new car and funds to move. As usual, they bailed me out. This was always appreciated, but in looking back I have mixed feelings about it. On one hand, if they let me sink or swim, I may have come to my senses a lot quicker and not have wasted so much of my life. However, I think my level of emotional disturbance and addiction was such that I would have easily gone off the deep end and either been killed or suicided rather quickly. By helping me along, they did enable my problems, but they also kept giving me a safety net that allowed me to eventually come out of the fog in one piece. I feel badly that I put them through it, but I still feel much of it was because of their lack of understanding to begin with. As you can tell, I still have mixed feelings about it. But, that never-give-up attitude is something I think I have taken on in my own work with others."

Here, John is aware of a valuable and positive aspect of his projective identification process in which he now, in his social-work career, tries to hang in there and help the underdog as his parents did with him. Indeed, John's creativity and personal growth through years of psychotherapy and intensive psychoanalysis, as well as his sobriety, have enabled him to offer a new chance to others, just as he has found a new chance. So, John does not just hang in there, but he tries to explore, understand, and master the underlying meaning of people's troubles, just as he has done with himself. However, as his story shows, he still confronts many old and new problems along the way.

John continued, "Anyway, I found a new roommate situation and off I went. This time, I moved in with three guys, two with drinking problems. One was an out-of-work drummer, and the other was a booking agent for musicians, but he never had much work. The third roommate was a conservative plumber who kept to himself and didn't get involved in our antics. Most of the time, I and the other two alcoholics sat around drinking, smoking, and trying to figure out how to get more weed. During the time I lived there, I kept trying to find another side of life, but it was hard. I wanted to be like the plumber who seemed stable and happy. I would sit by the pool on sunny days and read books suggested in some of my classes. At this point, I was taking a few courses at the community college towards a basic AA degree and looking at the nursing degree as a career possibility. I wanted to be interested in all these more healthy directions, but I also felt pulled away by a desperate loneliness, a horrible anxiety, and a crushing depression.

"Trying to get back into helping others, I found a low-paying job taking care of two kids while their single mother took time off for herself. This was a woman twice divorced who obviously had psychological problems. She was prone to partying and feeling righteous about 'respecting my body by not allowing birth control devices inside of me.' Apparently, this had led to her having four children, two of whom she was now sole caretaker of, since there were no men around except for her latest hot date. That is when I would be called in to babysit for her two kids. Her older daughter was no problem, but it was interesting taking care of her youngest. This was a six-month-old infant who was severely handicapped. I was told she had extensive brain damage and an abnormal digestive tract. So, in order to feed her, I would have to put a tube down her throat without choking her and then push a liquid food through a syringe to her stomach. This took a while and I had to do my best to soothe the baby while I did it. I was also in charge of changing her and trying to put her to sleep when she was ready for a nap. I had never held a baby let alone tube-fed one! So, this was an adventure. I felt proud to do it and felt love for this poor infant, but I also felt alone and uncertain.

"Another short-lived employment experience I had at this time was as a television delivery man. A television and stereo store offered free delivery, and the owner hired me to be the one who delicately brought your new expensive purchase to your home. I was very scared for several reasons. The biggest vehicle I had ever driven was my small, beat-up, used car. For this job, I was driving an old moving van that seemed enormous. I had no concept of how to navigate its large girth around tight corners or back it up driveways. Also, I was solely responsible for hoisting the large and heavy televisions into the van, out of the van, and into your home. Over the couple of months that I stuck with this low-paying job from hell, more than one customer looked very anxious when I, with my shoulder-length hair and alcoholic aroma, precariously made my way down their driveway with this old van, barely missing their mailbox, and began shoving their giant TV onto a small dolly to wobble into their living room."

The way John talked about these memories and this time in his life sounded very lonely and adrift. I asked him about this. He said he was indeed very lost during that time and tried to meet people but felt too anxious to make any real ties. He wrote poetry as an outlet but felt it was "a dead end." Interestingly, this creative spirit that emerged when John was in Sunny Acres, and when he was feeling so scattered as a teen, still helps him today. During a recent session, John came in and told me he had written a short story that he then submitted to a children's magazine. He said, "I'm pretty sure it won't get published, but it was fun to write and enjoyable to just do as a way to express myself." I read the story and found it amusing but also noticed that the sense of being lost, being abandoned, being in pain, and hoping to be rescued, found, understood, and loved that permeated John's childhood still resided in him as an adult. These aspects of his personality were fairly undisguised in his story.

John called the story "Stella's Prize," and it went as follows:

> Stella is a three-year-old black pug. Pugs are the dogs that look like little pigs with a squished in face. They are very affectionate but prone to laziness and loud snoring.

Stella the black pug had been part of a traveling group of eight show pugs owned by Betty and Bill. They traveled around California competing for prizes at the local dog shows. While Betty and Bill loved all their pugs and took very good care of them, Stella was never very happy. For one thing, she suffered from car sickness. So, when they drove from show to show, she felt quite ill and hung her head out the back window of the bus for air.

The other dogs in the group were cream-colored pugs, which is what most people are used to seeing. Black pugs are more unusual and tend to be mistaken for fat black tadpoles with buggy eyeballs. So, the judges at dog shows tended to see Stella as the oddball and never awarded her any points in the contests.

In fact, Stella had been in countless different dog shows since she was a puppy and never won any prizes. More and more, she felt no one must like her. She was so depressed she broke out in a terrible case of dog pimples. Her little black face had big red dots all over it. Now, the judges had another reason to mark her down.

Stella sat in the back of the pug bus and felt very alone and sad. She was convinced she was worthless, never having earned a single point in any category at any show and always being the only black pug around.

With her black face covered with red dots and a big F on her dog show report card, Stella was about to give up. The final insult was that Betty and Bill had put her up for sale! Since the dogs that won the competitions meant money and fame to the owners, pimply dogs with no trophies were unwanted. Of course, they wanted to find a good home for Stella, but nevertheless Stella was crushed.

So, in the summer of 2009, Stella was truly at her lowest. She hid in the back of the pug bus, depressed and car sick. As the bus pulled up to the Annual County Dog Show and parked in the big field where the show would be, Stella broke out in a few more pimples and cried.

Across the street from the show, there had lived two little dogs named Peanut and Popeye. Peanut was the smallest variety of poodle, the teacup. She was loved by her owners, Wanda and Peter. Peanut was now sixteen years old, which is more than 110 years old in human years. She should have had a small, teacup-sized cane and a tiny granny shawl over her tiny teacup shoulders. At this point, Peanut was blind, totally deaf, and quite forgetful.

Popeye was a cream-colored pug who had been Peanut's best friend and helper for many years. Popeye would use little Peanut as a pillow to sleep on and Peanut seemed to like her job as the official cushion. When Peanut was older, blind, and not sure what room she was in, she would follow Popeye around until she figured out where she was. Sadly, when Peanut was almost sixteen, Popeye died very suddenly and the family was devastated.

Everyone was sad, but Peanut was overwhelmed with grief. She would wander around sadly during the day and cry all night. A sad cloud hung over the home.

> Soon after the demise of Popeye, Peter was driving back from work. He saw the big dog show going on and pulled in. He found a black pug for sale named Stella. Peter thought she was so cute and thought Stella might help everyone over their grief from missing Popeye. An hour later he arrived back home with a new friend for Peanut. It has now been six months, and Peanut and Stella are doing very well together. Peanut uses Stella as a compass to find her way around the house and is glad to have her job back as official cushion.
>
> And, for Stella, life has become brighter. She has a comfortable pillow every night and someone who is happy to follow her around the house. For Stella, the best part of the deal is how much Wanda and Peter love her. They accepted her immediately and thought a black pug was a special and extra-wonderful thing. Over time, as she felt more confident and loved, Stella's pimples went away.
>
> Every once in a while, Wanda and Peter surprise Peanut and Stella by bringing out big blue prize ribbons and proudly announcing that Peanut and Stella have both tied for first place in the monthly Best Dog Contest. The whole family cheers and then it is biscuits for everyone. For the first time in her life, Stella feels she is truly a winner. The End.

Obviously, John's story is a thinly disguised version of his own life experiences. The story describes the same sense of rejection, loss, abandonment, and depression that John felt growing up and the same difficult history of constantly moving around and never fitting in. Perhaps even the dog's pimples are a reference to the awkward and painful adolescent years John speaks of so often. But, interestingly, John has also included a happy ending to his story in which Stella/John is found, rescued, appreciated, and loved. So, this is an example of a positive and creative growth-orientated side of John's reliance on projective identification. He was able to envision a better object that understood him, and in his mind he created a better relational outcome for himself via his projection onto Stella. He was able to break new ground internally instead of simply repeating the angry, hurtful trauma over and over through more pathological projective mechanisms.

Going on with his story about his new roommate situation, John told me, "I continued my sad ride into oblivion with drinking all the time and drugs whenever I could get them. I fancied myself a nature lover, so I would take long walks in the hills behind our house. I would smoke as much pot as possible and bring a six pack of beer with me. Then, I would just wander around in the woods looking at the trees and feeling free and easy. A mellow nature lover was an easier identity to take on than to admit to myself I was a lonely loser with a drinking problem. My roommates grew to not respect me, as I would have black outs and say or do things that offended them. They grew to see me as the kids in high school did, a drug addict out to get high at everyone's expense. I had nothing to give and only wanted what I wanted. I was not able or willing to be social so I seemed very withdrawn and selfish.

"During this time, I was with a couple of women for short periods. One example was a prostitute I picked up when she and her eight-year-old daughter where hitchhiking. They were homeless and poor, and I invited them to stay at my place. Another time, there was a sweet younger girl down the street who was smitten with me, but after I kept having sex with her without pursuing the deeper relationship she obviously wanted, she took her sister's advice to stay away from me. There were numerous women I brought home from the bar after we both had closed it down. This was always followed by the awkward morning ritual of trying to figure out who they were and what their names were.

"I was back at college, barely keeping up with my undergraduate courses and working part-time at the pet store I used to work at when I was at Sunny Acres. Only now I realized the owner was a cocaine addict and an alcoholic. I was part of his drama of divorcing his wife and co-owner of the store after his affair with another girl working there and his descent into alcoholic oblivion. I would wake up in the back room of the pet store, after we had spent the night drinking and snorting cocaine. Without a shower or a change of clothes, we would slug down another beer and open the doors for the customers who asked us questions about bird food and wanted to buy tropical fish. Again, my other, more healthy side was struggling along for the ride. I was actually very interested in the pets and, having read through all the books the pet store had, I was very knowledgeable about any species of tropical fish we sold and any underwater plant, goldfish, or flea product you could imagine. I liked my job and I was very good at it, even though I was probably a very scary person to deal with. My hair was down to my waist at this point, and I always stunk of booze and cigarettes. Yet, the customers always asked for me because they knew I cared and was honestly trying to help them. Again, my giving nature was trying to stay afloat throughout my selfish, destructive spiral downhill.

"It was while living in this roommate situation that I ended up with hepatitis. I managed to meet up with one of my old heroin buddies and we shared a needle while doing some of the drug. I remember feeling extremely ill the next week or two and having a stiff neck along with the worst possible flu-like symptoms. But, it wasn't until some ten years later that I found out from a blood test that I had Hep C. What I did find out during this time from blood tests at a physical exam prompted by dizzy spells and an ache in my side was that my liver was now damaged by very high enzyme levels. This was, in the doctor's words, a classic sign of severe alcoholism. I was drinking at least a six pack of beer a day, but when I had the money, it was always more. A typical day when I had enough money was more like six shots of whiskey, six to ten beers, lots of pot, and any cocaine I could find or afford.

After we could not afford to pay the rent anymore, this band of roommates broke up, and I found several other misfits to move in with in another town in Marin. At this place, I ended up with a girlfriend who was twenty years my senior. She was a forty-year-old alcoholic on disability for mental health problems. She was prone to fits of rage and violence when drunk, but we loved to have sex and drink together. Eventually, I moved into her house when I was kicked out of this house, but I had to experience my first overdose before making my exit."

At this point, John told me a detailed story about one of the many scary, emotionally torn moments in his past that showed him, again, to be frantically struggling for life among his death-seeking behaviors. John told me, "Imagine my delight when I talked my drug dealer into fronting me $500 of cocaine. In 1985, this was quite a haul. I told him I had 'an eager customer' to sell to and promised to pay him within 48 hours. I felt guilty lying since he was one of my only friends, plus it seemed crazy that he would trust me, given that I was one of his best customers.

"This period of time was part of a thirteen-year low. I was moving through life without ever thinking, just grabbing and digesting all the drugs and alcohol I could find. I was anxious and depressed, to the point of being suicidal, and I did my best to blot those feelings out. Nevertheless, I was aware enough of my chaotic reality to end up feeling like I was watching myself careen through a sad series of events without brakes or steering wheel. Like when watching a scary movie, you want to yell at the character to 'watch out for the monster around the corner,' but you know they won't hear you.

"My drug dealer was a really nice guy, a noted musician 'back in the day,' whom I would sit around with and chat with for hours—fairly easy when you both are high on a stimulant. I was at his house so often I felt like family.

"He and his girlfriend were interested in my college endeavors. First I was enrolled in a nursing program, but now I was studying psychology. On the surface it seemed we were having nice scholarly discussions about academic matters, although I never let on that my life was completely out of control and that I was barely passing my classes. In school, I was usually hung-over, trying to stop a drug-induced nosebleed as the teacher called on me to answer a question about something I knew nothing about, since I had chosen to go to a the bar instead of the library. The quizzes seemed so foreign they might as well have been written in another language. I felt ashamed to be sitting there smelling like stale beer and pretending to take a test on a subject that I knew nothing about.

"So, on one level, I felt cool to be hanging out and discussing my psychology program with my friend—the famous rock musician—his beautiful hippie girlfriend, and their cute five-year-old daughter. But my mind was still hanging on to enough bits of reality to painfully notice the other side of this study in denial.

"In fact, my friend/drug dealer was the former drummer for a famous sixties band that hadn't really done much in twenty years. He lived in a house bought back when he had money and fame. It looked like a quaint cottage at night when I went to pick up my goodies, but in the light of day, it was a rundown dump with a sagging roof and a rusted washing machine sitting in the front yard. He hadn't recorded anything in over a decade and only practiced occasionally in order to jam at the local dive bar once a month. He still knew other luminaries from the sixties' music scene, so when they came to buy drugs I got to meet people I had seen in *Rolling Stone* magazine. But most of them were still making records and were buying cocaine for recreation, not dealing it for a living. When I saw my dealer's five-year-old daughter watching him prepare the scales to weigh out the cocaine, I knew something was terribly wrong. But that is the painful life of a drug addict. You know you are living ugly but you don't walk away, you hang in there over and over, becoming part of a sick distortion.

"My dealer's girlfriend was a quiet woman who looked like the stereotype of a California flower child, now a bit wilted. She seemed to be drawn to me, and over time we developed an unspoken attraction for each other. It was clear that if her boyfriend wasn't in the picture, we would have become involved. One day, when driving around town, I saw her walking along by herself. I stopped and we talked for a while.

"I had two distinct feelings. I wanted to ask her to come home with me. She would have said yes, and we would have gotten high, had sex, and had a great time. I envisioned the union of two hipsters, I the bright college student and she the sophisticated older woman who used to be married to a famous Berkley beat poet and now living with the rock star. The other part of me realized that this would probably get back to my drug dealer/rock star, ruining my chances for any more 'bindles' of blow on credit.

"But, the sober little man that lived in the back of my head was whispering in my ear. I was painfully aware that here on the side of the road was a washed up, aging woman who lived with a drug dealer and looked like a bunch of dried flowers, a faded remnant of what used to be vibrant and alive. Chatting her up was a terribly confused drug addict, completely adrift and desperate for love and comfort. So, I said goodbye and made my way to the liquor store for my nightly six pack and half pint, with the hope of ignoring the empty void that was tunneling into my soul.

"Remembering I had this large pile of cocaine in my pocket made everything else in my life very unimportant. All I wanted to do was race home and start consuming. Of course, I was madly justifying and rationalizing how to use 'only a small amount' and then figure out how to sell the rest in order to pay my dealer back. The truth was I didn't know anyone who would want to be a part of this scheme, so I had to figure out how to either come up with the money myself or give the drugs back, which was definitely out of the question. I had a syringe from the last house I lived in where I and a group of crazy tree trimmers shared a love of heroin. These were guys who drove pickups, carried knives and guns, ran chainsaws for a living, and relaxed with a stiff shot of 'China White' in the evening. They taught me the love of opium and the pleasure of the needle. So, now I was racing home with a giant bindle of cocaine in my pocket to a lonely syringe waiting at home.

"Once I got there, I went straight to the bathroom and began shooting up some of my on-credit bonanza. Very quickly, I was in wild negotiation with myself. 'I will only do this much and then that's it! OK, I will do a little more, but after that I am done! Well, there is a little more than two-thirds left, so I might as well make it an even half. Oh well, I will figure out how to come up with the money to pay him back somehow. Fuck it, I am doing some more! Oh, the hell with it. Let's do it all!'

"This last idea was what must have done me in because the next thing I recall is coming to on the floor with blood all over the bathroom, as the more whacked I became the sloppier I was with the needle. I heard someone banging on the bathroom door and yelling my name. I crawled up off the floor and managed to put the last of the drugs in my pocket right before a fireman kicked down the door. I was too weak to say much so they took me to the hospital to monitor my heart. Off I went in a blaze of red lights.

"At the hospital, I went through all the emergency procedures and an hour of observation to make sure my heart was functioning properly. Apparently, I had shot so much cocaine that my heart had gone from overload to not working well at all. This left me so weak that I talked in a whisper. There were two moments that stayed with me. One was being told I was lucky because 'another minute or two on the bathroom floor and [I] would have been dead.' The other was overhearing two nurses talking: 'It's just another Marin County kid overdosing. They must have nothing better to do.' I felt some shock but mostly humiliation. I was already scared and alone, but now I felt I was part of a group everyone looked down on. Sitting in the hospital waiting to be released, I was embarrassed, scared, and ashamed. I was also excited and amazed. I still had the cocaine in my pocket, and no one had searched me or taken it away! I could do some more! I was ecstatic. The fear and shame were quickly buried with the thought of another high.

"But, my party had to wait. When I got home, I was still very weak and almost unable to speak. My roommate Karen had called the fire department, and she was there for me the moment I stumbled back in the door. She brought tea and sat with me for hours. I was still physically drained and in a state of emotional shock. Karen held my hand, taking care of me late into the night. Up to now, she had been my roommate, not much more.

"I already had a sense that Karen was interested in me romantically because whenever I had my crazy, alcoholic girlfriend over, spending all day in my room drinking and having sex, Karen seemed a little jealous. My girlfriend was twenty years older than me. She was an ex-model who drank from the moment she woke up. She was funny, nice, and interesting until about the tenth glass of wine, and then she turned vicious and violent. We moved in together a year later and put a modern spin on some of Tennessee William's more depressing plays.

"Karen was very quiet and withdrawn. The only thing I knew for sure about her was that she was always depressed and acted peculiar. She was on heavy medications and looked lost and lonely, spending most of her time locked in her room, rarely saying much when she came out. Karen was one of the characters in my dysfunctional reality show. She was on disability for depression and schizophrenia and hadn't worked for years. Down the hall from Karen was Ann, the responsible one in the house. She made sure our rent was paid and dealt with our 'last chance' notices from the utility company. Grossly overweight, she chain smoked and had a dog that shed more than seemingly possible. To keep up with the daily rainfall of dog hair, Ann was constantly vacuuming. When not in the kitchen cooking and eating enormous amounts of food, Ann was in the living room vacuuming up endless amounts of dog hair. We also had a friendly guy from New York crashing in the living room, always singing loudly to Billy Joel tapes. He paid us with food stamps and unemployment checks and brought home donuts on Sunday mornings. Not nearly as nice or fun loving was the creepy guy who slept in the garage. He kept to himself, acting very edgy and suspicious.

"What was my unfortunate character choice in this sick movie? I was the college student who never seemed to have any homework, only a driving focus to drink as much alcohol as possible and scrounge around for the next drug score. Out of my roommates, I had the only car. However, it barely ran and I added a dent every week by driving in a perpetual blackout, often ricocheting from guardrail to guardrail.

"So, after spending the day recuperating with Karen by my side, I felt better and went about my business. I could tell she felt we had bonded and she hoped that we would become more intimate. She looked like a shy little puppy that had come out of hiding in the hopes of being petted and loved. But, this shift in our relationship seemed unimportant as I got back to the business of pursuing the next high.

"About a month later, Karen jumped off the Golden Gate Bridge. Everyone in the house was stunned but not surprised. She had attempted it before. In cleaning out her room, we came upon her diary and I was sickened to read about her feelings for me and her hopes for our relationship. I felt she saved me and then I turned my back on her. I didn't want to be her boyfriend or rescue her, but she paid attention to me and tried to help me through a terrible moment. I wish I would have done that for her. Thirty years later I still feel guilty about it."

At this point, John started to share a wide variety of stories of his painful experiences during his addiction. The seemingly random and scattered expression he began to use seemed to parallel the sense of scattered confusion and psychological chaos that he had survived. While fragmented in terms of time and sequence, John's stories still were a sharp recollection, a meaningful reflection, and a painful memory of a life of dramatic internal struggle.

John went on to tell me the various details of his life for many more months but his story continued to be more disorganized. He started going back and forth from one period of time to another and from one location to another location. This disorganized state of recall was matched by his increased anxiety and reluctance to share these events with me in treatment. He said, "It just gets worse and worse as I try to share it with you. It is too painful to go through. It becomes just another gut-wrenching story of another wrecked car, another failed relationship, another blackout, another arrest, another sexual disease, another time I stole money and ruined a friendship, another time I lied to my parents, and another time I hated myself and felt so lost and completely alone that I wanted to drag a knife over every inch of my body till I *bleed* to death. There was even a point where I lived in an old cabin in the Marin countryside right by a large creek. There was a historically devastating flood that year and I literally got out five minutes before the cabin and about half of everything I owned, including some of my pets, were washed away for good. I was walking through a foot of water that was rushing under my front door. I just had to get to the refrigerator to get the beer out of it before leaving. I knew I could be electrocuted because the water was past the height of all the electrical sockets in the place, but I needed to get my beer. I feel traumatized recalling these events. It leaves me overwhelmed. I have these sick images I lived through, many humiliating, devastating, and terrifying moments that I haven't begun to share with you yet. But, what I have told you must give you an understanding of what I am still trying to move past. The first thirteen years of my life were very difficult and full of loss, anxiety, and anger. The next thirteen were a long ride down to emotional hell. Since then, I have been trying to build something new."

I pointed out to John that his use of the present tense in his "till I bleed to death" comment about wanting to cut himself indicated he was currently feeling that way. He agreed.

Over the next few months, John continued his life story with me. But, his sequence of events was now more of a blurry, messy, erratic tale of misery and the limping efforts of someone who wanted to change and give to others. But, that more positive aspect of John was constantly overshadowed and beaten down by the chaotic and destructive actions of drugs, alcohol, and mental illness. Over time, we understood these patterns, and the way he shared his story with me was a valuable window into what John's emotional state was actually like back then and the traumatic fallout that still exists today.

John told me, "After the flood, it really got worse. Over the course of the next few years, I collapsed emotionally and physically. I drank as much as possible every day and searched for any drug I could find. I tried my best to find the fullest state of oblivion possible. My parents tried in their own way to be supportive and caring by paying all my bills. They now lived in Washington and came out to visit me on Christmas and usually one other time during each year. They were horrified to see me in such a state but kept going with a steady combination of denial, fear, sadness, guilt, and hope."

At the same time, there continued to be many examples of how John struggled to grow into a more productive adult who gave to others and had creative interests. He continued to work on his poetry and various art projects. He continued to volunteer with various needy children's groups. He tried to join a local singing group but quit after feeling too anxious. He did some work with an environmental agency but didn't feel interested enough to continue.

John began to do quite well in the psychology classes he had to take for his nursing program. He felt particularly interested in them and received good grades and compliments from the teachers. John attended meetings and workshops for a local "death and dying" caregivers movement that later would become famous throughout the country as a new way to understand and assist the dying individual. It was similar to the hospice movement but more in line with the human potential movement and the holistic healing approaches that were popular at that time.

But, there were countless situations in which drugs and alcohol were the driving force to divert John from these more positive and life-defining paths to this more destructive and desolate position.

Recently, John told me he was driving through an area of Marin County that he hadn't been through for years. He was taking the back way to a golf course, one of his creative hobbies he now involves himself in, and found himself driving past the small studio cottage where he once lived. John was drawn to it and immediately had intense memories come back. He reminded me how this was the last place he lived before he stopped drinking and drugs. It was where he "hit bottom." After the historic flood of 1984 washed away the small cabin, John had spent time in a motel and then in a back room in his landlord's home. His landlord was an alcoholic in a wheelchair and they spent many a night getting drunk and doing drugs. When the cabin was finally rebuilt, John moved back in and continued his downhill descent.

In his own uniquely eloquent manner, John told me, "This little cabin is in a funky area of Marin County off a dirt road. I stopped and got out of my car and went over to the cabin. There is a yard all around it and then there is the creek. I was taking it all in and noticed hundreds of stones strewn about in the yard. They were peppered here and there in a random way. But twenty-five years earlier, they were all in nice straight lines and precise circles as part of a vegetable garden. They were like little soldiers guarding the vegetable plants they surrounded, a squadron of ten rock soldiers for every tomato plant and a team of rock troops for every squash. It was like a rock garden combined with a vegetable garden, but above all it was a victory garden." John was filled with emotion.

I asked John what he meant by a "victory" garden. He said, "After thirteen years of drugs and alcohol addiction, after cutting myself on a regular basis, after smoking two packs of cigarettes a day, and after living with a level of anxiety and depression that made suicide something I pondered every day, I finally gave in and quit. I had started feeling awful about myself and about life when I was very young. But, my actual acting out and addiction days started when I was thirteen. They officially ended when I was twenty-six when I was living at that cabin.

"My therapist at the time, probably the tenth mental health worker I had spent time with at that point in my life, told me she would not see me anymore if I kept using. My doctor told me my liver was going to shut down if I didn't stop, my parents were terrified and furious, my landlord was about to throw me out even though we still went to the bar together all the time to get plastered. I was peeing the bed and not caring about it. I had no friends whatsoever, and since I spent all my money on drugs and alcohol, I was broke to the point that I was eating dog food. The culminating moment for me was when I realized I was eating kibble out of a big bag of dog food and washing it down with a beer while my dog sat there skinny as can be because I was keeping the kibble to myself. This was truly the low point for me. My dog looked up at me and cried for food. I wouldn't give him any because I thought I could have more money for drugs and beer if I hoarded his food.

"So, I decided to quit and turn my life around. I stocked up on hot tea and cigarettes and stayed at home. I didn't get out of bed for four days. I drank water, pissed the bed, ate an old sandwich from the fridge, threw up, and smoked many cigarettes. I hallucinated the first two days, and the next day my body hurt so bad I thought I had broken some bones. I was later told by my doctor that I probably had a seizure from withdrawals.

"At the end of five days, I came out of my cottage and looked around. I was completely baffled about what to do with my life. But, I didn't want to get high anymore. I felt like crap, but I also had a burning desire to do something meaningful with my life. This was the empty emotional void that usually drove me to my dealer's house and to the bar, but I forced myself to channel it somewhere else. I had always liked the idea of gardening even though I wasn't any good at it. I borrowed a shovel and some other gardening tools from my landlord's garage and started digging up the large space behind my cottage. I got the idea that I could make it pretty by having all the plants lined with stones. So, I got a bucket and began trips up and down the banks of the creek.

"Every day was a busy trip to the nursery, hauling rocks up from the creek, digging holes, and carefully planting seeds and baby starter plants. This was a sizable plot and the whole thing took weeks to complete. But, that was the point. I needed something that totally absorbed my time and concentration. It became my substitute drug. After I was done, I entered the next phase of this new devotion. I had to water, feed, and protect. There was a virtual army of slugs that marched on my green shoots of faith, and I was out there to stab them with a stick or toss them into the creek. I and the rows of creek stones were to stand guard and make sure this garden was a victory. In doing so, I became a victory. I was clean and sober for the first time in many years, thirteen to be exact.

"I started going to twelve-step meetings at this same time. Again, like my drug and alcohol problem, I became fairly obsessed about the road to recovery. I went to a meeting every day. This was good because I wasn't doing anything else with my life and time on my hands was not what I wanted. So, it was the victory garden by day and meetings by night.

"Since I was a virtual recluse and hated being social, I went to the low-key small AA meetings they had in the rural area where I lived. No one demanded much, and I felt relatively accepted but also left alone."

This defined way of seeing the world and way of wanting to be accepted and involved but not too close or committed is a fluctuating set of emotions that seems to have solidified at an early age and followed John throughout his adult life. "Don't forget me but don't get near me," "I want to know you and be with you but don't ask too much of me," and "Let's do something together—maybe" are all ways that this hot/cold, desire/fear mindset seems to manifest for him. Indeed, John's drug and alcohol problems could be seen as a defense against these fears and conflicts as well as an emotional compromise. He got to feel a wonderful union with the euphoria of drug and alcohol oblivion but then faced the lost, alone, and barren life that came with it.

After John successfully stopped using all drugs and alcohol, life was immediately different but also very much the same for a while. He realized he loved all his psychology classes and didn't really enjoy the medical classes he had to take for nursing. So, he switched to another college and began to pursue a degree in psychology. He helped many people along the way in Alcoholics Anonymous meetings and Narcotics Anonymous meetings. As part of his college classes, he started to volunteer at a local rehabilitation program and conducted group therapy sessions for the recovering homeless addicts. John also became a grief counselor and a therapist for a local crisis center.

However, the first five years of sobriety continued to be an emotional jungle, with John feeling suicidal, needing heavy psychiatric medications, going to therapy several times a week, being unable to stop crying for weeks on end, cutting himself to the point of needing stitches, calling off an engagement to a new sober girlfriend, and feeling unable to envision any sort of viable future.

Yet, over time and with an enormous amount of personal work and determination, he did change and grow. He met a woman in college and married her. John says, "She is my true soul mate. She gets me and I get her. We are mated!" He graduated college and went on for specialized graduate training, winning many awards. He took up hobbies and found a source of creativity in photography, in teaching, and in writing. John has established a successful private practice in order to help others, and he feels fulfilled and stimulated. He has published many articles and books and is internationally known in his field. A special soul who was lost has been found. John finally found himself.

SECTION III

Analytic Observations and the Analytic Process

Eight

Taming Destructive Phantasies

While transference interpretations are usually considered the most effective and deeper method of making analytic contact (Waska, 2007) with patient's unconscious phantasy and conflict state, certain patients seem to require and do better with additional methods of therapeutic communication. With narcissistic and borderline patients who are prone to acting out internally or externally, the analyst may sometimes need to make more immediate restorative observations of the destructive nature of the patient's object relational phantasies. Specifically, these are analytic interpretations of the way in which the patient is using, abusing, controlling, demanding, or devaluing the self or other. The analyst is more so stating a fact about the transference and the internal landscape of the patient's unconscious phantasies than making interpretive links about causality, defense, or anxiety. These more traditional interpretations often will follow, but to define, contain, or ground the patient in the reality of their transference acting out with analytic observations must often come first. These more firm or containing observations translate the acting out into an object relational fact of how the self and other are being valued, de-valued, attacked, or abandoned. Without these more fundamental translations of acting out that create symbolic meaning rather than concrete action, the patient may escalate, fragment, or further devolve into their narcissistic or borderline state and the treatment may be at risk.

Gabbard (2004) considers analytic observations to be highly expressive methods of offering insight and understanding that are as complex and healing as a standard interpretation. Gabbard defines the analytic observation as a technique which stops short of a full interpretation in that it does not attempt to explain or link. The motive or explanation is left for later. To expand on this, I would add that it is vital with these hard-to-reach patients who make up much of our typical private practice caseload (Waska, 2005, 2010a) to highlight the specific nature of their object relational phantasy and the destructive, controlling, limiting, and rigid nature of how they view themselves and others. The analyst is stopping at that exact moment in the transference to say, "Take a look. This is exactly how you see our value and this is exactly how you are using us and placing us on the chessboard of life." This technical procedure is meant to match the immediate clinical need for symbolic translation, containment, and emotional definition. The linking to why the patient needs to do so and the patient's associated conflicts with love, hate, and knowledge are the next step in the analytic process. But, for many of these more primitive patients, especially when they are lashing out or acting out, the analyst observation paves the way to that more traditional interpretation. Before that can happen, we must assure the treatment is intact and that understanding or personal thought and meaning are not a casualty of the patient's acting out in phantasy or reality.

Analytic observation is helpful in promoting much needed understanding in chaotic and confusing cases with patients who struggle against understanding and being understood (Joseph, 1983). Of course, when analytic observations bring about new relational modes and the potential for change, this new state of relational openness is often experienced as a threat to the patient's psychic equilibrium (Joseph, 1989) and as such, they experience change as danger (Waska, 2006). They feel in danger of losing their control and omnipotence, leading to persecutory dependence and an overwhelming lack of definition and identity (Shafer, 2005). To give up the false self is to have no self at all. Since it feels like we offer nothing in return, we are seen as merely stripping them naked and leaving them alone and cold, vulnerable to the world's cruelty. This is the psychological feelings state of being taken out of a familiar psychic retreat (Steiner, 1993) and towards the depressive position (Klein, 1935, 1940) this primitive state of loss (Waska, 2002, 2005) creates a renewed level of acting out and psychological retreat.

The types of transference acting out that analytic observations are meant to define and translate vary widely. But, the theme is a destructive, controlling, aggressive withdrawing, or defensive entitlement that is rigid and concrete. In the realm of the death instinct, it is either predatory, as with destructive narcissism, or defensive, as with libidinal narcissism or thin-skinned narcissists. But, in both cases, it is always unbending, defiant, and absolute.

Envy often plays a role in the narcissistic acting out we encounter. Cairo-Chiarandini (2001) has noted that for some patients, the recognition of difference between self and other creates such envy and loss that the patient feels incomplete at a very fundamental and disturbing level. Turning back to familiar states of mind within primitive narcissistic organizations (Spillius, 1983) or pathological organizations (Steiner, 1993) is felt to be essential to regain a sense of safety, power, and identity.

Analytic observations point out elements of phantasy and transference, such as the patient's fear of dependence, the patient's devaluation of the analyst, the patient's identification with the idealized vision of the analyst, the patient's masochistic control, and projective identification evacuation of all unwanted knowledge or affect. Another such element of acting out that analyst observation can help define and contain is the concrete grievance resistance that Spillius (1993) speaks to when she describes patients who demand we agree with their sadomasochistic view of the world and the concrete ways they feel injustice as occurred or we become yet another grievance and insult on their lifetime list of hated objects.

By using analytic observations and hopefully finding a way to follow them up with more traditional interpretations that link to the underlying conflict and defense of the phantasy state, we can eventually help patients through the extreme anxiety they have regarding loss, mourning, and grief. These narcissistic and borderline patients are more comfortable being angry about what they never receive and more in control waiting to one day receive what they never had than they are mourning and grieving the failure and loss of hoped-for objects and the desired vision of self and other from long past that have never come to pass (Carpy, unpublished).

Another aspect of envy that takes over the analytic situation if it is not corralled and managed properly is noted by Lopez-Corvo (1999). He describes how an idealized object is internalized and felt to be unreachable and withholding to another aspect of the self, creating unbearable anger, hurt, loss, and envy against the self, but then is often projected. Lopez-Corvo recommends interpretations that speak to the intra-psychic conflict as primary and transference conflict as critical but secondary in these cases of extreme self-envy. This is very similar to how the focus of analytic observations is to describe the nature of the patient's in-the-moment object relational phantasy and the narcissistic elements of that phantasy. How the object is viewed and how the object is used are the immediate concerns of the analyst, and linking to symbolic meaning and underlying anxiety and conflict is brought in afterwards. Only when a more defined or contained climate is reached without the acting out threatening the stability of the treatment can more predictable transference interpretations be possible and helpful.

Analytic observations translate the concrete acting out of internal phantasy into the facts of symbolic interaction between self and other, internally and externally. The analyst offers the patient the knowledge of what the patient is doing to and with others in his mind, shifting the action of acting out into a description of emotional interaction. Hard-to-reach and slow-to-thaw patients often have a fundamental fear of and hatred of knowledge and of having to learn or not to know everything already (Taylor, 2004). Indeed, as Roth (2004) notes, the most painful fact we must all face is that we will never learn or know everything about ourselves or our objects, and in that sense, our patients struggle with having to grieve never being complete, never finding the answers, and never being in control, all pertaining to both self and other.

Analytic observations are designed to provide what Feldman (2004) sees as the essential task of the analyst, that being to assist the disturbed patient to find resolution and integration to their internal chaos and sense of despair. With analytic observations, the analyst follows the elements of the patient's acting out with enough clarity to translate exactly what the patient is doing with himself and with the analyst, internally and externally. The analyst shares this knowledge with the patient to provide containment, definition, and a sense of understanding. This engenders the patient's experience of a helpful, functioning container (Bion, 1959) that is able to and willing to tolerate the patient's projections without rejecting them or collapsing under their toxic intensity (Hinshelwood, 1999; Waska, 2010b, 2010c).

Analytic observations serve as a pre-alpha function for the desperate or angry narcissist seeking or demanding a container for immediate discharge of their unwanted and toxic aspects of self. Analytic observations serve as an organizing tool for the patient who is acting out on his object and in desperate and immediate need for a reflective surface to find understanding. Analytic observations provide a reflective surface that also does not allow for any further destruction or abuse of self or object. It is a clinical movement towards the life instinct that stands up to and defines the death instinct motives of the patient's destructive phantasies.

Grotstein (2000) and Cartwright (2010) have examined the differences between holding and containment. They note that some traditional interpretations offer the element of holding as a therapeutic measure in more intense and aggressive projective identification attacks on self or other. Other more standard interpretations offer more meaning-making and mental links that promote the experience of alpha function from a caring object. Analytic observations are a technical method of offering something of an in-between or hybrid of both.

These therapeutic observations are more encompassing and insight-giving than a holding remark but not quite as a transformational as the alpha function that traditional interpretations offer. Perhaps we can use the formula of Holding←→Analytic Observation/Pre-Alpha Function ←→Interpretation/Alpha Function. This shows how the analytic observation serves as an early stage alpha-function container and translation of object relational phantasy which provides immediate functional containment while interpretation proper provides symbolic meaning or full containment with links to unconscious meaning and purpose. Another way to state this is that analytic observations name the phantasy by action taken on self or object and interpretation tames the phantasy by decoding the reasons behind the actions taken in unconscious phantasy.

Analytic observations can be and are often made in both an analyst-centered and patient-centered (Steiner, 1994) manner, but the communication must be not only how the patient sees his object but also what he is doing to it. Over time, this hopefully creates an atmosphere of exploration of otherness, healthy separation, and peaceful difference. In such a new world, otherness can be respected, autonomy is of value, and the self is still powerful and important even when not ruling over all or forcing fusion between self and others. This then creates a bridge of increasing self-ownership, leading to responsibility for what one feels and thinks instead of blaming others or feeling persecuted and powerless. It means we are the authors of our needs and can fill them ourselves some of the time and can rely on others in a fair and kind way for the rest. We can face incompleteness, lack of control, and the inability to have the imperfect past restored (Spillius, 2007). We can know and accept that we will never know. We can learn that we will never finish learning. Thus, the object no longer provokes such envy, persecution, or guilt and can be considered the imperfect source of love, learning, and understanding in a three-dimensional symbolic world that includes loss of love, lack of learning, and failure to be understood, but with whole-object functioning the emotional experience is also of enough love, learning, and understanding that at the end of the day all is still well.

CASE MATERIAL: PATIENTS M AND W

I have been meeting with M for about three months. He came in to examine his long-standing problems with "anxiety and boredom." He told me he really likes to be around people and considers himself very social, but he went on to explain, "I hate to have to be alone. I get very bored and tend to just watch TV or do nothing. I lose all motivation and feel quite lost. But, if I can call a friend or organize a get-together with people, I instantly feel better." I said, "It is not clear if you really want to be with each person for whom they are or if you are in a way using them to stop this lost and bored feeling."

It was the very robotic way in which M talked with me, not quite callous but certainly aloof or disengaged from the thought of others as separate important entities, that made me elect this more direct and defined method of making analytic observations. In doing so, I was pulling no punches as to what I thought was taking place in his phantasy world. I spoke to the destructive or controlling object relational manner in which he seemed to engage with others and with me in the transference. M responded in a very matter of fact manner. M said, "Well, I think it is a bit of both. I need them to be with so I will feel better, but I also like them for who they are. They are my friends and they mean a lot to me." So, M revealed a mixture of relational and narcissistic motives in his answer. I replied, "So, you need someone to play with or you feel lost and alone. But, you have special people you like to spend time with too." He nodded yes. Here, I went with my counter-transference image of a lonely and possibly entitled little child, wanting someone, anyone, to come out and play with him so he might feel better. M seemed to understand my metaphor quite well.

M told me about the relationship he had been in for over a year. He explained that he met a woman and "started hanging out and having a real fun time. I enjoyed her company but I wasn't head over heels about her. On the other hand, I noticed she started to really like me and seemed to be falling in love with me. I thought this could be a problem since I didn't feel that way. But, we have continued to be together for over a year now." I asked, "You haven't wanted to clarify it with her along the way?" I asked this based on my complete counter-transference impression (Waska, 2011a, 2011b) of how he was talking with me, the way he was physically with me in the room, and the overall attitude he held. Based on these feelings of mine that were based on how he seemed to want to use his objects, I wondered if he was trying to have his cake and eat it too.

M said, "Well, I didn't want to hurt her feelings. But, I understand that it might hurt just as much or worse if I wait and tell her later. Things were really fun and enjoyable with her, and I thought I might have more feelings later so I just went along with it." I asked, "I wonder if you didn't want to give up the fun part so you kept your lack of feelings to yourself?" Here, I was continuing to follow up with M on my speculation that he was trying to have his cake and eat it too. I wanted to set the record straight, if possible, between us; otherwise, he would only be telling me a half-truth just like he was possibly telling his girlfriend a half-truth.

M said, "Yes. There was that element to it as well. I liked how things were going so I didn't want to have that disturbed." This feeling of having his world just so for his pleasure and control came out in various ways as we proceeded. I interpreted that M was anxious if he felt that control was taken away or in question. He told me he has always "liked things just so" and he wants to "be able to predict what is happening and to have everything be a known quantity." So, I worked with this obsessive, controlling need that combined with a more narcissistic profile by combining more traditional interpretations with some tougher or defined analytic observations. As a result, we slowly found our way towards what seemed to be a core of anxiety around the phantasy of being alone without control over the world.

After dating his girlfriend for over a year, she was accepted to advanced schooling in a distant city. She was quite upset about how they would be pulled apart and asked M if he wanted to go with her. They discussed the possibility and M told her he had to stay to continue his job and his current training. So, they began exploring the idea of a long-distance relationship. She was hopeful but worried, and he told her, "I'm not sure if it will work, but we can try."

M told me he has felt pressured to figure out how to make it work and said, "She is definitely more in love with me than I am with her, so I am having a hard time telling her what I think. I don't want to hurt her feelings. I told her I think the long-distance thing is going to be very stressful on the relationship so we may have to reconsider our plans and the future." Again, I felt he was holding back with me and not being honest with me about the plain truth of what he wanted. I said, "I think you are holding back from telling me about the more basic thing you want. Maybe you are worried about looking like a selfish person to me and to her. So, you are trying to make me think you are much more thoughtful. But, it looks like what you are really saying is that you want to use the moving away situation as a convenient excuse to break up with her." Here, I was making both an analytic observation about how he was using or manipulating his objects as well as an interpretive explanation of what I thought his anxieties were. So, it was a firm and containing analytic observation about his phantasies and his use of his objects, but also a more traditional interpretive remark about his fears and defenses in the transference and with his objects.

M said, "You are right. That is what I was doing. I didn't really want to go through all the hassle of a breakup. I don't like having to talk all about it, to have to help her with her feelings, and to end up feeling guilty about hurting her feelings. So, it was just much easier to blame it on the distance and be done with it. I want to have us be done and to move on to the stage of just being friends so we can continue to hang out, since I really enjoy her company and like doing things together. We have a lot in common and I don't want to lose her as a friend. I just hope she doesn't take too long to get to that stage."

This statement left me feeling surprised once again at the complete lack of empathy M had for his objects. I said, "You seem to want to have a playmate to escape feeling bored and lonely. And, you don't like it if someone is not operating on the same page as you. If she isn't over her grief on your time, you are irritated because she can't be your friend as soon as you need her to be. You need us all to do your bidding or you start to feel anxious and uncomfortable." I combined an analytic observation about his misuse of others and an interpretation about his anxiety over loss. While very difficult to locate, loss is often at the bedrock of such cruel ways of using one's objects but exists at a more primitive paranoid-schizoid level (Waska, 2002, 2005, 2006).

M replied, "I guess I have a timetable and I am over the relationship already. So, I don't like it that either I am supposed to act like I am still all broken up about it or, if I act like I feel, which is that I am definitely ready to move on, she will see me as a jerk and feel hurt. I don't want to hurt her but I don't want to have to wait around to get on with my life either." I reminded him that it had been all of two weeks since they broke up and he was already impatient and seeing her as an inconvenient obstacle in his way. This was an analytic observation of M's view of his objects. M said, "That is a good way to describe it. I do feel she is in my way and I want her to hurry up and just be my friend." M was demonstrating the intensity and rigidity of his narcissism and his desire to have people be like his chess pieces on a board he controlled.

This style of grounded analytic observation that translates the basic manner in which the patient is using or misusing their objects or themselves is very beneficial when working with certain types of borderline and narcissistic patients, especially those more thick-skinned patients such as M. However, it is usually not advised as a technique with some more thin-skinned patients and libidinal narcissists, specifically those individuals who are prone to persecutory collapse or fragmentation from chronic traumatic experiences not yet fully integrated or worked through. Such patients benefit more from the traditional analytic interpretations of unconscious desire, anxiety, and defense.

An example of this would be W, a patient I have seen in analytic treatment twice a week for almost two years. With W, I almost never use analytic observations. Instead, I favor more traditional interpretations that offer holding and containment and import meaning to his anxiety, conflict, and primitive defense. W was easily devoured by fears of total annihilation and bottomless emptiness. He was put into a religious cult by his divorced and alcoholic parents at age six. He only saw his parents from time to time for the next six years. During the years between six and twelve at the cult, W reports many incidences of sexual abuse and physical as well as emotional abuse. This was an extremely traumatic experience for him. As an adult, he was with a distant and abusive girlfriend for five years before she died in a horrible car accident. Since then, he has been in a relationship with a volatile alcoholic. After ten years together, she started to cheat on him. That was when he came to see me.

W is also an alcoholic and abuses drugs. He drinks a great deal to cope with is sense of emptiness, abandonment, and lack of direction.

Many if not most of W's sessions involve his recounting the horrors of growing up in the cult and how "lost and terrified" he felt during his adolescent years and in his twenties. He talks a great deal about his masochistic relationship with his current girlfriend and how, even though she seems to want to see him only for financial or sexual reasons, he still holds out hope for them to get back together in a committed relationship. But then he feels devastated when she again shows evidence of "not really being into [him] anymore." W often tells me of "new evidence" of her still seeing the man she cheated on him with. So, an example of my interpretive work with W is when I noticed that even though we meet on Tuesdays and Wednesdays, he would bring me a separate check for each session. After a long time of noticing this and thinking about it, I said, "I notice you pay twice instead of once a week. I wonder if you are so unsure about the future and our connection that you have to keep it all to one day at a time."

This type of interpretation involves my providing an alpha function, containing and interpreting his anxiety and his defensive posture. In doing so, I convey understanding and encourage reflective thought and self-containment, and propose gradual trust in self and confidence in others as a possibility worth considering.

At first, W took my comment about the checks as an accusation. He seemed flustered and apologized. He told me "I will make sure I always give you one bigger check. I am sorry!" I said, "I think you are worried you have broken one of my religious cult rules and now I will turn on you and punish you. So, you are really nervous and want to apologize. But, that is your fear. I am not angry. I am more wondering if you are so convinced that your connections with me, your girlfriend, your parents, and the world are so fragile that you can only count on what is in front of you. And, even that seems precarious." W started crying and said, "I am unsure about what is around the corner and if I will even wake up tomorrow. Most of my life, the next day always seemed to turn out so horrible!" So, I was focusing on the *why* of how he used us and placed us in the transference, rather than the *how* and *what* that analytic observations highlight. In doing so, I helped him to connect more and work through the intense uncertainty and anxiety he lived with so constantly.

In the next session, W said, "I thought about what we talked about and I think I will give you a bigger check next time." I said, "You are going to risk believing that we can be OK together in the future." He nodded yes with a great deal of emotion in his face. With W, there is rarely the type of intense narcissistic or borderline acting out that requires firm therapeutic observations.

With his more thin-skinned narcissistic anxieties, the more usual containing interpretations are most helpful.

Now I will return to the case of M, who does stir up much more dramatic, destructive, and chaotic acting out in the transference and in phantasy, internally and externally. During one recent session, M told me, "I put everything off. I have so much to do around the house and various projects from work as well as things I really want to do for fun. But, if I have to do something I don't feel like I will enjoy, I can't find the motivation to do it. I can't focus on it at all and tend to put it off till the last minute. I think it is a serious problem of procrastination. Maybe I have that attention deficit problem I hear about and need some kind of medication so I could be more focused."

Again, in the counter-transference, my experience of listening to M describe these problems left me picturing a spoiled child who doesn't want to do his chores or homework and would rather go out and play. I felt he was, in a sense, telling me how little guidance he had and how much he needed some kind of help or mentoring. On the other hand, it seemed like he simply didn't want to do anything he didn't want to do. In trying to sort out these two elements of my counter-transference for clinical information, I came to think that this was the mixture of libidinal and destructive narcissistic qualities Kleinian authors have described in certain more difficult to reach patients.

So, I interpreted by saying, "It sounds like you are describing a little kid who only wants to do what he wants to do. He doesn't want to do homework or chores and only feels comfortable when he can do what feels like fun. He hates everything else and feels trapped and anxious when he has to do all the adult stuff."

M replied, "When I have to face all those things I don't want to do, I immediately want to call someone and hang out with them. If I can find someone to be with, I will always put off whatever it is. I don't like to have to be alone and then do all this stuff I am not interested in. It's boring, it makes me anxious, and I feel dark and gloomy. But, if I can find someone to do something with instead, I feel great." I interpreted in reply: "You sound like you feel lonely and lost all by yourself and can't handle it so you want to run to someone for comfort. Also, it sounds like you are using people as a filler when you feel bored and lonely. You want to go out and play and call around until you can find a playmate to have fun with. So, maybe you use other people to escape that horrible feeling of loneliness, the dark gloomy place."

Here, I was confronting his narcissistic manipulation and use of others to take away his unhappiness, as well as interpreting the more tender and painful anxieties underneath. Therefore, this was a hybrid of therapeutic observation and traditional interpretation. I started off interpreting the destructive narcissistic aspects and went on to add the more libidinal elements of his feelings and actions. M replied, "I tend to manipulate people. I have done that my whole life and I am quite good at it. I use people to get my way. I know how to spot people's vulnerabilities and weak spots and then I exploit them. I make it a point to size people up that way and then I take advantage of them."

In the counter-transference, I felt we were making a breakthrough on one hand but I also felt scared and shocked at the callous degree in which he was having this straightforward conversation without any apparent reflection or realization at how careless he was with the feelings of others. Therefore, I chose to introduce another analytic observation.

I said, "You are using us all to avoid having to be with yourself and face some kind of anxiety, but it also sounds like you are disgusted or sickened when you see others being weak or vulnerable. You are saying you pick out the weak one in the herd and pounce." Again, with this type of narcissistic patient, this more tough and direct observation is useful (Rosenfeld, 1987) and important in this exact moment in order to help the patient face the object relational reality of his actions on the other or on self rather than continue on in the transience as if all is right and normal, which would be a counter-transference enactment or collusion. A confrontational comment grounded in the intrapsychic reality of current phantasy material is an analytic observation by definition and helps to ground the patient in a less combative, confusing, and catastrophic internal world.

M said, "I exploit my friends and anyone I meet to get what I want. I look down on anyone who lets themselves be taken advantage of. If they don't see it happening, they deserve it. I feel I have the right to manipulate them if they don't have the brains to see me coming. My girlfriend was like that. She always was so sweet and always trying to be there for me. I saw that as a giant weakness and I definitely took advantage of that."

I said, "It sounds like you are very angry when you feel like others are open and giving. Something about that makes you want to attack us. You are being predatory when you see love or kindness. You are saying that we have it coming." M said, "Exactly. I sort of feel like, if they let me get away with it, I should do it. If you are not going to stop me, then why should I have a conscience about it? I know I should set that kind of limit for myself, but I feel like if others don't do it, then they have it coming."

I said, "So, I am confronting you on it. What is that like?" He said, "It actually feels good. I have never had anyone really call me out on it. You are the most honest and most confrontational therapist I have ever had. I like it. Some of my friends have told me I can be very cold, and some of them have gotten angry at me for me using them when I am bored. One time when I was bored I called a friend to go over and do stuff, and he said I only call him when I don't have anything to do. He felt used. But, you are talking about the bigger way I do it." I said, "Yes. There seems to be some very deep anger or vengeance you feel that makes you want to target everyone to do your bidding or else. I am having to protect myself by calling you out, and you respect that, but you don't like having to limit yourself by respecting me and others just for who we are. Instead, you are saying we have to earn your respect."

Here, I was interpreting the relational meaning of what M usually does and feels nothing about. The narcissistic manner in which he used projective identification to make others an extension of himself and a pawn in his game of life took away any impact or relational meaning to his interactions. My meaningful comments attempted to bring life back to his actions. Again, these last comments were a hybrid of analytic observations and standard interpretations that both spelled out how he was using us and viewing us as well as why he might be treating us that way.

M said, "When you said 'protection' it made me think some. I do everything I am talking about because of my parent's divorce. When I was seven, they divorced after years of yelling and fighting. Then, they used me for the next ten years as a fucking Ping-Pong ball to fight with each other. They put me in the middle and went back and forth year after year fighting about visitation rights, custody issues, and money problems. It wasn't that either one of them wanted to spend more time with me. They just saw me as a weapon in their fight with each other. I never felt they loved me. They just used me. If they can do that to me and feel fine about it, then now it is my turn. I will just do the same to everyone else. Why not?"

I said, "And no one drew the limit with them. No one said stop it. No one told them to stop being so selfish and start paying attention to their son. So, now you have no limits and don't pay attention to the humans around you who might need love or could love you." M said, "I hate coming here and never look forward to it. But, I notice that I leave feeling very good. I have been thinking about the things we talk about and it makes me feel better, less anxious. I also went home last time and actually did my projects that I hate. I felt lonely and wanted to not do them. I wanted to call someone instead and go have a beer. But, I thought about how I had to face the darkness or the gloomy feelings that come up. I didn't really enjoy it but I felt better later."

So, this was a breakthrough for M. He was starting to reflect on himself and was considering himself less superior and more human. As a result, the humans around him had more value and weren't merely pawns in his kingdom. M had made a critical link to his history and his sense of being merely a weapon in his parent's selfish fighting. Now he had a foothold in life, and we could work more on the life-affirming aspects of his experiences instead of fighting off his death-instinct manipulations and destructive withdrawals into himself.

CASE MATERIAL: PATIENT H

H is a thirty-year-old woman I have been seeing in psychoanalysis four times a week on the couch. She has had problems with severe depression and anxiety. In relationships, she feels unwanted, unheard, and toxic. H feels she is to blame for all problems and is sure of my imminent disgust or rejection. Then, she flips to feeling angry with me and all others for never being enough or never understanding her just right. H is a patient who seems to fluctuate rather quickly between thick-skinned and thin-skinned, between paranoid and depressive, and between more severe pathological organizations and more integrated states of mind. This oscillation was more jagged, unpredictable, and severe when we first began treatment. Now, the shift is more healthy and hopeful, leaving her with longer periods of time exposed to the real world and relating as an equal in a less cruel world in which she gradually feels more accepted and more accepting. However, this is still a very iffy process and prone to breakdown.

The period of time I want to concentrate on occurred recently, in the sixth year of analytic work. For several weeks, H had been describing various situations in her life about which she was unhappy. Over and over, the theme seemed to be that, angrily, she thought most of her objects should be doing something different from what they were doing, and she was angry that they were "not doing it right." Also, she felt she should step in and rescue them in some manner to save them from the dangers of not doing it right. Overall, H described being surrounded by objects that were not operating in the manner she saw fit, and she wanted to take over and make sure they did it right.

So, it might be that her friend needed to seek help for her financial problems but never got around to it. Therefore, H thought she could step in, "be helpful," and set up an appointment with a financial advisor for her. Or, H was sick of how her boyfriend always seemed to want to hang out with his family and seemed to like them more than H's family, so she wanted to have yet another talk with him about it. As a result, he was "sick and tired at having to stop and talk about that topic almost every damn day." He felt H was "far too sensitive and not letting other people do their thing without taking it personal." H was also unhappy with how the special training program at work was being run, and she ended up debating with the supervisor about how it should be changed.

I tried to explore these states of mind in which H appeared to be anxious, angry, and extremely controlling. She seemed to feel that her objects were either not treating her well enough and should make major changes, or her fragile objects were in danger or not organized well enough, so she wanted to set them straight and make things better for them. Of course, no one was ever asking her for help. In several instances, she ended up being told off and asked to essentially mind her own business. Some of the disagreements were over things that might not even take place for a year or two, but H said, "I couldn't get them out of my mind and had to find an answer to them now."

I tried to interpret that she was very anxious about those around her when they seemed not to be operating as she expected or as she thought best. I said she seemed anxious about her own safety or the safety of others and wanted to fix it all immediately. However, this meant that she was trying to orchestrate and control many people and many things, and that was always doomed to fail so she must feel she is always losing ground and not able to steer the ship properly. Therefore, I suggested, it must feel like it is just a matter of time before things go completely out of control and either she, me, or others are in harm's way.

Here, I was making a standard interpretation regarding her transference phantasy, desires, conflict, anxiety, and defense. I was also thinking about the pathological way H was using projective identification to place aspects of herself into her objects and then either attack them and/or try to rescue them. She took both actions by trying to control others and, via projective identification, often felt controlled by her environment. I also gave her this interpretive communication from both an analyst-centered and a patient-centered point of view (Steiner, 1994), which in my mind provided a balanced and non-accusatory way of communicating with her.

H, however, was unhappy with me for this line of interpretation and said I was calling her "controlling" and "some kind of nasty person." She then outlined the concrete details of each situation and each of her grievances as if to say, "Given the actual circumstances, you would have to agree with me. I had good reason to criticize them." Here, H seemed to show the type of "agree with my anxiety and grievance or else" standoff that Spillius (1993, 2007) speaks to. In fact, that is what I felt in the counter-transference. I felt I could only agree with her or I would be immediately branded as not on her side and against her. I felt controlled and as though I were yet another object in her world that needed to be under her control or it was out of her reach, against her, or in danger. My being in danger was the result of her assaultive projective identification and was evident in how, fairly often, H would ask me, "Are you OK?" or "Is everything all right?" If I asked her for details she would say I looked tired, I seemed angry, or I sounded bored.

So, I interpreted that she would only allow me to be one way. I was restricted to a one-dimensional way of existing. She would not allow me to be caring, concerned, or confused. And, in the case of the controlling topic, she would not allow me to have my opinion. She was now controlling me in that I had to simply listen or agree, but if I were to say anything out of line with her view or that challenged her view, I was automatically hurtful and blaming. This was more of an analytic observation.

H said I was too quick in telling her what I thought and that I didn't listen to her before "sticking a label" on her. I replied, "That is my experience as well. So, I wonder if you are not sure who is who here. I try to say something to you to help make some sense out of things for you, but before I can really finish you are very quick to size me up as blaming and not understanding. I think we have to sort out how it is that you so quickly lose yourself in me and others. It looks like it is uncomfortable for you to let me and others have our opinion even if it looks different from what you expect or think is best. When we are two individuals, separate, it looks like danger and you try to fix it as soon as possible by making us all one. But, then I think you feel swallowed up in that and want to be your own person, and it becomes a vicious cycle."

I was interpreting the narcissistic phantasy of oneness in which H forced us together by intense projective identification and splitting. Fusion was the solution to her anxieties about difference. But this led to a sense of suffocation and lack of value. This was projected as well. This cycle of projective identification was a pathological component in an ongoing psychic retreat (Steiner, 1993) in which there was always a right and always a wrong, and never any way for us to be together except in this controlled, forced manner. This was a very difficult therapeutic impasse, typical of borderline or narcissistic issues in which existing closely together but still apart as unique beings is very threatening and triggers the types of acting out and repetitious defense systems that H demonstrated. Lasting analytic contact became very delicate, hard to reach, and hard to hold on to for any length of time.

In the last few weeks, H had been complaining bitterly about how most of the important people in her life had been falling down on the job of meeting her expectations for someone supportive, understanding, and caring. H found fault with her boyfriend for always criticizing her, her hairdresser for always talking about herself, her physical therapist for not being empathic enough about M's chronic back condition, her teacher for seeming to overlook her efforts and hard work, and her analyst for "not getting what [she was] saying" and for being "obviously angry" with her. She would take me to task over and over again when I would use a certain word, and she would then pounce on the word as being "hard evidence" that I didn't like her.

After her telling me "how irritated" she was with her landlord for weeks on end, I said, "You are irritated with your landlord quite often. It seems like you feel he is never willing to give you the time of day or tend to your requests. From what you say, you feel very defeated and fed up." While I was trying to explore the underlying sense of betrayal, of being ignored, and of wanting something and being denied, H grabbed the word *irritated* and started a feverous debate and accusation process with me.

She said, "It is obvious with how you called me 'irritated' that you hate me. I am sorry that I have made you feel that way, but I can't believe you see me that way. All I am trying to do is to explain some of the problems I am having. I can't believe you would end up saying that I am so irritated. You don't seem to get me. I want to believe that you can help me, but it doesn't feel like you get me." Now, in the counter-transference, I felt completely misunderstood, blamed, and twisted around, which was exactly how H said she was feeling. I used this information to try to gain my balance and think about the intense and targeted projective identification process that was shaping the transference and counter-transference.

I said, "You are taking my words and twisting them around so you feel attacked and I am the bully. You are telling me that you feel irritated with the landlord and not being cared for or understood by him. That is exactly how you feel right now with me too. I think that with me, you are wanting me to understand you and help you, but at the same time you are fighting me off and twisting things around so we have very little room to be together. Instead, we are very far apart, and whatever I say next will only be heard as a further division. So, we have to figure out this pull-and-push way you feel with me."

Here, with a more analytic observation, I was pointing out the destructive death instinct as it operated in the transference and how H was doing damage to our ability to be together. I was also interpreting her conflict and struggle between the life and death instincts and how that was affecting our work together. So, it was a direct or tougher analytic observation that said, "Hey! Look at what you are doing." But it was also a life-affirming interpretation that said, "Hey! We have to figure this out so we can improve things and make sure you feel understood."

During the next few sessions, H continued to bring up what seemed to be an endless list of grievances around her disappointment and irritation with various authorities and important people in her life. After a while, I said, "You want to look up to, rely on, and trust us all, but you end up disappointed and let down by all of us and that leaves you lost and angry." H became angry upon hearing this interpretation and said she felt I was blaming her for being disappointed in everybody. I felt handcuffed and unable to say anything without being told I was wrong and insensitive. I said this to her and she said, "Well, I may just be an angry person. That is the common denominator. I had a dream the other day. It was after I saw you and had that disagreement with you over all this crap."

H went on to tell me of her dream about an angry man confronting an authority. In the story, the man has come back to be with his daughter after being away at war. There was a trainer at a local gym that had become a kind mentor to the daughter and had helped her enter a number of local marathons. She had won several prizes. But, when the father came back into the picture, he found out about the relationship and warned the trainer to back off and not have anything to do with his daughter or else. H said it made her nervous in the dream how rough and intimidating the father was and how his threat seemed genuine and scary. She said it was "powerful and intimidating. It scared me!" I said, "Given what we were just talking about and your feelings about my comments, I wonder if this is a warning to me to back off and stop telling you my opinion about things."

Now, I also thought the dream was a reference to elements of her envy over my helping her to change, and now she wanted to take over and do it herself. I thought it could also be about primitive oedipal issues around who got to be with whom and who was off limits. Finally, I did think she was afraid of her own angry, possessive self. But, given the current nature of her transference phantasies, I choose to make my interpretation more in the direction of her anxiety over my having my own opinion about what she was doing. H wanted me to back off and mind my own business. This was keeping with the Kleinian approach to the here and now and the total transference.

In response, H became very upset and angry with me. She said, "You are not listening to me and once again blaming me and telling me I'm just an angry person. What have I done to make you see me in such a poor light? You keep telling me I am an angry person. Didn't you hear me say how scared I was of this man? What about that?"

I said, "Yes. You did say that. I still wonder if you are scared of your own anger and how, when others don't do it the way you want, you feel very disappointed and angry. Sometimes you blame yourself and other times I think you end up angry but also quite guilty or anxious about it." H said, "I can't believe you say that kind of crap. I feel terrible. All you do is tell me I am an angry person!"

Here, I felt she had escalated and put us into a no-win zone; therefore, I made a more grounding and defining analytic observation. I said, "You are the one who said you are an angry person. Practically the first thing you said today was that you think you are just an angry person and then you went on to tell me about the dream. So, I am simply following the trail and think you are still talking about your view of yourself as an angry person. I think it scares you to be angry, so you don't like it when I point it out as a possibility. It's very complicated and overwhelming but we can slowly sort out who is who and who is feeling what. Otherwise, it is like a ricocheting bullet—it is unclear who fired it but somebody is bound to get hurt."

H said, "I am pretty sure I know what you mean. I get pretty worked up and start to feel like you don't like me and that no one understands. But, I feel better now, and I think we might be able to work this out as long as you don't leap before you listen." I said, with a smile, "As long as you can do the same!" H smiled and left. So, the analytic observation helped to reduce her anxiety, translate her object relational phantasy regarding what she was doing with her object and how she viewed it, and contain her borderline acting out. Of course, with this type of case, it is often a temporary victory.

Indeed, I was not surprised when H arrived for the next session and told me, "I am shocked and worried you feel I am shooting bullets at you. I feel uncomfortable if you think one of us will be hurt." It is this shifting from primitive depressive back to paranoid, and from a more structured or whole-object moment back to a thin-skinned narcissistic experience, that is characteristic of her pathology. However, over time, my combination of analytic observations and traditional interpretations seems to be helping H find a gradual transition from a frightening paranoid-schizoid experience (Klein, 1946) to a more mature and stable depressive position with the resulting slow move towards trusting her objects and believing in herself.

Nine

Translating Destructive Acting Out

In working from a psychoanalytic perspective, we notice some patients acting out their phantasies and anxieties in a very narcissistic manner or in a way that suggests a rigid pathological organization (Rosenfeld, 1987; Steiner, 1987). Sometimes, in the heat of this paranoid-schizoid (Klein, 1946) mode of relating, we encounter transference states that require something a bit stronger than our normal style of interpretation. By making a more defined and containing analytic observation of our patients' acting out, we can draw attention to the relational nature and impact of their phantasies, both internally and externally. Once we have helped patients be more in touch with and more directly face their deadening or entitled stance with themselves or their objects, we can more easily move towards a more traditional interpretation in which links between anxiety, underlying desire or need, and unconscious conflict can be made. However, without the more observational and sometimes stricter, firmer, or even confrontational communication, it is difficult to find a way to work with these harder-to-reach and tougher-to-thaw individuals.

The case report offered in this chapter focuses on a couple in which both individuals were prone to narcissistic acting out as well as more thin-skinned borderline volatility. They had built a mutual psychic retreat (Steiner, 1993) based on envy, rejection, revenge, and entitlement that prevented more depressive (Klein, 1935, 1940) functioning and symbolic thought (Segal, 1974, 1977b, 1981). Ordinary interpretations seemed to do no good until more direct analytic observations were made about their transference acting out, their destructive narcissistic phantasies, and the object relational results of those controlling and demanding standoffs.

In the course of this treatment, I was drawn into various enactments (Waska, 2010a, 2010b) in which I unconsciously took sides, was pulled away by the patients' forceful projective identification attacks and provocations (Waska, 2004), was prevented from establishing ongoing and stable analytic contact (Waska, 2007) by their mutual defensive reactions to underlying fears and anxieties, and, as a result, was sometimes unsure of how or when or why I was being used and placed in their internal landscape. It was a stormy process that moved back and forth with volatility, but little by little I saw a predictable transference theme emerging which I tracked with analytic observations and interpretations. These less than perfect circumstances are not unusual when working with more disturbed patients (Waska, 2005) who see change as danger (Waska, 2006). These are patients who rely on excessive projective identification to constantly destabilize the container function of the analytic environment and are unable or unwilling to engage in their own internal containment for a variety of object relational conflicts involving life-and-death struggles between love, hate, and knowledge between self and other.

CASE MATERIAL: ANALYTIC OBSERVATIONS WITH A COUPLE RESIDING WITHIN A NARCISSISTIC RETREAT

Nick and Nancy related to me and to each other in very particular ways. How they acted, how they dressed, and what sort of arguments they were quick to get into left me with a few immediate impressions. My counter-transference image of Nick was of a demanding, spoiled little boy who liked to tell everyone what a generous martyr he was. Nancy seemed like an obsessive, demanding, histrionic woman, dressed like a teenager despite her age of fifty-one. She wanted Nick to constantly provide sex, money, and attention, while at the same time she didn't want to share much of herself with him either emotionally or financially.

Nick and Nancy came to see me after ten years of arguments over money, sex, commitment, trust, and dependency. When they married, Nancy told Nick she had a legal agreement that enabled her to keep her ranch and livestock as her sole property. She came from a family of horse breeders and had inherited a sizable ranch with many horses. She did not want to have Nick be a legal partner in any of those assets. She felt it was all her property and she wanted the right to do with it as she pleased.

Nick had agreed to this, but he has always resented it and has brought it up many times over the years. He told me, "It is her way of showing how selfish she can be. She clearly does not want to be a team." Nick was also quick to tell me how he wasn't like that and, in fact, how "generous and sharing" he was. Nick told me many stories of his sacrifice of time and money on Nancy's behalf and that if he had a ranch, he would "immediately share it" with Nancy. Nick insisted, "That is just how I am. I give anything and everything without any thought of myself. I don't keep score. I love and I give. That is who I am!"

In response, Nancy would quickly shake her head and tell me how "absurd" this was. She said, "He is always watching out for himself and always making sure he has plenty of time for himself and his car racing. Nick is never home. He is usually off with his car-racing buddies." Nancy told me she was often alone on the weekend because he leaves for a car race. Nick interrupted her to accuse her of "never respecting [his] interests and lying about the weekends." As counter-evidence, he would bring up all the vacations he took her on and all the dinners he has bought her. Nick emphasized that he would spend his own "hard-earned money to pay for each and every one of those dinners." They had kept separate bank accounts throughout the entire marriage and this was also a point of contention. They didn't respect each other's ideas on how to spend or save, so they both felt it worked better to simply keep everything separate.

Besides their constant conflicts over money and the constant argument over Nancy's ranch property, they immediately pulled me in as a judge over their grievances around sex. Nancy said Nick was never in the mood and added, "He always leaves me without the proper stimulation a normal woman needs. He doesn't seem to understand it is not normal to only have sex every two or three months."

Nick raised his eyebrows and said, "She simply makes things up or grossly exaggerates. We have sex at least twice a week, every week. There was a period of a few months when I had whiplash from a car accident, and I was in a great deal of pain. So, of course, I wasn't in the mood. But, that actually proves my point about her. She is selfish and demanding. Is it too much to ask that she consider the other person's needs? She is only wanting what she wants and never considering the two of us or my needs." Nancy rolled her eyes and said, "I just think it is strange for a middle-aged man to not want to have sex on a regular basis. I think he must have some type of psychological hang-up!" And, on it would go.

I noticed that Nick and Nancy sometimes smiled or laughed when they were in these heated and accusatory cycles. So, I interpreted this by saying, "You both seem to get something out of this back and forth. It seems like you have more verbal intercourse this way than actual sex. Maybe there is a way you are both playing with each other but it is also in a hurtful way that leaves you upset or unsatisfied." They both agreed and said they had a history of "needling each other and each person always wanting to be right." I asked for more details. They agreed they both wanted to be right, to "run the show," and liked to be independent and in control. I commented, "Perhaps all that covers up the desire you both have to be more dependent and vulnerable to each other. Perhaps you both wish you could be more of a together team but something makes you anxious about that intimacy, sharing, and trust." They both agreed that "it could be."

As part of this line of interpretive investigation, I also brought up the transference position they seemed to want to put me in or the way they seemed to want to mutually utilize me (Joseph, 1983; Waska, 2010c). I interpreted that I have to be the one that brings up the feelings or lack of feelings they are experiencing inside themselves and in relation to each other. In other words, I spoke to the fact that they both would rather debate and fight over matters of money, sex, or time together instead of having to show me or share with each other how they might be hurt, lonely, scared, or angry that they were not finding the love they wanted. This was an interpretation I first made to them as a couple. It was an interpretation of the projective identification method they used to jettison, discard, and smuggle their unwanted anxiety and vulnerability into me.

Then, I also made interpretations to them individually. I told Nick that he used stories of Nancy's being demanding and selfish to shield himself from having to share with me his sense of not being wanted, of being used, and of not being included in Nancy's life. I told Nancy that I thought she was afraid or ashamed of telling me about wanting to depend on Nick, so instead she told me all about how he failed her over and over. Here, I was noticing the feelings that were placed into me and then stripped from the couple's interactions. I interpreted this evacuative and defensive aspect of projective identification they both used in the transference. This led to both of them speaking, for a while, about these more vulnerable and exposed aspects of their inner world.

However, as with most volatile couples in the beginning phase of treatment, they felt anxious and quickly shifted back into a feelingless state of debate and accusation. I thought to myself that their mutual laughing and smiling during these fights and bickering was their mutual relief and camaraderie over helping each other to not have to face their internal conflicts and fears and instead disguise them with arguments.

During the first month of working with Nick and Nancy, there were different transference states that emerged around scheduling issues. As I tried to find them a place in my calendar and discussed various possibilities of different dates, they both reacted in particular ways. Nancy was very detailed and had her calendar ready to go. She was willing to engage in the discussion with me. But, very quickly, I noticed that it was just she and I discussing our schedule. Nick was not interested in participating and seemed to delegate the calendar chores to Nancy. I pictured her as the secretary in the relationship.

So, we gradually worked out some possible dates and times for the future. As we were doing this, I could tell that not only was Nick not engaged or interested, but he was starting to be more and more agitated. I asked him what the matter was. He said, "Everything is fine!" But a minute later, he interrupted us and said, "Can't you do this some other time? Do we have to waste our time doing this?" I said, "The only way we will be able to meet another time is to schedule another time. What makes you so irritated about this?"

Nick said, "I don't think I should have to waste my time talking about the schedule. I don't pay any of my other doctors to sit around talking about the schedule. I don't think I like this at all. You are wasting my time. Nancy can call you at another time and figure this all out!" I said, "There is no other time or place. You want Nancy to be your secretary and figure this out on her time, but this is something all three of us have to do, here and now, because it is important for all three of us. But you seem to be angry and want to not participate and instead have your own agenda to get to. You seem to feel I am taking something away from you, but you are not willing to give something to us right now. If you want to be here, you have to put the work in, including figuring out when we can meet." This was a confrontational, limit setting, and containing analytic observation of how Nick was experiencing his objects and what he wanted from them. It was a therapeutic observation of his narcissistic acting out and his turning away from a mutual task to demanding something for himself. This was helpful and calmed him down. We finished sorting out the schedule.

At this point, we didn't have the immediate opportunity to explore it any further. Sometimes, analytic observations can create enough analytic momentum to proceed with a more traditional interpretation about anxiety, desire, conflict, and defense. Other times, as in this situation, the analytic observation is the only and best technique possible at that immediate moment, given the degree of destructive acting out occurring.

At the end of the fourth session, Nancy looked at me as she got up to leave. She said, "So, when are you going to tell us what to do?" I said, acting out some of my irritation at her demand, "What to do about what?" She replied, "How to get along better. Aren't you going to tell us what to do to stop fighting and how to get along better?"

I said, "You are wanting or demanding a quick fix and instant cure from me without wanting to spend any time telling me about yourself and the problems you are having. At this point, I don't know much about you and I don't think you know much about why things are so messy in the marriage. Yet, you are demanding to have all the answers yesterday. You will have to be patient and participate in learning about the problem and finding the solutions. Maybe how you are demanding it all so fast and seeing me as not giving you everything fast enough is some information that helps us. It may tell us something about how you see the world and something about your unhappiness in the marriage. We can talk about it next time."

Here, I offered an analytic observation that was containing yet translating of her reluctance to give and take, and pointed out how, instead, she wanted everything for nothing and was turning me into a disposable dispenser of relief and her into a demanding consumer.

This seemed to calm Nancy down and provide some containment and guidance to what might be fueling her internal impatience and forceful hunger for immediate gratification. I thought to myself that Nancy's demanding and demeaning transference to me was very much like the demanding and demeaning way she spoke to Nick when he didn't deliver sex, attention, or money as quickly as she expected.

At other times in the treatment, similar transference states arose between them and me or between each of them. At those times, I said, "Both of you seem to struggle with wanting a great deal from each other and then feeling frustrated that the other is withholding or unable to give that to you. You end up feeling you are with someone who frustrates you and isn't living up to what you expect. We need to understand where all that expectation comes from, since you feel so let down by the other person much of the time, whether it be by me or by each other." This was a helpful line of exploration, as it seemed to be a main theme in each of their phantasy conflicts. This communication was more of a hybrid between an analytic observation and a traditional interpretation.

Another moment of transference emerged when Nancy told me she would be retiring soon from her job. "It is a place I have grown to hate where they don't respect me. I am tired of the whole thing." She went on to tell me,

"I have plans about what I will do in my retirement." I asked her what she was thinking. She went on to speak to me—not to Nick and me, but just to me—about how she plans to go back to school and train as a nurse, something she had always been interested in. As she told me about this, I began to think about how she was excluding Nick and making this a private conversation between the two of us, just like with the scheduling. I wondered how Nick was feeling.

Before I could make this interpretation, Nick blurted out, "You never wanted to share the ranch with me. You are very selfish. I have helped out with the horses for years, but you don't seem to see that effort. I consider all my property our property. But, you always have to have things of your own and hold on to them without sharing!" Nancy yelled, "What the hell! Why are you bringing that up for no reason!" Turning to me, she yelled, "See! He is always having some kind of issue and blaming me for things!"

I interpreted to Nick, "I think you are angry and bringing up the ranch problem right now because when Nancy started having this one-to-one conversation with me and told me how she was going to live out her retirement, you felt left out. You felt she left you out of this conversation and she never pictured you in her retirement. You were left out and hurt so you are lashing out by bringing up the ranch problem." Nick said, "That is right! I do feel left out. She was talking about *her* retirement, not *our* retirement. That is one of the biggest problems in our marriage. She is selfish and always thinking of herself. It is never about me and never about us. It is only about her. I, on the other hand, make a great effort all the time to share everything with her."

Nick went into a long list of things he has done for Nancy and many examples of how generous and sharing he has always been. In the counter-transference, my sense was that he was grandiose and was now trying to prove he is the most generous person in the couple as a way to combat his despair and hurt over feeling left out and ignored. So, I made that interpretation.

Nick said, "Well, yes. I do feel hurt. I want her to treat me like I treat her." Here, he seemed to step just a bit away from the grandiosity and began to talk about his desire for a more mutual, give-and-take relationship. Unfortunately, Nancy became defensive about this and started to tell me about "all the things I do for him that he never notices and takes for granted."

I interpreted, "Now, you both are trying to convince me who is the biggest martyr and who has the longest list of generous acts towards the other. It looks like you both would rather argue and debate then have to speak about your feelings of needing more, feeling left out or ignored by the other person, and how that could be changed." This interpretation brought some calm to both of them and they managed to start talking about their hurt feelings and the history of a "who owes whom" mentality that has gotten in the way of love. This showed their mutual capacity for being together in a more mature, whole-object mentality, at least for a short period of time. However, this was a fragile commodity easily broken and forgotten.

The dynamics of feeling left out, feeling entitled, and feeling anger at not receiving but also refusing to give much back continued to play out in their relationship as well as their transference to me. The day before we were scheduled for one of our sessions, I had a message from Nancy. She was the person who kept the calendar for both of them, while Nick went about his business and only seemed to care about the things he wanted to do. The rest was for Nancy to keep track of. I had made this analytic observation earlier. In response, Nick had said he was more than able to keep a calendar but "she is controlling and likes to be in charge of everything." Nancy had said, "He is right. I do like to have everything in its place and know what is going on. But, he never seems to want to help even if I ask."

So, Nancy's phone call right before our scheduled session was to convey Nick's message that his best friend from college had come to town for a business meeting. Nick wanted to meet with him for dinner and then go to a car race the next day. Therefore, Nancy said Nick was canceling our scheduled session. In response, I left a message stating that we had agreed they would provide forty-eight hours' notice when canceling so they did need to still pay for the session. I also said I hoped he could work around his friend's arrival because I in fact would be away for the following scheduled session myself. So, it would be even more important than usual for us to meet. I also mentioned that while I was sure Nick felt it was important to see his friend and go to the car race, perhaps our meeting was as important for him and the marriage so he could consider that.

In the counter-transference, I had several reactions. I felt Nick was using Nancy as his secretary and I too felt used as an unimportant item that could easily be discarded if something better came into town. I also thought, "I have seen this before. He is a borderline with narcissistic patterns who wants what he wants. If something gets in the way or if he has to give to the other person, he reacts and rebels. I know how this one will end."

This was a thought that came from nearly thirty years of work with borderline, narcissistic, and psychotic patients who often exited treatment under these types of abrupt, jarring, and non-negotiable circumstances. It was also a sign of my counter-transference frustration with Nick's way of not valuing me or the treatment. Interestingly, that was the very thing he seemed to complain about in the marriage, of being taken for granted and not given value, except usually in the concrete way of not having his name on the ranch property.

Nick left me another message, responding to mine. He said, "I don't know why you would charge me for not coming in. That is not fair and I have never heard of anyone doing something like that. It seems outrageous. Also, if you are going to charge me for changing things, then I should charge you for the times you have changed our appointment." This was a reference to one time when I called four days before our scheduled time and asked if we could change the time. He went on, "If you are going to operate in this kind of unfair way, then I don't think we will be coming back. My friend is in town and I would think you would be able to respect that and not pull this kind of crap."

So, I called back and left a message stating, "I received your message and I hope that you will still make our scheduled time. As far as it being unfair, we had all agreed that you would give me forty-eight hours' notice if you needed to change something. Also, I did not call you the day before to tell you I wasn't going to see you because I had something better to do. I called and asked you four days ahead if we could change our time. So, it is not the same thing. Finally, it seems pretty radical for you to say you will never come in again if I charge you for a late cancellation. All these feelings you are having would probably be helpful to discuss in person and for us to understand together. I hope I see you tomorrow."

Then, I called Nancy and told her that I felt she should be a part of this problem, as it affected all three of us. I explained Nick's messages as well as mine and asked for her opinion. She was quite reasonable, offered to send me a check, and said, "See. That is the same problem I have with him. He will never commit to anything and will change everything if he has something better to do. So, I don't know if he will want to return. I could come in by myself, I guess, but I don't think he will want to. I can try and ask him to, but I don't want to make any promises."

I said, "It would definitely be better if you both come in, but it sounds like you would still want to have a chance to talk about your feelings with me even if he doesn't want to continue. So, let's plan on both of you showing up next time but if he doesn't want to make it, then I will plan on just meeting with you."

This is, in fact, what happened. Nick refused to continue so Nancy started to see me on her own. She told me she wanted to find out "if she really had a relationship or just a person who takes advantage of her." She went on to tell me, "I have never felt in love with Nick, but I dread the idea of being alone." She also told me that all her family and friends have been telling her for years to "dump Nick." So, I began exploring this dread and also how she contributes to feeling used by always catering to Nick, as well as this idea that she is with someone whom she knows is a bad choice but she remains loyal to him and her empty relationship with him.

No doubt, the reader can see how I was pulled into acting out with Nick and Nancy in these phone messages and in continuing to see Nancy by herself. Unfortunately, with these types of stormy and turbulent patients, this is not uncommon, and I felt it better to continue under less than optimal conditions than not to continue at all.

These individual sessions with Nancy were productive, but I noticed that in the counter-transference I felt like telling her she should wake up and see what a loser her husband is and how she should move on to better things. By the way she spoke to me, she seemed to want to align me with her devalued view of Nick and leave me with a very one-dimensional perspective of him. Also, it was interesting to notice how I started to see her as a victim who was helpless against Nick's nastiness. Given these sudden counter-transference reactions from what I understood to be Nancy's projective identification–based transference, I was very interested to hear Nancy tell me, "My friends and family have told me to leave Nick and realize I have been wasting my time with him. They all tell me how I could do so much better." So, my counter-transference informed me and helped me interpret her transference.

I interpreted her push/pull relationship with me in which she presents reasons I should come to her defense and side with her against Nick. But, then, if I do move in this direction, she is quick to tell me why she needs to stay and make no changes because of her financial problems and fear of loneliness. Therefore, by noting my counter-transference, which has been shaped by her transference projections, I was able to make these types of interpretations about her conflict and masochistic methods of justifying her unhappiness.

As mentioned, to have a couple begin treatment and then have one party quit while the other continues is not that unusual. With many volatile couples, one party may be so fragile, aggressive, defensive, or unwilling to give of themselves that they are one foot out the door when they first show up and then quickly exit altogether. The prognosis for the person continuing as an individual is mixed. They usually feel torn and in conflict that they are turning against their partner and seeking out something for themselves. So, guilt and anxiety can overcome them and they too will exit. Other times, they are able to maintain a sense of how seeking help for themselves would be beneficial to the relationship as well as to themselves so they don't feel so selfish. But, they may feel persecuted or fearful that if they seek help for their own feelings, they will be punished in some way by their partner, so they may still exit prematurely.

With Nancy, I was in touch with, containing, and interpreting a variety of intense narcissistic projections that I felt in the counter-transference. I interpreted her role in the transference, which seemed to be part of the complex couple's dynamic continuing to be repeated with me. So, the emphasis on the couple's issues remained, even though we shifted to an individual treatment setting. The way they argued with each other, demanding to be given to, feeling denied, insisting on being right, and seeing the other person as solely wrong, all within a sadomasochistic bond, was still being played out in the transference and counter-transference even as Nancy continued seeing me and Nick had stopped.

Of course, the way Nancy set aside Nick and created a special one-to-one dynamic with me around the scheduling issues and around retirement issues was repeated in her now seeing me without Nick. As Segal (1962) has noted, we must strive to keep the analytic setting stable and pure. However, especially with more unstable and acting-out patients such as Nick and Nancy, this is often impossible. We often have to accept being in the midst of or in the thick of some degree of enactment (Waska, 2011a). As Steiner (1984) notes, this is unavoidable and can help us find direction in the analytic work if we step away from our own acting out. Also, these unsettling dynamics are usually the result of the patient's excessive reliance on projective identification. So, bit by bit, the analyst must try to ascertain if the patient is using this mechanism to get rid of unwanted aspects of his or her self, control the analyst, attack, or try to communicate in some primitive manner (Bion, 1963; Rosenfeld, 1971).

I think it is often a combination of these elements. The case of Nancy and Nick show the gradual unfolding of multiple ways they both relied on projective systems to relate or act out with their objects. In the process, they entangled me (Joseph, 1983) in various ways that seemed to be designed to both communicate their conflicts to me but also prevent me from fully understanding them, and as a result none of us could easily speak about these issues, as we were too caught up in them. This was the thorny and complicated nature of the total transference situation (Joseph, 1985; Waska, 2011b). However, as I mentioned, I was slowly able to notice my counter-transference feelings and use them as a compass to exit this state and gradually make sense out of what was occurring.

Over the course of the next two months, I met with Nancy to discuss her own personal struggles as well as her continued problems with the marriage. During this time, she told me many stories about how she felt "used" by Nick and how he "never listened" to her. Over and over, I felt she was giving me examples that were meant to have me side with her against what sounded like a man who was selfish and somewhat of a bully. Of course, I had to watch my balance in the counter-transference, as this was exactly my experience with him when he left his phone messages and broke off his attendance. In other words, I had to be careful to not blurt out to Nancy, "I know exactly what you mean—he treats me that way too!"

Over the course of several sessions, I listened to how Nancy's friends and family told her to "leave the creep" and how she "could easily do better." Bit by bit, however, I noticed that Nancy laid out these stories about Nick regarding how he always ignored her and did whatever he wanted as if she had told him what she wanted or as if she had said no to something and then he ignored her requests or pushed his agenda over hers. Yet that wasn't the case. I interpreted that she was telling me she was a victim to his bullying when, in fact, she never really expressed to Nick what she wanted or didn't want, but then was resentful that he went ahead and made all the decisions in the relationship.

I interpreted that she was trying to have me see her as standing up for her rights and being kicked down by a bully and then have me rally for her against this bully. Then, I would be doing her dirty work, her talking for her. So, I interpreted that she was withholding her needs, differences, and desires from him and instead hoping that I would rescue her as this silent victim. Here, I was interpreting how she was using me in the transference (Joseph, 1983) and how she utilized projective identification to rigidly shape herself and her objects according to certain phantasies (Joseph, 1988).

In response, Nancy said, "I know what you mean. It is true. I usually don't say much because I am afraid of what will happen. I am scared to ask for anything and even more scared to say no to something because he starts yelling." I told Nancy that the way she described the "yelling" sounded quite scary and intimidating. I asked her if she felt this was indeed how Nick was or if she might also have some sort of sensitivity or extra fear about the possible conflict that could occur if they had differences. Here, I did not want to be pulled into seeing Nick as this scary fellow without investigating it a bit more. In response, very quickly, Nancy referred to her upbringing. She described how her father was an "angry drunk who had to have his way and if anyone got in the way there was hell to pay." She said growing up was a "very unpredictable time and a scary one too." She said, "I remember the many times I watched my mother become silent and passive, sort of fading into the wallpaper, when father had his moods."

I said, "It sounds like you are now feeling and acting like your mother and seeing others as potentially being like father. So, you stay silent and passive just in case. I think you do that with me as far as not sharing the full extent of your wants and your opinions, and it certainly sounds like that could be the case with Nick." Nancy agreed and said, "I rarely say much or disagree because I assume it won't go well."

So, now that we had discovered one aspect of the historical profile she brought to the projective identification–based transference with Nick and me, I asked Nancy to say more about whether she saw me as scary or not. Nancy said, "On the contrary! I feel I can be open with you and really express myself. It is a breath of fresh air. I wish I could do that with Nick, but I rarely get the chance." Aware of her quick idealization of me and quick assurance of how positive and safe I was to her, despite her obvious censorship of certain feelings and thoughts, I still set this aside for the moment to continue understanding more about her distortion of and censorship with Nick.

I interpreted by saying, "Maybe that is because you are not talking about what is actually on your mind. You are not being totally honest with him." She said, "That is right. I don't think I can. I think I might have to wait this out and bite my tongue until I can quit my job and find a better one. But, that could take a year or two." I asked her what she meant. She explained that she had often thought, "If I could just find a great paying job with good benefits I would have no reason to stick around."

I said, "Well, it now seems like you haven't been forthcoming with me or Nick. From what you are saying, you have simply been using him for your financial security, and if you can find a way to make more money yourself, you will be out the door." Here, I was making an analytic observation, which was a concise translation of her object relational phantasy and how that phantasy played out in reality. This technique of therapeutic containment and confrontation helps the more thick-skinned borderline or narcissist (Rosenfeld, 1987) patient to face, turn towards, or consider an element of him- or herself more than they usually do. Sometimes, it is possible to follow up these firmer comments with more traditional interpretations of the unconscious desires, anxieties, aggressions, and defenses that are taking place. Other times, it is important to let the dust clear and see what the patient can do with what the analyst has brought up. Carefully listening to how our patients have heard us, ignored us, understood us, or misunderstood us is critical to notice.

In this moment with Nancy, I choose to follow up my analytic observation with "I think you feel scared of conflict so you find a way to manipulate things without others knowing. That way, you still feel in control but avoid the possible tension or fallout. You are not telling me everything so you can avoid my judgment or any conflict about what you are doing. But, the price for that is that we don't have very good communication and you are in it alone instead of together. Is that what Nick means when he says you can be controlling or wanting everything a certain way?"

Here, I was not only working with Nancy's transference to me, but I wanted to make sure to continue to include Nick in the conversation, even though he wasn't present. Otherwise, I would be colluding with Nancy's tendency to ignore him or set him aside while she tended to her priorities.

Nancy said, "That could be. I guess I haven't brought all that up before, but I don't really want to have to look at it. It is kind of sad or pathetic that I am using him that way. It is not much of a marriage!" I said, "And, in the process of using others and not really talking with us all in an honest way, you are confirming your idea that you are helpless and need what we have to survive. In that way, you seem to feel you have to be in situations you don't like but you try and control anyway and get what you can out of them. Like telling me how you need Nick's money. You must feel very poor and helpless, resenting having to rely on him."

After a moment of reflection, Nancy said, "I think you have a good point that I never thought about. If I really consider it, I don't need to wait to find a better job. I need to really sit down and look at my bank account. But, I think I would be just fine right now on my own. So, what does that mean? I think I am also fearful of being alone and by myself. I feel old and I don't want to end up old, alone, and with no one to take care of me. What if I can't take care of myself because I am too sick or crippled? I am worried about that." I said, "Well, since you are only in your fifties, I think you are really talking about a deeper fear of being emotionally lost and all alone, and some horrible feeling of being sick and never rescued or helped. If that is the case, it makes more sense that you would tolerate all these things you say you hate and stay instead of leave."

Nancy said, "I think it is that, the emotional stuff!" Here, Nancy showed the ability to think for a bit about more symbolic matters without having to retreat into concrete issues she felt she could control. As Steiner (1984) has noted, our more difficult patients rely more on actions as a way of interaction and less on symbolic communication. Steiner goes on to say that the analyst must find a way to contain and translate the action into symbolic terms, then the patient can begin to contain his own actions and practice and risk using symbolic communication instead.

With narcissistic and borderline patients, the analytic observation is meant to do just that, provide a bridge from action to symbolic function and a way for the analyst to set the therapeutic stage for a deeper interpretation. First, we make our way through the counter-transference, using it as a compass to orientate ourselves to what the patient's principal phantasy is at that moment.

Then, we translate the object relational dynamic, which usually is fueled by death-instinct attacks or domination on the object, the relationship, or even the self. Once in place, the analytic observation breaks the ground for a more traditional interpretation, which this type of patient would otherwise usually ignore.

In the next few meetings, we talked more about these more emotional matters, and at one point, Nancy told me, "I have taken what we are saying to heart in a few ways. I have started telling Nick more about what I need and what I want. I have brought up a few things around house chores, around paying bills, and around how we spend our time together. Actually, it was around how we don't spend our time together. We never do much together. He always is off at the races, and I have no idea when he will be home. But, I told him we have to start having better communication. I asked him to come back to therapy here with me and he has agreed."

So, Nick showed up with Nancy for the next session. He said hello and settled in as if there was nothing to talk about regarding our last encounter. I said that to him, and he said, "Oh, that. I just think there was a misunderstanding about the time to meet. No big deal." I said, "You seem to be ignoring what actually happened. You had set up a time with me and didn't show up because you found something better to do, and then you were angry that you had to pay me for the time." He said, "I guess I see your point. I don't want you to think that is what I do all the time. I apologize, and hopefully we can move forward. It wasn't really that big of a deal, so I am thinking we can just move ahead."

I felt like Nick was sidestepping the way he had treated me and wanted to ignore it or quickly forget about it by "simply moving forward." I said, "From the way you are quick to dismiss it, I think you don't want to take ownership of what happened, so I will set the record straight. You ended up treating me exactly the way your wife says you treat her. We need to understand that better and find out why you are like that. At the same time, we need to find out why Nancy seems to have such a hard time expressing herself to you or me about whatever she is unhappy about. In a way, she has invited me to do her dirty work for her today by having to tell you what I am unhappy about." Here, I was making an initial analytic observation, in a grounding manner or confrontational manner, and then following it with a more explanatory interpretation of how I thought the transference and projective identification processes were operating in the moment between each of them and towards me.

Nick responded, "Nancy does express herself. She is always telling me what I am not doing. I never give her enough sex, I never do enough around the house, and I never spend enough time with her. But, you know what? She doesn't realize how great she has it. She is so selfish and controlling about her money and her property, while I am always sharing everything with her. Every time she asks me for something, I am right there delivering. So, she has no clue how good she has it. I am so in love with her, and I will always be around to do things for her. But she seems to just want to use me for my money and sees me as just someone to do her housework or errands. She can't see what a great husband she has because she is too busy counting her money and property and thinking of what she needs and wants."

Predictably, this led to an immediate and loud defensive response from Nancy. She began with, "You must be from some other planet! I don't know what you are talking about. You don't ever spend time with me unless I demand it, and then you resent me. All I ever hear from you is how you resent my property and how I am bad for not giving you half. I told you that from the start and you won't let go of it. And, when have you ever offered to help out financially? You say you are there for me, but I don't see it!" In the next ten minutes, they both devolved into back-and-forth arguments about money, bills, and who did what for whom. I said, "You both are way more comfortable trading accusations than talking about what you actually need and what might make you uncomfortable to give to the other person." Here, I was making more of a standard interpretation, exploring the unconscious anxieties that led them both to these sorts of blaming and circular defensive systems.

In the next session, Nick and Nancy started off saying all was well, that they had talked about their fighting over money after the last session, and they decided "to put it all aside and move on. We think it is best to never talk about that kind of stuff again" I said, "You seem to want to pretend something painful isn't there, and now I have to be the one to bring it back. I am sure the problem is still here today, so we need to find a way to understand it and then solve it. Then, you both will feel closer in the end." So, Nancy spoke up and said, "I am happy to hear that Nick is not going to bother me with all his feelings of being cheated around the ranch property. But, I think it is important for a man to show his woman he cares by buying her dinner and taking her out to shows and paying for it. That is how it always was when I was dating. When I was dating, the men would always pick up the bill."

Nancy seemed to be quickly retreating from the dependency I had spoken about and was suddenly acting out by being entitled, demanding, and devaluing. I said, "Well, the difference today is that you are not dating. You are married, but you seem to want to have things still go your way and have the man cater to you." This was more of an analytic observation. Nancy replied, "What is wrong with that?" Here, her underlying narcissistic view of others was emerging. I said, "So, you don't see a problem with it. But, you seem to have a very hard time feeling comfortable being an equal with Nick and sharing yourself emotionally. You seem to want to have special attention, and you have a hard time dropping all that and just being vulnerable. When you told me you were thinking of leaving Nick but you didn't want to be old and without enough money or someone to care for you, you were not thinking about him, only thinking about yourself. It must be hard to let someone in."

Before she could answer, Nick said to Nancy, "You are just superficial. It is all about how you look and what you get. I am not like that. I remember when you decided to spend all that money of mine on your facelift. I told you I loved you just the way you are. But, you went ahead and spent it anyway. It's OK because whatever you want I give you, and I don't care what bank account it comes out of. But, you don't appreciate what I good guy I am." I interpreted to Nick, "You are saying you don't care and what a good guy you are, but what you are hiding from me is your resentment and anger. I think you feel used but you never set limits with her or never say no. You only pretend to be OK about everything but on the inside you are angry and resentful."

Suddenly, Nick started to choke up and began sobbing. Turning to Nancy, he said, "I feel so used! I can't believe you treat me this way!" He was silent and cried for several minutes. Nancy tried to console him. Finally, he went on to say, "I don't think you understand how much I am here for you. I always give you whatever you want, but you always talk about everything as *yours, yours, yours*. It is always about you!"

I asked Nancy to respond to that, especially considering how, while she says she wants to share and doesn't need his money, she has told me she would divorce him if she could afford to and that she just needs to be with him until she can get a better job. I said that she is giving me and him a very contrary message. I said that she does not seem to see them as a team who shares things; instead, she sees him as someone who should be taking care of her and picking up the tab. Yet, she makes sure she has her own retirement account, her ranch property, and a facelift.

Nancy said, "I just have never thought of men in any other way. I see them as there to take care of me. I guess it is cultural, but I don't see what is wrong with that." I said, "I think that is what Nick means when he says he is feeling used." Nick said, "I do feel used. I feel that all the time. She only wants me around for chores or money. But, I have never been like that. I am generous and I don't care about all that. She can have all my money. I am here to love her. I only think of how I can take care of her and how to give her whatever she needs. We are very different that way. From day one, I wasn't in this relationship for money or anything else except for love. I just wanted to have somebody to grow old with." Nancy said, "See! You just want *someone*. It could be anyone. You don't really care about me. You just want *someone* to be with so you don't feel lonely. I think you are very needy and want things *your way*. So, I don't see you as generous at all. I think you are often very selfish."

The session then evolved into a debate between Nick and Nancy with Nick saying how Nancy never shares any of her money and property and with Nancy saying how Nick is selfish and never home. But then Nick backtracked into how generous he always is. I ended up coming back to an interpretive theme that I have used throughout the analytic work with Nick and Nancy. With analytic observations, I had been more directly or firmly commenting on their mutual acting out of these narcissistic and borderline methods of sadomasochistic debating and concrete thinking to avoid any emotional pain or vulnerability. Here, I interpreted that Nick was saying he is just fine with everything and doesn't want anything, but in fact, he is always resentful, envious, and feeling used and cheated. He tries to be a boastful martyr, proving how generous he is, but he really is always feeling hungry and lonely. Here, I was pointing to his borderline emptiness, neediness, and masochistic acting out. Also, I brought up that they both have found pleasure and a way of hiding from facing themselves by focusing on money and a million variations of how each other is getting shorted.

Finally, I brought up that they had told me of a supposed agreement, which sounded perverse to begin with, in which Nick would "pay Nancy's way to retirement and fund her until the day she cashes in her ranch property and takes over paying the bills." Nick confirmed, "Yes. And, then, she will start paying for *my* dinners!" Nancy was shocked to hear this and told him so. She said, "I have no plans to roll out the red carpet for you. I need to protect my savings and make sure I plan out my financial future so as to not spend down my money." Nick said, "See! You keep saying YOUR money; it is never anything about us. I can't believe how selfish you are." Then, they both quickly escalated into their usual yelling match about money and who was being unfair to whom.

I told them to stop and interpreted that they were both killing off any emotional expression or vulnerability with me and instead hiding behind these concrete money fights. I said it must be very uncomfortable to allow any life or love into the room and have to face what that might mean. To depend on each other and to give in to the other's needs to some degree seems very dangerous and unacceptable. I interpreted that Nick tries to make me see him as a wonderfully generous man who only cares about love, when he really feels used, left out, and resentful. I interpreted to Nancy that she wants me to see her as the victim and be on her side against him, but it looks like she never wants to share or feel how she will be very vulnerable and out of control if she depends on us or shares her feelings with us.

Another example of their continuous acting out, their splitting of various internal conflict states, and their mutual reliance on pathological projective mechanisms came out in a phone message I received from Nancy after this last session. In the message she said, "I just wanted to let you know that after that last session, Nick and I have done a lot of talking and we both want to really make this marriage work. We both love each other and think it is worth it. I am looking forward to doing whatever it takes to work on this marriage and really figure things out to improve our relationship, as long as the insurance coverage is in place." Of course, I was struck by the contrary and entitled message of "I really want this and will do anything for it" contrasted with "until I have to pay for it myself." This was particularly striking since they only had another ten visits under their insurance plan.

So, the next time I met with them, I noticed they hadn't given me my partial payment and I asked for it. Nancy went back and forth about how she thought this session was covered completely because we had just been given ten more visits. I told her "No. You owe for this session just as you do for all the sessions. You pay a portion and the insurance company pays the rest. But, this situation reminds me of something important. I listened to your message the other day and was really interested in one part of it. As I have said before, the both of you seem to present one thing and then say something quite the opposite. In your own ways, you both are constantly contradicting yourself. It seems you say one thing and even though you might really feel that way, you also feel another way that comes out later. So, Nancy, in your phone message, I heard you first sound very loving and all about the marriage no matter what, but then you ended with 'until the insurance runs out.' So, it looks like you care only as far as you don't have to pay for anything. That makes you look selfish and not really wanting to work on the marriage unless you get your way." This was an analytic observation.

Nick shouted out, "Oh my God! That is exactly what she does to me all the time. That is the same message I have always heard. She will only give if it doesn't cost her a dime. But, if she has to give something in return, forget it! She has received ten or twenty thousand dollars in stock payouts almost every year from property-related holdings, and she has never asked if I need anything or never said she wanted to put that money towards something for the two of us. There is never a word about us as a couple. I don't resent it because I believe that love is the highest priority for me but that is the way she is. I accept her as is, but that is her flaw."

I said to Nick, "You are quick to say you don't care because you only believe in love. That is one of the ways you contradict yourself. I think you are actually angry and resentful that she doesn't share more. Now, one way that this happens over and over is you feel resentful about it but you never ask for much. I have not heard you ever ask her to have a joint bank account, to put some of her money into something for the two of you, or any other thing you might want. So, by not ever asking, you make her either offer on her own or you can resent her as being selfish." Now, I was shifting to make a more traditional interpretation.

Nancy said, "I agree that he is always saying nonsense. He always wants to do everything his way even though in here he talks about wanting to be in love and doing everything together. He is never around to do anything together. Just this week, he was out once again playing poker with the boys. I kept asking him if he was going to be home for dinner that night and he wouldn't tell me. He never wants to tell me anything so he can stay in control and call the shots. But, then I don't know if I should fix him a dinner or not. That is inconsiderate and selfish."

Nick started to argue with her about that particular night and how his poker game was possibly going to be rescheduled due to some problem his friends were having and he didn't know until the last moment. I said to Nancy, "Did you ask him to not go to poker that night and have dinner with you instead?" She said no. I said, "It looks like you both have a difficult time asking for things and instead just want it delivered to you. If it isn't, then you feel resentful, hurt, and convinced the other person is selfish. But, it sounds like you wanted Nick to be with you and have dinner with you. Maybe, you and he are both very uncomfortable with allowing yourselves to be vulnerable or needy and with asking for love and caring from each other. To have it be a shared bond, you both have to ask for what you need, instead of never asking for it but always demanding it." Here, I was interpreting the narcissistic standoff they often have and the resulting masochistic and entitled reactions they exhibit and fight over.

Nick and Nancy continue to show up and act out. However, by using analytic observations that help them face the reality of their destructive phantasies and the exact manner in which they use, abuse, avoid, and control their objects, externally and internally, we are gradually carving out more and more space for analytic contact and symbolic thought instead of acting out. This firmer, containing, and grounding approach of analytic observation allows for more traditional interpretations to follow when patients are ready to take in deeper links regarding the meaning of their anxiety, desire, and defense. Analytic observations are allowing Nick and Nancy to see the results of their acting out and their narcissistic and borderline phantasies.

While they continue to use pathological projective identification to maintain a strained and delicate psychic equilibrium (Joseph, 1989; Spillius, 1992), analytic observations are providing them with more of a chance to work with their underlying narcissistic anxieties of loss and rejection (Waska, 2002). In such a complicated and in-motion treatment, I still struggle to maintain my analytic balance and not sink too deeply into various states of enactment (Steiner, 2006) but instead utilize them as helpful clinical information about the nature of this particular couple's unconscious phantasies and conflicts (Waska, 2011b).

The more Nick and Nancy allow themselves to face the reality of their constricted and deadening phantasies, the more they have a choice in how they feel and think about themselves and others. In doing so, they can establish a momentary truce in their projective identification battleground and peace talks can begin.

Ten

Pre-Interpretive Containment

Some patients present rather challenging narcissistic or borderline transferences that threaten to take over the analytic space and quickly eliminate any chance of exploration or learning. Their acting out negates symbolic communication and the opportunity for effective analytic contact (Waska, 2007). In working with such patients, I often find myself with counter-transference images of wild animals needing to be tamed, of ticking time bombs that need to be defused, and of spreading toxic spills that need to be contained and decontaminated.

In this chapter, I will discuss how a more confrontational or direct therapeutic observation is both helpful and necessary during the rougher moments with such patients. These are moments of acting out that involve desperate states of anxiety, anger, envy, or entitlement that need to be enclosed, contained, and translated with words.

Specifically, I think it is essential for patients who are exhibiting both destructive and libidinal narcissistic patterns (Rosenfeld, 1987) to hear what they are doing, in the moment, to their objects internally and externally as a way of limiting or managing their wild and desperately defensive or aggressively entitled acting out. Without the analyst stepping in to provide this immediate and direct therapeutic observation, an overbearing or devouring projective identification process takes place in which the patient dominates the analytic situation with their demand for power, love, revenge, or control.

The death instinct, as defined by an attack on difference, dependence, growth, learning, and vulnerability, is a core element in these hard-to-handle cases. The destructive narcissist will use projective identification to mobilize the death instinct to take over his or her objects. Analytic observations are pro-life translations of the here-and-now, destructive, object relational phantasies the patient is acting out in the transference.

In these clinical firestorms, the analyst must clearly define and translate the nature of the patient's object relational world with tougher or more boldly outlined observations, because in those moments patients have lost their own sense of definition and are only able to meagerly identify themselves by these more outrageous or intense methods of relating. In the process of acting out within the transference, in either a narcissistic or borderline fashion, patients will increasingly blur the nature of themselves and their objects, distorting the therapeutic relationship, the purpose of the treatment, and the very character of the analyst. The projective identification process, as the vehicle for a patient's death-instinct conflicts, is so overused and aggressive that the patient becomes empty and without any sense of internal value or definition. Analytic observations help to halt and gradually reverse that process.

Without these verbal limits and tougher definitions of what is what, the analyst will become the psychological property of the patient, an emotional dump site, and an extension of the patient's gradual absorbing stance in which the patient works to claim himself and others as the same, entities without difference or conflict. If this confrontational emotional corral is not available, the patient will tend to assimilate the analyst into his world of clone objects, or if he decides the analyst is too different or not in agreement with him, then the offending object is devalued or discarded.

Of course, through excessive reliance on projective identification, the more thin-skinned patient (Rosenfeld, 1971) will often feel judged, misunderstood, or persecuted by the analyst. No matter what is said, borderline patients will usually feel alienated, persecuted, and prone to counterattack. The sooner a protective netting or boundary is drawn by firmly translating the object relational phantasy that is being acted out and the nature of the destructive attacks on the self or the other, the sooner the core anxieties can be worked through and reduced.

The more thick-skinned (Rosenfeld, 1971) patient may seem fairly oblivious to this on one level but sometimes able to stop and consider the meaning of the analytic observation on another level. When the patient seems to only become wilder and more demanding or continues to be entitled and dismissive of others, we are witnessing the workings of the death instinct. The death instinct is often clinically observable through a violent and unrelenting projective identification cycle that rules the transference and easily contaminates the counter-transference, pulling for a variety of enactments (Waska, 2011a, 2011b).

This chapter highlights moments in which the patient's narcissistic acting out, internally and externally, crates such turbulence that the symbolic function of the analytic endeavor, so precious to change and growth, is at risk. In these unstable situations, the analyst must find a way to drop anchor in a sea so stormy that the ship could end up sinking if left to meander about without direction.

The analyst must offer an immediate containment and clear symbolic translation of the elements of the destructive death instinct taking place in the transference and in phantasy. A pro-life, pro-containment stance must be taken to redefine the collapsing, controlling, fragmenting, or predatory direction the patient's inner world has taken, in which the patient is struggling to assert power and control but only manages to take himself down in the process.

Some of these turbulent or difficult-to-thaw patients are high-functioning and show a good deal of depressive position (Klein, 1935, 1940) capacity; however, this is fragile, prone to erosion, and can easily shift to more primitive or paranoid-schizoid relating or non-relating (Klein, 1946). Taming or tougher analytic observations are often necessary with these patients. This technique can prove helpful to patients in their anxious, angry, or chaotic moments of acting out and can prove stabilizing to the overall integrity of the treatment. As a rule, borderline and narcissistic patients can benefit from analytic observations that help them to face their method of destructively organizing the world, internally and externally. This helps patients gradually tame, train, and contain the more fragmented and broken aspects of themselves. Once the more destructive, death-instinct aspects of the transference and the patient's core phantasy conflicts have been swaddled by the analytic observation, then the more libidinal struggles can be reached and addressed with traditional interpretations that explore underlying meaning and motive.

Also, the forceful, jarring, and disorganizing types of transference acting out that is typical with these more disruptive and difficult patients can be effectively herded together, as well as temporarily bounded with analytic observations, to allow for some reflection to take place instead of escalating power struggles, persecutory meltdowns, or entitled proclamations.

At the very least, therapeutic observations can put the brakes on transference acting out that is derailing treatment or perverting the nature of the way the analyst is seen or treated. In turn, it helps patients view themselves in a new and more respectful or reflective light. Well-defined or tougher analytic observations that call patients' attention to their object relational ways of using or abusing themselves or others may be very helpful to patients who internally feel very formless, volatile, or uncertain. They may find new objects that can stand up for themselves or objects that can survive the other's aggression. Such therapeutic feedback can provide a vision of connection and peaceful coexistence rather than a view of the object as resorting to immediate combat or retreat, just as patients are prone to do.

Some more thick-skinned narcissists need stronger, more direct analytic observations before they can allow themselves to relate on a more human level, acknowledging their own feelings to some degree and acknowledging that others exist and deserve recognition. The more thin-skinned narcissists or borderline patients do better with therapeutic observations that are immediately linked to containing and explanatory interpretations that speak to anxiety, desire, conflict, and defense.

With both types of patient, if the level of projection is so aggressive, overbearing, grandiose, or destructive of the analytic situation, an analytic observation that names the predatory or destructive nature of the patient's relational moves is often necessary to keep things alive and on track. Sometimes, we have to say what feels like too much. The more acting-out and thick-skinned narcissistic patients, or even some borderline patients, do not take offense. In fact, we may be the holding, the sense of firmness and definition, or the sense of limit that they psychologically need at that moment.

As mentioned, most of the time, these sorts of patients are long to emotionally thaw, volatile in mood, or quite oblivious to the value of others and, therefore, are aided or contained by the tougher or confrontational analytic observations that speak to the value of life and relatedness. When the transference takes the analytic situation hostage and meaning is the victim of the patient's mind, then there can be a real benefit to introducing more direct or confrontational observations that work towards reestablishing analytic contact and advocate for life-affirming mental and emotional links instead of de-linking, death-instinct neutralization or elimination of self-worth or object-worth. Analytic observations hold the self and object as needed and valued yet still see independence and autonomy as vital. Indeed, the idea of tolerating difference and sharing without an overwhelming sense of defeat or loss is very foreign and threatening to many narcissistic and borderline patients and they will embrace the death instinct to combat this threat or flee from it.

CASE MATERIAL: PATIENT G, A LIBIDINAL NARCISSIST

G came to see me after he was laid off from his company. While G had known of the termination well in advance and was going to be given a generous severance package, it was clear that G felt humiliated or powerless to some degree. He didn't say this, but he seemed hurt and embarrassed. G told me, "I felt a little uneasy even though it was something I have known about for a while. It was just a bit odd having to go get my things and not return." The way he said this, I had a counter-transference image of a shamed and slinking man trying to run out of the building with his box of things before his coworkers might see him and laugh at him or feel sorry for him. I said this to G and he said, "Yes, I guess I do feel somewhat ashamed and like I don't want to have others see me that way. Yes! I think you understand exactly what I am saying." Here, I was glad he benefited from my comment but I also thought he was tossing me a bone far too quickly.

While G wanted to talk about his loss of employment, he said he had "other matters" that felt "more pressing." He went on to tell me, "I've been having a terrible problem with something that makes me feel like I will never succeed." G told me he had been trying to take the entrance test for law school for the past two years and had failed every time. He explained how he would study a great deal but often became distracted "by thoughts of myself involved in grand heroic undertakings where others were amazed and grateful. They would admire me and I felt heroic. But I also had these other thoughts about times when I have let people down or when people were disappointed in me or even angry with me. I get lost in all that. Then, the next thing I know, the time is gone and I haven't studied anything."

After exploring these daydreams of greatness and despair in greater detail, I interpreted by saying, "You want to be our hero and have us love you, but you worry you are failing and we don't like you." G repeated my comment by saying, "I want to be your hero, but I worry that I am failing." Then, he continued, "Yes! That is exactly how I feel. Why is that? I really want to pass the test and get into law school, but I feel so stupid that I keep failing. I have consulted with a company that tutors people for the test, and they said I have great aptitude and should be able to pass with no problem but that I get bogged down in trying to answer every question just so."

I said, "You won't let yourself fail at anything. You want to ace every question before you will allow yourself to move on. Maybe, when you don't know one particular answer or feel you have made a mistake, it is very uncomfortable to move on and feel OK about the next question." G said, "I do want to make sure I answer all of them correctly. I don't like the idea that I may have failed at one or may have misunderstood one, so I spend way too much time lingering over each question." He added, "And, I lose my concentration when I drift away thinking about feeling like the hero for everyone but then also thinking of how I might have let them down."

Based on my counter-transference of listening to how he said this and his affect around it, I thought that G was more concerned about how he looked bad than the sense of guilt for letting others down. The guilt that was present seemed more of a persecutory nature (Grinberg, 1964). So, I interpreted: "You are mostly worried about looking bad. You want to appear as the hero, and it makes you anxious when you think you might look like the loser instead." G said, "You seem to know exactly what I am thinking! I love feeling like the hero, and I think it is important to me to have others look up to me and need me. I really like the feeling of being there for them when they need someone and then they remember me as the person who fulfilled that need. But, as you say, I really don't like it if I think they see me in the opposite way. That was very interesting, Doctor!"

Here, I felt G was applauding me instead of actually internalizing what I said. He did seem to consider what I meant for a moment and in that moment let it be helpful, but then he quickly turned it into a parroting cheer. I said, "You were listening and taking in what I said, but then you suddenly are trying to make me the hero just like you want to be. I am now the hero and you are my cheering audience, but we no longer can think or feel anything about your problems." G said, "Oh. I see. I am making you into a hero too. OK. Well, let's get back to what you were saying. What was it?" I said, "Maybe it is too painful to think about being a loser and not having anyone love you, so instead you run off in this other hero direction." G said, "To not be loved, that would be painful, indeed." So, here I was following up my initial interpretation about his splitting and projective identification with an interpretation about the motive of his defensive move, the pain of feeling worthless.

G was still fending it off by speaking in a removed, third-party sort of way about my interpretations, but he still allowed some of me and some of my interpretations into his mind. He let himself feel something genuine about it and began to respond and allow himself to share with me in a more honest and vulnerable manner.

G's method of parroting me was a pattern throughout the analytic treatment. He would ask for an extra session, and when I was able to accommodate his request, he would say, "Wow! That is fantastic. That is just supreme. Thank you." When I would give an interpretation, he would often repeat my exact words, as if he had just been told the winning lottery ticket number. After noticing this for a while, I said, "You seem to want to put my words on an altar, to praise them, and make me feel good. You are in awe, but I think you lose out on the meaning of my words by trying to inflate them so much." He replied to this interpretation by saying, "Ah! Very interesting! How I inflate them and lose out on the meaning!"

So, again, my sense was that G was able to digest a few of my interpretations but eradicated the rest with this deadly narcissistic inflation. It was a combination of mockery, narcissistic control, and devaluation alternating with idealization. As a result, there was not too much genuine relating left to hang on to or benefit from.

In getting to know G, I thought his childhood and his current connections with his family were important to understand, as they seemed to directly influence his present psychological predicaments. G told me his father was "a very angry man who has to always have it his way and always commands the attention and admiration of everyone. He will do things like overhear my mother talking about wanting to surprise a cousin with a gift. Then, my father will scream at my mother for daring to waste his money on some worthless person. But, later, my father will buy a gift and surprise that cousin with it so he gets all the praise and looks like the thoughtful one instead of my mother. He is so selfish that way! It has to be all about him all the time. I have tried to win his attention for my whole life, but it is near impossible. And, I feel very bad for my mother. She has been treated so badly for so long. I don't think my father really loves us for who we are, but if we provide him with some attention or help him feel great and grand, then he gives us a moment." I said, "It seems you are still trying to win that fleeting moment of love but you must feel sad since it is only for his gratification and never really about you." After a moment of silence, G said, "Yes. That is the way it is." Here, he was suddenly much less grandiose and much more grounded in his pain and loss. We established a point of analytic contact (Waska, 2007) in which he momentarily stepped into a more depressive experience.

As we worked together over the months, there were quite a few moments of significant analytic contact, but it was still a rocky ride. Understanding the deeper source of his narcissistic acting out and assisting him to move from this rigid psychic retreat (Steiner, 1993) to something more human, real, and reachable was slow going and easily kidnapped by his controlling narcissistic transference. G had a very specific way of trying to be the grand master and be admired, and while he wanted help and intellectually could take in my interpretations, emotionally he often remained encased in his narcissistic shell. However, I found that using more direct and defining therapeutic observations of how he controlled his objects gradually allowed opportunity for other more symbolic interpretations that explored the deeper conflicts and psychological issues with which he grappled.

Throughout his analytic treatment, G continued to act out in provocative, controlling, and narcissistic ways. In the transference, he anxiously hoped I could be a healer and truth finder whom he could depend on and look up to for guidance but he also wanted to be the idol and use me as an adoring audience and force me to give him a quick fix, to be his fast-food servant who provided him with immediate gratification and instant answers to external problems. In this ongoing transference acting out, I found it useful to make regular analytic observations that offered containment, confrontation, and firm but supportive translation of the object relational havoc of his narcissistic acting out.

One such situation involved G's going to a funeral. He told me about the death of a college friend that he knew, but only casually. The way G told me about going to the event was in a narcissistic and provocative manner. He went on and on about the camaraderie of college and the "deep ties that people find under such important circumstances and the lifelong connections that become established." He said, "It is a matter of respect and support to show up and do what I can for everyone involved."

In the counter-transference, I felt like G was describing the death of a war buddy he had fought with for years in the trenches of some great battle. He was now going to be reunited with his squad to celebrate their eternal dedication to each other and their country and mourn their fallen brother. I said that to G, highlighting how he seemed to want me to be in awe of his compassionate nature and use me as his audience. In doing so, I also told G that it seemed such a grand and serious story that it was more and more about someone else, a superhero that is a model of moral and emotional strength for others. As a result, more and more, it was about an ideal hero figure and less and less about G and whatever feelings he might have. I said that he was trying to convince me of his greatness and how he was showing up to save the hearts and minds of all the funeral-goers and really make a magnificent impression. So, this was mostly a direct analytic observation of how he was using his objects in the transference and the nature of his phantasy. It did not go into the usual detail of an interpretation that might address why he would place himself and his objects in that particular way on his internal chessboard.

So, it was striking when G said, "Yes. That is what I want to do." He agreed with everything I said and had no qualms about it. G was so concretely attached to this hero phantasy that he could not see the reality of what I was saying. So, I made another direct observation of his narcissistic transference mode. I said, "You want to hijack the funeral so you can enlist some more fans into your club. You want me and them to see you as the hero. Their sadness gets pushed aside so you can look like the most generous one there." So, here I was using an analytic observation to focus on the narcissistic intent and object relational impact his acting out has. In response, G said, "I guess it sounds pretty awful. I do want them to see me as the most generous and sympathetic person there and to like me for being so attentive and helpful."

Now that G was more in touch with himself and the impact of his phantasy, I followed up with a more traditional interpretation. I said, "I think you are worried that without that special position, no one will notice you. You will be just a regular guy at the funeral and feel forgotten." G replied, "Feel forgotten—yes. I feel like if I can't be special I would just be this regular guy, and that feels less than or insignificant. I don't want that. I want to be paid attention to. I can see how that sounds really bad, especially since it is a funeral. But, I do feel like I need that special attention."

I said, "Without special love you feel completely invisible, but since you keep that as the only way to feel loved, you are always chasing it and always feeling invisible." Here, I was interpreting the vicious cycle of destructive narcissistic projective identification in which everyday life is choked and dismissed in pursuit of eternal life. G said, "Maybe I can just go to the funeral and offer my support and realize these are my friends. I am not there to have everyone like me. It is not my funeral. It is supposed to be something for the person who died and his family."

I said, "That is a new and difficult point of view for you. Given how you describe your father, it is probably hard to allow someone else to have the spotlight without feeling forgotten, hurt, or resentful." Here, I was making more of a generic interpretation and a suggestion about his identification with his father's quest for attention. G said, "Wow. That is certainly the case. No matter what the situation, he manages to make it about himself." I said, "So, by making the funeral about you, we can see you trying to be like your father. Maybe that is the only way to be close to him, but in the end it backfires on you and you feel empty all over again." He nodded, paused, and then asked, "I know you will tell me I am after the instant fix again, but what do I do?" I said, "Yes. You do want me to give the quick fix so you don't have to look within and find yourself. We are here to find a way to fill that emptiness inside you but you are anxious about having to face it and fill it so you want me to do the dirty work and do it now. You are ignoring the fact that we are doing the work together as we go." He said, "I got it."

Another similar situation arose when G came in and told me about having to fly back to his family over the weekend to go to the hospital where his elderly aunt was dying. She had suffered with cancer for over a year but had deteriorated recently and had a few weeks to live. So, the family had gathered to say their goodbyes. G told me, "Just like with the funeral, I tried to get everyone's attention. I know it is not a good thing, just like we discussed, but I felt it was an opportunity to get people to see me as the central person who played the greatest role. I want that feeling." Here, G demonstrated the traits of a libidinal narcissist who was thick-skinned and wanting to use and abuse others for his profit. But, he also was able to reflect on that predatory intent and had, in part, come to me for help with that. At the same time, he seemed to want me to give him special points for realizing his narcissistic intent and win me over that way.

G said, "I wanted to appear as a very admirable and helpful person. I know it sounds not so great, but I made sure that I was the only one holding her hand when she actually died. I tried to act like I was talking with her as she passed and helping her to make that transition. Everyone was very moved by how compassionate I was. Several family members thanked me for taking the lead in such a difficult time and said they were grateful I could help so much in her last moments."

I said, "You took advantage of a dying person to win points with everyone else. You found a way to make them see you as extra important and special. You manipulated them to be loved and admired."

Here, I was making a therapeutic observation that spoke to his narcissistic actions and narcissistic aim. I focused on the target and the goal of his narcissistic acting out. The therapeutic observation translated the nature of how he used his objects and his phantasy about that. G responded, "Manipulated them so I could be loved and admired. Yes. I don't like that word *manipulated*, but I see what you mean. I do that quite often, and I am usually successful. But, then I find myself always searching out the next chance to do that." I said, "It is a hunger that will never go away, like a vampire. You are empty inside and as long as you don't attend to that, you have to fill it up artificially, over and over, from the outside."

G said, "From the outside. Yes. I have read much about that. The inside must be filled with true feelings that come from deep within and can be gifted to others as they, in turn, can gift you with their true selves. I think it was called the endless loop of love and devotion." I said, "You have now destroyed what I said and replaced it with mumbo jumbo from some self-help book. You are running away from being with me on the inside. You are attacking our work with silly slogans from the outside." Here, I interpreted the death instinct and his destructive efforts to replace our life blood with artificial plasma and to take over control instead of having to be vulnerable and dependent. This was more of a traditional Kleinian interpretation that followed my analytic observation made with containing directness about the nature of his object relational acting out.

G said, "I realize that it is very strange to be trying to steal the thunder at someone's deathbed, but I really wanted to have everyone see me as special. I want to feel needed and respected as that special person." I interpreted by saying, "But you are convinced that just being your real self would only get you ordinary praise and love, and that is never good enough for you. So, you throw away the chance for real, regular love and chase after special false love."

Here again, I was making an analytic observation of the narcissistic acting out, but I combined it with a more symbolic, deeper linking to the unconscious conflicts and anxieties with which he suffered. In particular, I was addressing the vicious cycle of projective identification that he was lost in, always wanting more and never utilizing what he had. Devaluation of what he was led to an endless search for what he wasn't but wanted to be and never would be.

G replied, "Yes. It seems ordinary and not enough." I said, "You are afraid I will see you as regular and ordinary or, even worse, like a loser, so you keep trying to impress me with these stories. But you shy away from exposing the lost little boy who feels unloved and never enough." G said, "I always feel that way. I feel I never get enough attention and I am always searching for more. I don't want you to think poorly of me. I want to be your best, most favorite patient!" I said, "So, you destroy our bond together by not letting me see you as a good person. I can only see you as the best patient I have ever had or you are a loser. That is a terrible bind you put us both in." Here, I again used an analytic observation to regain the balance of the clinical situation and to show G how he was taking us hostage and demanding that we be only one way or else.

G has a very long history of buying every possible self-help book and new-age CD as well as attending countless self-help seminars and workshops. He tries to fill himself with the quick fix, the golden answer, and the wisdom from the ages. But, he simply parrots whatever he reads or hears, and nothing ever really sticks or makes a difference. He uses it all as a way to feel good, look good, and sound good but never as a way to think for himself or learn anything.

With me, he constantly is recycling phrases and slogans he has heard at these workshops and tries to fake a real connection or insight by using these pieces of someone else's advice. So, during one session, G said, "I always want to feel better and improve myself. I don't want to be ordinary. I think it is healthy to strive for excellence in every realm of life. I believe it was on a CD from a top Buddhist teacher that I heard about how to find the pockets of emotional opportunity for new ways of bringing excellence into daily life and to transcend the binds of daily normality. We can find excellence; it is only a matter of understanding where it hides and then finding it."

I said, "That is fake improvement. You want to push us aside and fill the space with more empty slogans from someone who is getting rich selling you CDs about harmony and inner peace. You are running away from yourself and from having to share what is really inside you, the good, the bad, and the ordinary. You don't trust that those things inside you do make you special and you don't believe I will like you if I really get to know you."

G replied, "Well, the last workshop I went to on finding your inner potential talked about searching for the window of opportunity for love and friendship and to either take it or make it. If it doesn't appear, you have to make it appear. I thought that is what I was doing at the hospital with my dying aunt." I said, "I think you have no idea what you are saying right now. You are chanting a bunch of self-help phrases to stop us from looking at the emptiness inside you and how much you ache for love but how unlovable you feel. You use the self-help stuff to hide behind and to justify using people to get your special attention. Deep down you want to find real love but are unsure if you want to give up all your special power and claim to fame."

G said, "I don't want to give it up unless you can guarantee me something as good or better! I know what you mean, I really do. But, I don't know if I can give up this other stuff. As a matter of fact, an example of that is this workshop I am thinking of signing up for. I know you will shake your head when I bring it up. I thought about not bringing it up at all because I thought you would tell me I am being shallow, but I think I might really get something out of it."

I asked for details. G told me about a workshop "put on by the king of the smooth talkers called 'The Art of the Pick Up.' It is a workshop all about how to become a successful pickup artist, and it promises to teach you how to manipulate women into going out with you instantly." I said, "You pitch it to me in a way that invites me to judge you and tell you how much of a loser you are. I think you want my advice on many things but set it up for me to either give you the golden quick fix and thumbs up or to call you a loser. You don't let us have much room to do anything else." Here, I was interpreting his splitting and projective identification of the all-special or all-bad role with which G struggled.

G went on to try to justify why the workshop would be helpful for him: "I am somewhat shy with women and need to seek help in how to properly socialize." I said, "You are hiding your fear of being rejected by women with this justification so we can fight over it but never get to really talk about your fears of being rejected for who you are. You want the protection and weapons of manipulation the workshop offers so you don't have to show your vulnerable self to me and the women. You never feel like you are enough, but you end up putting on so much armor you can barely move." G said, "Doctor! I love the analogy. Like I have too much armor on to move. Interesting." I said, "There you go again, trying to butter me up!" G laughed and nodded yes.

There were other ways G seemed to try to use me in the transference (Joseph, 1983, 1988; Steiner, 1984, 1998). I felt like he was constantly provoking me to put him in his place, manipulating me to praise him and be his audience, and courting me to pull him out of his narcissistic quicksand. I interpreted that he wanted me to be a good guiding father, but he quickly dismissed that in favor of heroic adventure and immediate control rather than unknown possibilities of attachment and growth.

So, I thought all these factors were at work in the way he used projective identification to shape the transference. The fact that he mostly used his narcissistic desire for greatness and control in his projective efforts made it necessary to first use analytic observations before focusing more on traditional interpretations of anxiety, conflict, and defense.

One example of how these dynamics played out in the transference and his acting out took place in my office kitchen. There is a hallway off the waiting room for patients to walk down to get to the bathroom. Along the hallway are three doors. The first leads to my kitchen. It has a big "Private" sign on it and the door is kept closed. Next is the bathroom door. Finally, there is a washroom with a sink. Before my session with G, I came out of my office and went to the kitchen. I opened the door to find G washing his hands in the kitchen sink. I took a look and said, pointing to the "Private" sign, "You have to leave. You can't be in here."

I was responding to my counter-transference feeling of having someone seem too deliberately and defiantly trespassing, using my private property as his own. This was interesting in that, in over twenty years of being at this office location, only a few other patients have ever done this. And, those few times never engendered these same types of intruded on and invaded feelings in me. I felt G had absolutely no sense of my needs or rights in that moment, so I felt I had to immediately place some boundaries on the setting. I felt it was critical to define the situation as soon as possible.

At the same time, I wondered about how forceful I was sounding and what might have pulled me into that role. In response to my telling him to leave the kitchen, G said, "Oh. OK. I see. Sorry. Is there another place to wash up?" I said, "Yes. Right next door. But this room is private." He said, "OK. Sorry." During the course of the session that day, I brought up this incident and interpreted it in several different ways. I interpreted that he once again seemed to think nothing of others, except as a thing to use for his convenience or pleasure. I said he seemed to shy away from noticing his impact on others. This was an analytic observation.

G responded, "I think I see what you mean. Recently, I have been told off by some other people for the same thing. I took a date out to dinner and then told her I wanted to swing by this other girl's apartment to pick up some clothes I had left there when I spent the night. My date and I were on the way to the dance club and I thought it was no big deal. I had left some clothes over at this girl's place when I had a one night stand with her a few weeks ago. When my date realized what was happening, she told me it was really rude. I didn't get it for a while but then it made sense. And, recently, I offered to help my neighbor move some stuff in his garage, but I really was offering so I would look good in front of him and his family. When he kept changing the date he needed help, I called him and yelled at him about it, and he said he was really offended. Actually, there have been a fair number of such situations."

I followed up with a more traditional interpretation. I said, "So, you have been busted for using and abusing others. It is similar with me. You seemed to create a provocative moment in which I could easily judge you and yell at you, much like you want to tell your father off for his selfishness. Also, you seem to want me to have to work at figuring out what is really going on underneath for you without your ever doing much work. I think that, down deep, you want to feel close, feel loved, and want to share my kitchen like we are one big happy family. But I think you don't want to have to risk that hope or vulnerability so openly, so you have me do all the heavy lifting."

G was interested in what I said and agreed to most of it. He said, "I wish I could do that but you are right. I end up getting people angry after I try and use them to look good or bolster my reputation. Anyway, I am sorry about the kitchen. I didn't see the sign and I had to wash my hands." So, he became concrete with his apology and stopped speaking more about his feelings and his emotional struggles. I said, "Getting concrete about the kitchen door is easier than having to look at the messy emotional parts of all this. Maybe you feel guilty using me and needing me so much. Maybe you are worried about how I will react."

G agreed and said he felt the same about our schedule. He said he worried that I would be irritated when he called for additional sessions, as he often does. I usually see him twice a week, but when I can, I see him three or four times a week. He often cancels several weeks of appointments to go traveling, to go visit family, or to have fun with his friends up north. But, then he calls to see if I can fit him back in and see him "extra." So, I brought up that he was fearful of needing me too much but at the same time discarded me when better things came up. So, he must feel guilty when he wants to come back and see me. He agreed.

I also thought to myself that when he comes back, it is a combination of honest desire to see me for help with his issues and partly a return to me as the vending machine where he can get a quick fix before he tosses me aside again and goes off to have fun. G said, "I don't want to wear you down or make you angry that way. I hope you are OK. Are you Doc? I don't want to be too much!"

Here, G was showing advancement into more depressive anxiety and the ability to talk about it as well. This fear of wearing me down and creating a crisis or rejection was intense. G used me and his objects like throw-away Band-Aids, but the more we worked together, the more we discovered his strong need for attachment and intense dependency on his objects for love, approval, and reassurance. This search for a nourishing attachment was camouflaged by his destructive narcissistic system of using others for immediate praise or fame.

Over the course of our work together, G was one foot in the treatment and one foot out, both literally and emotionally. As I just mentioned, he sought out fusion or attachment with me and others but perverted it into a vampire-like draining of other's love by means of manipulation and demand. So, he keep coming back with genuine desire for change and insight, but his destructive narcissism eroded that and perverted it into a stage show where he wanted to be acclaimed and applauded.

Literally, he was only partly available. G was planning on moving out of the city and back north where his family and friends lived. He was going to use them as a staging area for his planned six-month trip around the globe "for fun and opportunity." Of course, this would mean the end of our relationship. On one hand, G was cold and callous about this. He said nothing about it, and when I brought it up he said it was "just an eventuality." But, if I told him he seemed to not value himself and our work together, he said he was contemplating "sticking around just for our work time."

Indeed, the last two months have involved G's being in town only to see me. He no longer has an apartment or any other real ties in the city. He has moved six hours away to be around his family and friends, yet he stays in the city for weeks at a time to see me. Obviously, this is a sign of how much he looks to me for help and how much he feels the need to change. But, as I said, it also speaks to the quick way he can turn on his needed object and walk away towards something else that has caught his attention as a faster, easier, and shinier way to feeling like the master of his universe.

One way in which our work together was having an impact on G was through a slow internalization of my analytic observational approach. During the last few months of our work together, G started to tell me more about how his father was so "self-centered and cold" and how G wished that one day he might stand up to his father on behalf of both his mother and himself to tell his father off." He talked about how angry, dominating, and arrogant his father could be. As a result, speaking up was something no one ever did in his house. G told me he often pictured the day he might be able to confront his father on his selfish ways.

I interpreted that G was very angry at his father for ignoring him and very hurt that his father seemed so uninterested in him and who he really is. I had said many times throughout our sessions that I thought G had internalized his selfish, ignoring father and that now G ignored his own real self and wanted something bigger and better than who he already was. He approaches life trying to build up his fake hero profile and ignores the goodness or greatness that he already has. I have told G he turns away from my current respect and appreciation for his real self and waits instead for me to adore him as a superhero. I interpreted that he has made an eternal and lonely wait out of something warm and good that he already has but devalues.

When G spoke of wanting to confront his father, I told him that he often acted like his father, which invited me to confront him. I interpreted that I was put in the position of telling G that he wasn't being real with me, wasn't paying attention to me, and was always wanting to be the shiny hero in the room and how that completely tarnished our relationship. So, the very thing G felt had hurt him with his father over the course of his life was now being repeated in the transference. Likewise, G felt the urge and necessity to confront this narcissistic toxin in his father, just as I had to draw G's attention to his own version of that toxin within himself. This was more of a traditional interpretation that spoke to his desires, fears, loss, conflicts, and defensive use of the projective identification processes.

So, it was striking to hear G tell me what happened on a recent trip to visit his family: "I had a real standoff with my father. I said something I have never said to him. It was amazing." I asked what happened. G said, "I was trying to tell my father about how difficult it is to fail the law school tests over and over again and how I am not sure when I will try to take them again. He interrupted me to go on and on about how he will be able to brag to all his friends about having a famous lawyer son who will make lots of money and make the family the talk of the town. He said he will be envied by all his friends and that once again he has proven what a great father he is. I was stunned by the degree of self-absorption he showed. It was all about him and nothing about me. I was furious. Normally, I would just walk away and try to ignore it or feel resentful for days, but I decided to do it differently this time. I said, 'Father, please stop. All you are doing is talking about yourself. Don't you care about me? Don't you care about my feelings? I was talking about all my difficulties with the law test and you started talking about yourself. I need you to pay attention to me and realize you have a son who matters!'"

G said his father was silent and then said, "OK. I can do that. I think I already do that," and walked away. G said it was unclear if his father would change but that it "felt fantastic and important" to say what he did and to "be honest for the first time and feel like it mattered."

In reflecting on G's actions with his father, I think he had slowly internalized my role as one making analytic observations that drew an interpersonal limit and translated the object relational impact of narcissistic acting out. The implicit request for respect and consideration, as well as the firm and direct articulation of what is being done to the object and how the object is being manipulated, used, or abused, are elements of the approach I took with G when he acted out from his narcissistic framework.

I think he had taken this in and tried to identify with me as the one who stood for life, respect, and love of the genuine, instead of the more destructive, narcissistic one who trashed what was, in favor of the ultimate perfection that never is. For him to have experimented with considering himself worth something "as is" and wanting his father to love him simply for being his son and a good person showed a promising start to the resolution of such a self-hating narcissistic burden.

As Kavaler-Adler (1993) states, we must renew our love in the face of the hate we have for our withholding or less-than-ideal objects. The envy we have of the love we feel deprived of must be tolerated, contained, and worked through so as to not constantly deface or destroy the love and attachment we can have with our objects.

For G, he was unable for most of his life to stop his demanding search for something better, something his father might love. He envied that others seemed to have more, and, compared to that ideal, he had less. So, he always sought a way to appear greater and to be the hero that others envied. He tried to outdo his father and to provide his father with the ideal, shining son that he seemed to want. This was crushing enough to G's soul, but when he internalized this ongoing cycle of expectation and disappointment, he became his own worst enemy.

Searles (1978) has written about the need to integrate a sense of hope in exchange for the previously held sense of omnipotence. Searles notes that a parallel line of gradual hope is necessary to help the patient through the line of necessary disappointment, despair, grief, and rage that emerges as the strands of narcissism are unraveled. This is difficult and is still a work in progress for G that he struggles to embrace. He reaches for hope but flees from the internal hopelessness that has plagued him and that he tries to deny through his constant narcissistic acting out.

Most of our more difficult narcissistic patients are a combination of destructive and libidinal narcissists (Rosenfeld, 1971). Analytic observations are designed to work with the destructive aspects and the death-instinct elements of patients' phantasies, which seek to eliminate any threatening aspects of the life instinct within themselves or others. As Tuckett (1989) points out, Herbert Rosenfeld is still one of the primary Kleinian voices in the area of narcissism and the death instinct. Rosenfeld believed that helping the patient become aware of his immediate psychic reality is vital to the healing process. Analytic observations are meant to focus and translate the very nature of the patient's narcissistic phantasy and to show the patient exactly how he is attempting to use his objects and position himself in the world, including, of course, in the transference. Analytic observations help gradually contain, manage, and reduce the patient's acting out, which Rosenfeld (1987) has noted is caused by the omnipotent defenses, such as projective identification and other primitive conflicts the patient feels trapped by and attempts to overcome and to triumph over.

Tuckett (1989) has also noted how important the analyst's counter-transference is to getting a clinical understanding of the intense reliance the patient has on projective identification. The case of G shows the ongoing and severe reliance and self-destructive results of such pathological projective mechanisms. For the more narcissistic or borderline patient, such rigid reliance both provides a distorted pathological organization (Steiner, 1987) and psychic retreat (Steiner, 1993) that feels safe and omnipotent but is actually claustrophobic and kills off any possible emotional nourishment from the object and deadens any appreciation of self or other that is so needed in normal development and daily living.

Such death-instinct fueled use of projective identification tends to corrode and eventually topple any functioning container capacity in the self or in the object. Analyst observations help to provide the containment and translation of such desperate and destructive phantasies that Gold (1983) describes as so important for eventual identification by the patient. Analyst observations help to define and stop the hateful, abusive, or neutralizing effects of the death instinct, mobilized via excessive projective identification. And, the strong and aggressive envy that narcissistic patients tend to exhibit in which they ignore or attack any goodness in themselves or in others leads to what Bion (1962) felt was a deadening of thinking itself.

So, analytic observations are important technical tools in achieving psychic change. Steiner (1984) notes that real emotional change results when the analyst can identify the current psychic reality or the unconscious phantasy which is occurring for the patient in the total transference situation (Joseph, 1985). Because the borderline and narcissistic patient has such rigid, violent, two-dimensional, and desperate phantasies of actions that must be taken and taken immediately, analytic observations provide a net of sorts for the first stage of translating the patient's inner struggles.

Analytic observations verbalize *what* the patient is doing internally. Once these elements are worked with in the transference, a more standard interpretation of *why* and *how* can follow. But, initially, we must make the therapeutic observation a first-line method of reducing the acting out, internally and externally, manage the anxiety and aggression, and regain the stability and container function of the analytic moment. Analytic observations help the patient reach a place where he or she can actually think and feel, instead of react, retaliate, or retreat.

Analytic observations have helped G through some of his more destructive narcissistic conflicts, and more standard analytic interpretations have been useful in working with his libidinal narcissism. Analytic observations have helped him face his external and internal acting out and have provided a bridge to where he and I can begin to understand and repair the damage underneath.

Eleven

Name It, Claim It, and Tame It

There are times in analytic treatment when our patients demonstrate the destructive elements of the death instinct by a variety of actions, phantasies, and transference modes. There are many ways this acting out in phantasy and in interpersonal behavior can take place. This includes severing ties with others, killing off meaning, attacking self-knowledge or identity, preventing difference between the self or others, claiming control over the object, denying dependence, or eliminating any value in others around them.

Such patients are usually borderline or narcissistic, but there can be instances of such pathology in highly defended and rigid neurotic patients. All of these hard-to-reach and slow-to-thaw individuals are exhibiting ways of relating or non-relating intended to break off the life-sustaining aspects of relational connections and to erase the meaning of the object. Or, in some more masochistic and depressive cases, they seek to void the value of the self. Therefore, establishing analytic contact (Waska, 2007, 2010a, 2010b) is very difficult. Ultimately, when their pathological projective identification mechanisms are understood, what we see clinically is that the value and meaning of feelings or thoughts in the self are the ultimate targets in this destructive approach. But, through projection, the acting out so common with borderline and narcissistic patients is usually aimed at the object.

In these difficult clinical situations, the analyst must make ongoing life-affirming interpretations that have to be firm, forceful, and direct. After these more confrontational analytic observations have engaged the destructive aspects of the patient's narcissism, the analyst can follow up with more traditional or tender interpretations. Kernberg (1975) has described confrontations as preludes to interpretations that simply point out contradictions in the patient's actions or speech. This is not what I am examining. When I speak of the confrontational aspect of therapeutic observations, I mean the manner in which the analyst helps the patient face the narcissistic motivations, the destructive death drive, and the object relational impact of his acting out. This is done by verbalizing the *how* of the patient's phantasy. While usual interpretations describe the why of a patient's view of self and others, as well as unconscious motives behind the internal or external acting out of phantasies, analytic observations speak to exactly how the patient is using, placing, controlling, or viewing self and object. This has an important holding, containing, and symbolizing function that interrupts the deadly, concrete, and destructive nature of the object relational acting out that this type of patient so frequently brings to the transference.

So, it might be that the patient has so strongly neutralized his feelings that he is relating like a robot and thinking nothing of it. Or, it might be that the patient is constantly blaming the analyst for a variety of things in a way that is meant to never allow the analyst to have a say, only to have to silently suffer the pain of blame and persecution. Or, it might be that the patient is describing others in such a devalued and cruel manner that unless the analyst steps in verbally, the patient is left to be a ruthless dictator in the transference.

When the narcissistic or borderline patient acts out his predatory, desperately retreating, or ruthlessly controlling phantasies, the transference must be addressed in a much more confrontational, grounding, and containing manner before a more traditional interpretation can be heard or be helpful. The death instinct can dominate the transference in such a manner that unless deliberately life-affirming comments are made that describe the lifelessness of the transference, the cruelty of the patient's mindset, or the deliberate attacks on love and loss in the clinical moment, the destructive drive will take over and not only dominate but overtake the analytic situation.

The term *analytic observation* describes the need for the analyst in special moments with the narcissistic or borderline patient to face off in the transference, directly and verbally, with the way the patient is attempting to neutralize, deaden, or overthrow the therapeutic relationship by controlling, eliminating, or dehumanizing all or parts of his object, including the potential of analytic contact with the analyst. This death force, this move to kill off, deaden, or eliminate any need, dependence, meaning, or value, must be directly defined in a containing yet defining manner to ground or stabilize the analytic situation and stop the patient from escalating the destructive or life draining projective identification processes.

When the analyst makes firm and direct analytic observations, the unreachable, acting-out narcissistic patient is more reachable and open to hearing or taking in more traditional interpretations. Bateman (1998) and, more recently, Britton (2004) have stated that real psychic change only occurs when the patient is in transition from a more thick-skinned narcissistic state to a more thin-skinned state. I believe these more formed, defined, and tougher analytic observations can facilitate that movement and create an atmosphere in which the deeper interpretations regarding core conflict and anxiety become possible and eventually are helpful. The destructive narcissist, in his thick-skinned pathological organization, fends off the more traditional method of talking. This type of patient doesn't let in our ideas or inquiries about the inner self. So, the initial interpretive move must address the workings of death drive that sweeps across the analytic space. These more pro-life therapeutic observations can help transition a patient from a well-defended paranoid-schizoid state to a more semi-depressive outlook, at least temporarily and long enough for the patient to begin feeling something and to consider his conflicts from a more whole-object and reflective mode. At least for a moment, the patient is in a better position to potentially work on core anxieties instead of relying so much on extreme splitting, denial, manic command, or pathological projective identification.

Betty Joseph (1985) has noted that many of our more borderline or narcissistic patients have had trouble in their upbringings with finding good objects that were able and willing to hold, cherish, and protect their most basic projections regarding love, hate, and knowledge. Joseph thinks the analyst's task is to utilize the transference and the analytic situation to locate the conflict and anxiety within these patients. By doing so, we can help bring alive again feelings regarding others and the desire for relationships that have been deeply defended against or even deadened and nearly killed off. Then, we can help such patients become more deeply rooted in these pro-life strivings. So, I am extending Joseph's idea by stating that we must cultivate the struggling and fragile life instinct within our patients, and part of that is facing off with the their reliance on the death instinct and its destructive methods of relating and non-relating.

This approach can be crucial with the more disturbed patient, particularly the narcissistic individual but also the borderline patient. It can also be useful and important in the treatment of rigid and emotionally one-dimensional neurotic patients. The idea of using more grounded, direct, and confrontational observations that strongly examine how the patient treats his objects, including in the transference, is a way of gradually inviting the patient out of encased and tightly drawn psychic retreats (Steiner, 1993). This approach to interpretation is meant as a technical tool when encountering pathological organizations (Rosenfeld, 1964; Steiner, 1979) that have become permanent retreats and psychological control centers for the embattled and brittle ego, overcome by its own reliance on the death instinct for dominance and power.

Methods of interpretation are critical to examine when faced with the variety of emotional blizzards or emotional firestorms that we usually find with borderline or narcissistic patients. Rosenfeld (1964) and Bion (1959) have discussed the severe alienation and relational severing that occurs in these patients' omnipotent projective-identification phantasies. Indeed, the degree of pathological projective identification present is parallel to the narcissistic blockade, the impasse, and the death-instinct defense we find in the transference.

Rosenfeld (1971) has been a pioneer in discovering the way conflicts with the life and death instinct are at the core of severe narcissistic disturbances. In conjunction with excessive reliance on projective identification, there come to be pathological organizations that congeal into libidinal or destructive profiles. These are the thick-skinned or thin-skinned personality states we find so complex and confusing to analyze.

Analytic observations are meant to be technical tools to better work through the destructive and controlling aspects of a patient's death instinct–driven phantasies and make our way towards the more accessible libidinal aspects of his narcissistic state. At that point, more traditional interpretations are important to introduce.

ANALYTIC OBSERVATION WITH A NEUROTIC PATIENT: THE CASE OF N

N had met with me for four years in psychoanalytic treatment, on the couch. Over the course of our time together, he had made many changes and elected to decrease from twice a week to once a week and finally to every other week during the last six months. So, it was not a complete surprise when N came in and said, "I want to let you know that this will be my last session. I feel very positive about it and want to thank you for everything you have done for me. Since I moved last year, it takes me an hour to get here, and now that Liz and I are starting the adoption process with the agency, I won't have a lot of free time. But, that is only part of it. The bigger part is that I feel ready. I feel good. I feel like I can finally stand on my own and make it."

A good deal of the transference work had centered around N's fear of conflict, fear of hurting the other with his own needs or opinions, and fear of the consequences in terms of either crippling guilt or anticipated punishment. So, I asked N what he was feeling about his announcement. N said, "I used to be afraid of saying the wrong thing with you or making a mistake. I tried my best to be a good patient and make you happy. But then I moved through that and found out I could be myself without it being the end of the world. I am no longer worried about hurting you or making you angry. Before, I never let myself even think about what I wanted. It was always what the other person wants or needs and how I can facilitate that."

I said, "Or what you *think* I need or want. Often, you are so anxious to please me and others that you are the one that makes up what we need and then you rush to fill that need." N said, "Good point! Yes. I am really only dedicating myself to what I *think* everyone one wants, which is even worse. Well, now I am turning my attention to myself and what I *actually* want and need! That feels so different. At first, it felt different in a dangerous way. Later, it felt different in an awkward and foreign way. Now, it feels different but sometimes in an exciting way. It makes me curious and interested. I still may take forever to check it out, but I am intrigued and curious on my own behalf. I used to look to you to be my mentor, and we talked for years about how I wished someone would step in and be my mentor, the mentor my father never was. I now accept that isn't going to happen and that actually I don't really even want it. I think I am a pretty smart fellow and in a lot of ways I am able to be my own mentor now!"

These changes in N's internal life are reflected in N's external life. He operates in a much different fashion from when he began his psychoanalytic treatment. N finally left a career he felt bored and stifled by. He had kept with it for years because he felt like he should have a regular job that paid the bills. He told me he felt he had to stay with it "even if it is something I don't like. We can't all be happy all the time, right?" I interpreted his fear of pursuing happiness and making moves towards something that had meaning to him instead of placating the looming authority he anticipated around every corner. We examined his reluctance to have his own desire and to want something for himself, something he might actually like instead of merely tolerate. In the transference, I interpreted for years that he was fearful to show his feelings to me especially if they involved desire or difference. Instead of taking that risk, N was very quick to engage me in a highly intellectual, controlled, and logical discussion of varied topics, but all stripped of any emotional value.

Over time, N was able to let himself investigate what he might want, and he realized he would have to go back to school to earn a degree in a new field. This meant months of obsessive debating and neutralizing of his desires before he was able to risk really owning his dream to go to school and learn something he enjoyed. He used whatever detour possible, including what he pictured I wanted, what he pictured his girlfriend wanted, and the disappointment his boss and coworkers might show when he told them he was leaving. Fear and guilt bled through almost everything in which N tried to be involved.

By the time N terminated his analytic treatment, he was married and starting an adoption process. He had earned a certificate in a school program that allowed him to land a new job that he found interesting. More important, he was able to tell himself and me that, overall, he saw it as a temporary stepping stone that he would use to land another job that he would actually enjoy even more. So, he could feel OK about not liking something completely but choosing to essentially use it for his own benefit as a way to something better instead of something he had to tolerate without any hope of change.

When I first met N, he was crippled by his past and the ways his past still distorted and choked off any breath of life or growth in his adulthood. When he was five years old, his father left the family, and N's mother and N's two brothers were left to struggle with poverty and a complete lack of resources for the next year. Then, N's mother remarried to a violent, sadistic alcoholic who routinely beat and terrorized the family. N has many traumatic memories, including being yelled at to eat all of a cold dinner he didn't like; and then when he vomited on the bathroom floor, he was kicked and forced to lick it all up off the floor. N witnessed his brother being sexually abused and the other brother humiliated and beat many times over. N told me, "When my step-father beat me, it was really bad. But, what was worse was not knowing when he would suddenly turn on you. I tried to find a way to hide. He might be laughing one moment and turn into a firestorm the next."

N tried to cope with this severe abuse in several ways that were repeated in the transference. He felt very sorry for his mother, and he has tried to save her and his brothers over the years by providing them with money, advice, and any favors along the way. However, they all continue to be adrift in an endless cycle of drugs, alcohol, poverty, and lack of self-care. We have worked for years on his denial of how they use him and abuse him and his overwhelming sense of guilt and obligation to sacrifice for them. No matter what, N tried to please everyone and always avoid or deny any negative feelings, desires, or ambitions of his own. Any assertive or self-defining thoughts were quickly attacked and felt as dangerous to either him or the object. Instead, he tried to blend in and avoid conflict at any cost. This resulted in his spending many sessions simply talking at a rapid pace about nothing but logical, intellectual facts that, more and more, had nothing to do with him or anything else.

So, over the years, in the counter-transference, I consistently found myself in a numb, thoughtless state when listening to N's words. I felt like they were just words without any meaning. They were not connected to any feelings, conviction, or disagreement. They were simply words that made up sentences that made up a story about something that occurred. It was data. There was always a point in the story but overall it seemed like a useless and unimportant story that only filled time and space. That was the defensive death instinct operating clinically. N tried to suffocate us with words and take the life out of our time together as a way to avoid the risk of showing his urge to live, love, and learn.

When talking with me, N seemed animated, but over time I noticed that this was more a state of automation, like a machine that keeps a certain speed no matter what. Alerted by my counter-transference trance-like state, I began interpreting this wall of suffocating logic. When I made a more standard interpretation of him using intellectual jargon to guard against his guilt around being more of a man or to guard against his anger or hurt, he was helped a bit and felt a bit less anxious, but only temporarily. Then, he resumed his automation. What worked much better were more direct and firm observations of what he was doing to me and to us in the transference. I translated his efforts to deaden us and pull us away from any sense of discovery, autonomy, or assertive thinking.

In other words, I observed him identifying with the intimidating father and preventing us from feeling safe to be ourselves and think, feel, and talk freely. I had to stand up to that internalized force. Over time, we examined how N wanted to please me and how much he certainly did not want to displease me. This double anxiety, pressure, and threat lead him to try to control us with this automated stream of neutralized logic designed to deaden any life or growth. But, initially, I had to verbalize the *what* and *how* of his phantasies rather than the *why* of them. So, I made more confrontational or life-affirming analytic observations, such as "You have taken the life out of the room," "We are not allowed to grow or explore," and "You are making sure we can't think or feel." Over time, and very gradually, these types of analytic or therapeutic observations allowed N to risk being more assertive, to think more independently, and to embrace life more fully. Once the more destructive level of death-instinct defense was contained and translated, the deeper meanings of his inner conflicts were reachable with more traditional interpretations regarding anxiety around love, hate, and knowledge.

PROVIDING ANALYTIC OBSERVATIONS TO A DIFFICULT COUPLE

A and B came to me in a point of crisis. However, the more I met with them, it was clear they were always in some level of tension, crisis, or sense of "being overwhelmed and falling apart." They described themselves like this: "At least one of us is often feeling pretty out of control and sometimes both of us. It is rare that we both feel stable, strong, and happy, or if we do it is short lived."

They had been married for ten years and lived in a neighborhood that they found "appealing at first and one we could afford five years ago." But, shortly after they bought their home, a series of disputes with the neighbors on both sides of them ensued. With one neighbor, it was about the constant loud parties, the late night drinking, and the music that kept A and B up at night. With the other neighbors, there was an ongoing dispute about their dogs. The dogs barked constantly and defecated on A and B's lawn. After about a year, B told A he wanted to sell the house and leave the area. A said she was not as uncomfortable as he was and also, because of the economy, she did not want to have to sell the house at a loss. Over the next few years, B became more and more upset over the situation and was involved in several verbal fights with the neighbors. As a result, the police were called. B said, "I have a temper problem to begin with, but they made it so much worse. I felt trapped and unable to have any freedom, choices, or even a sense of privacy. Nothing is mine. I have no say and no respect. And, I feel A never backs me up. I feel I am always on my own."

Having no control and being trapped was something they both also felt with their jobs. A and B worked at the same local gym and both felt "completely overworked, disrespected, underpaid, and stuck in a dysfunctional family from hell." They had met each other there years ago, started dating, and then married shortly after. Over the years, A had tried to be promoted and tried to find ways of enjoying her job but felt "shoved aside every step of the way. They only like you if you are their buddy. They don't care if you do a good job or not. I have no value to them and they treat me like shit."

B felt the same about the job but told me he "tolerates" it. "I just put in my time. I hate where I live and I hate where I work. With the house, I still have enormous anger that I am trying to manage. But I think I have given up at work. I just stay in my little office and play on the computer to waste time, but I can see how A isn't able to do that. She is really down about it." That last remark was a hopeful indication of some ability to imagine the plight of the other instead of being completely spellbound in either a paranoid or narcissistic state of mind that never considers the other, except as something to avoid, use, or attack.

B was raised in a household where he was the oldest and had four sisters. He said, "I felt I always had to honor whatever my sisters wanted. What I wanted was ignored. I felt castrated at a very early age, and my sisters got to run the show. I still get very volatile if I think someone is trying to tell me what to do." In the counter-transference, I took this as a warning. B's volatility had certainly been a problem in the marriage. A had called the police on B twice when he started to become violent or threatening because he felt he wasn't getting his way someone was trying to impose their way on him.

A was raised in a home where she was sexually abused from age five to age ten by her uncle and also verbally abused by her mother and intimidated by her alcoholic father. As a teen, she retreated into heavy drug use and was an addict for many years. She has been off of drugs now for thirteen years and goes to support groups on a regular basis.

The reason they came to see me was that B had punched a hole in the wall and screamed at A after they had a fight about their financial budget. They had bounced several checks. B said, "I felt completely humiliated and out of control that we had sunk to that level, on top of all our other problems." A told me, "At that point, I realized I have been tolerating a great deal of anger and intimidation from B for years. I grew up with that from both my parents, and when B punched that hole in the wall, a light went off and I realized I can't do this anymore. I told him I will be divorcing him in six months if there is not a radical turnaround!"

B replied, "I'm definitely aware of my issues and want to work on them," to which A responded, "I want to work on mine as well. I read through some old diaries and was shocked to see how, over and over, I have a pattern of feeling upset over being treated poorly and then ignoring it. When it happens again, I protest at first but quickly forget about it or deny it until the next time. That is what happened when I was molested, and I realize I am still doing that to myself. I want to stop."

Here, A was demonstrating some valuable psychological strength in reflecting on herself, having some insight, and then trying to use that knowledge to better herself. These are all hallmarks of the depressive position (Klein, 1935, 1940). Given the overall way A and B related to each other over time and in my office, I also thought their respective abilities to remain firmly planted in the depressive position was unstable and probably prone to fairly easy breakdown and collapse into the paranoid-schizoid position (Klein, 1946). So, we began a psychoanalytic treatment and met twice a week to explore these issues.

The way their insurance coverage worked was that they received the first visit free and then had a small copayment each session afterwards. In the second session, I asked for their share of the payment and B said, "I thought we were covered 100%." I said, "You are but only for the first session." B said, "The insurance company told me otherwise!" I told B what I tell all patients: "They may have told you one thing. But, I always have to go on what they tell me when I call in. They told me you owe after the first visit, so I need you to provide a check today." At that point, B sprung up in his chair with an angry look in his face and spoke very loudly and forcefully, "I don't think we have to do that. You can't tell us to pay for something that we don't owe. We know what we have covered. We don't have to pay anything!" B is a large man, almost twice my size, so with his posture, tone, loud voice, and overall verbal and physical stance, I felt intimidated and wondered if he was about to punch another hole, this time in my wall.

I said, "Why are you so angry? What is going on that makes you so upset?" B yelled back, "I am not angry! Why would you say that? I am simply frustrated that you want to have us pay money after we were told we would not pay anything. Anyone would be frustrated!" I replied, "Like I said, I have to go on what I am told, not what you are told. That is how it works. If it turns out there was a mistake or misunderstanding with what the insurance company told me, we will work it out down the line. But, right now, I need the payment. So, please pay so we can talk about this anger. I think that is the most important thing to figure out right now."

B yelled, "Why are you telling me what I am feeling! I am not angry and I don't know if I want to be here anymore. I didn't feel good about this in the first place!" Again, B was sitting up in his chair and now looking like he was going to pounce on me. His eyes were bulging out and his face was red. He was very angry.

I said, "Please sit down. We can sort this out, but first you must sit down and calm down. I want to find out why this has created such tension in you. You said you are not angry, but everything about this shows you are angry. You are showing me exactly what your wife said she is about to divorce you for. This is called anger. So, please sit down and write me a check. Then, we can proceed." Most of what I was saying to B up to this point was about limit setting and a very basic protection of the analytic environment. This included my physical well-being.

With a great deal of tension in the air, and B barely able to contain himself, he wrote me a check. Noticing how anxious A was looking at this point, I asked her how she was doing. A said, "I am speechless. I thought he might hit you. This is the same kind of emotional stress I have been experiencing. He doesn't think anything is wrong with it." B looked at me and said, "I don't like you telling me what I am feeling or what I can't feel. I am a very emotional person, and I feel better after I let off some steam. I was frustrated with you, and I have the right to be that."

I said, "I am telling you that what you are doing here in my office is anger, and it is not your right to unload whatever is inside of you. I can help you figure out what is in there and how to process it better, but you can't just pour it out. It sounds like you feel either you have the right to do as you please with your emotions or if I tell you no, then I am taking away your rights. I have the sense that is happening everywhere, with the neighbors, with your wife, with me, and with work." B said, "Yes, it is. I do feel that way a great deal."

Here, I was shifting from a more parental limit-setting role with his acting out of narcissistic rage to a more confrontational analytic observation that provided containment and translation of his narcissistic entitlement. My therapeutic observations included telling B that he had to respect me as a container that had value and that he could not use this deadly, rageful, and expulsive form of projective identification in which he attempted to unconsciously use me as a toxic emotional dumping site. This firm analytic observation lead to a reduction in his anxiety and his acting out. It also encouraged or enabled him to reflect on my comment about how this phantasy of humiliation and being controlled is so pervasive in his life.

Over the next two or three sessions, we continued to debate, talk, and explore his experience of himself as "just frustrated and expressing my feelings," and I continued to interpret his entitled rage. He tried to tell me he was not having any problems with anger because he was currently in an anger management workshop. I said, "Well, at this point you should get you money back or make sure you keep going for a while. You are still having anger management issues." I had to draw the line and stand up to him. Over the course of several sessions, it became clear to me that he genuinely did not understand that anything was wrong with his behavior. He was really clueless about how he was treating his objects and thought that it was a good thing to simply express whatever he felt without any censoring. Indeed, I interpreted that he felt that to censor himself was to again be emotionally castrated, as he felt he was when he was growing up.

So, we continued to explore this pathological form of projective identification (Waska, 2004) involving B's emotional entitlement and his destructive, deadening abuse of my container function. I also interpreted the defensive use of the death instinct when I told him it seemed he has decided that anyone who tries to control him will be defaced and, in revenge, will be controlled with fear and intimidation. He said, "I will not allow anyone to control me or take anything away from me. I know that is a trigger point for me, but I also don't care because no one has the right to try and make me be or do what I don't want to. I will say anything I want when I want." Here, he showed the more paranoid aspect of his narcissistic entitlement and the more destructive narcissism (Rosenfeld, 1987) that existed alongside his more thin-skinned (Rosenfeld, 1987) and libidinal narcissistic state (Rosenfeld, 1987).

Around the second month of treatment, A and B came in and sat down. All the sessions before this one were highlighted by the tension between me and B, as well as by a great deal of conflict, fighting, and tears between A and B. Our last session was a stern standoff between the two of them, and we eventually worked with and through a few core resentments and anxieties they both had towards each other. Things were certainly still up in the air and their mutual emotional state was still very much fragmented. So, it was striking that after sitting in silence for a minute, A said, "I don't have much to say today. Not too much going on. I am not sure what to talk about. Everything seems to be going pretty good. Things are fairly smooth and we are getting along pretty well. So, I am not sure if we have much to talk about."

Here, I felt I was being given the conflict, darkness, and trouble they have been burdened by and they could now feel free and not have any sense of trouble. This was an example of projective identification being used by her and by both of them to deposit any conflict or unhappiness into me and then claim to feel fine and not need me. This was an important moment in the treatment because projective identification is often the most critical aspect of the transference (Grotstein, 1994; Waska, 2004, 2010c, 2011a, 2011b). As Joseph (1985, 1988) states, projective identification is often used this way to get rid of unwanted conflict and to invade or control the object. Joseph (1989) also emphasizes projective identification as a tool used to maintain psychic equilibrium and, in the case of A and B, they used it to maintain their mutual pathological psychic system that was now unfolding in the transference. The difficulty in interpreting this is that some volatile patients, such as A and B, attribute or evacuate (Britton, 2004) so much into the object that they will not tolerate any mention of their projected material, let alone consider ownership of that toxic material. Therapeutic observations can work better in these more layered, rigid, and sensitive situations.

I made a firm and defining observation, followed by a more traditional interpretation, by saying, "It may help us to understand how you could feel so fine and not have anything to talk about when last week you were thinking of divorcing him for his violence and you were in tears about the years of trouble in the marriage. Suddenly you have nothing to say and everything is smooth. Maybe, you are trying to ignore some uncomfortable feeling and now I am the person who has to bring up the ugly stuff." So, I confronted her denial and projection into me as well as interpreting anxiety as a possible motive. A replied, "Well, I think I know what you mean. Actually, that is a pattern for me. I was reading some diary entries the other day from long time ago and realized there have been some pretty bad moments in our marriage. But, reading the diary, I also realized I tend to ignore it all until or unless it gets really bad and I have to respond to it. So, maybe I try to pretend there is nothing wrong and hope it all just gets better. I think that is what happened around my being molested. I am glad we are in therapy so I have a chance to look at my part in the marriage and what problems we are having. Now that we have made a commitment to being here for six months and working on things to see if we can stay together, I think there is a chance of things getting sorted out. We can both find out what is going on and what we want to do about it." Here, A was able to make some important links, reflect in a deeper way about herself, and look at how she was relating to her husband.

While this was going on in the session, B had taken out a notepad and was scribbling some notes. I asked him what he was writing down. B said, "I'm surprised to hear that I *have* to be in therapy for six months. That is a bit of a surprise." I said, "The way you say that shows us something. A said she was glad the two of you agreed to being here for six months, but you sound irritated that you are going to be stuck with me in something you didn't agree to and now you will have to tolerate being with me for six months. Those are two very different viewpoints. You are once again dreading me or her controlling you or having us rule over you without your having a choice."

We went over this for a while and it was clear how easily and quickly B felt persecuted and controlled. I made a link to how he felt I was controlling him and telling him how he felt when he had insisted that he wasn't angry but only frustrated. He was able to say, "I know I have a tendency to feel like other people are telling me what to do and then I react strongly." He said, "I think that would be helpful to work on." So, with my transference interpretation about his sense of persecution, his anxiety was reduced and he was able to think productively for a moment.

As the session came to an end, we went over the schedule for the following week. We were set for two sessions, and as we confirmed the dates, A said, as she had once before, "Maybe we don't need to meet so often. Everything seems to be going well. I think once a week would be right." I said, "You are suddenly taking over and telling me what is right. You came here seeking my help and my suggestions. I have told you several times what I think is necessary and what would serve you best. Now, you are forgetting about that and saying things are just fine. Maybe this is more of the cycle of denying, minimizing, or forgetting that you noticed in your diary. We have to have time to work on the things you want to change."

A said, "OK. I see what you mean. I do feel we have a great deal to work on. So, that is fine. But, I think we don't necessarily need to meet so often. Our insurance will run out faster if we meet twice a week so I think it might be better to only meet once a week since then we will have longer on the insurance."

I said, "Once again, you are telling me what is best and ignoring my suggestions even though you want my help. And, you are paying more attention to your insurance policy than your marriage and what might save it. So, you are getting me to be the spokesperson for your feelings and your marriage while you are busy counting the sessions your insurance company gives you. Let's try and understand more about that next time."

Here, I encountered A's attempt to take control of the analytic situation, devalue me, and drain the importance out of the issues she was facing. She was also being quite provocative, as she probably was with B. I made a very containing, defining, and confrontational therapeutic observation that showed her I was not going to be beaten down or taken off my focus, but neither was I going to retaliate and beat her down verbally like B seemed to do over the course of their marriage. I was trying to be a consistent object that could stand up for itself, which was something she could not yet do. So, I think her acting out and draining the life blood out of the moment had both destructive and libidinal purposes. I followed the analytic observation with a more traditional interpretation about her projective identification attempt to put her desire to work on the marriage into me. So, I first verbalized the *what* she was doing with her objects and the *how* she was controlling her objects, and then I added the *why* she might be acting out like that with her objects.

By making more direct analytic observations combined with standard interpretations in the sessions with both A and B, I was able to keep the treatment afloat and maintain a fragile but usable degree of analytic contact in which we could attempt to discover the source of these ongoing anxieties and mutual attacks on the vitality of the marriage. Slowly and against great resistance, we are moving forward towards understanding their mutual and individual ways of feeling so stagnant, depressed, and angry. Hopefully, these ongoing transference face-offs with their pathological patterns will lead to more of a bridge to possible growth, change, and love for life in the marriage, rather than the more deadening and predatory approach they tend to have towards each other.

SUMMARY

Using case material, I have shown how narcissistic and borderline patients, as well as more entrenched or severely neurotic patients, will prove impossible to reach by standard interpretive means. Unless the analyst can find a more direct, firm, and confrontational manner in which to speak to these impasse-prone individuals, the treatment can stale. Specifically, analytic observations seem to be what is needed before more standard interpretations make a difference. These therapeutic observations provide a focused translation and containment of the narcissistic acting out in the transference and provide a way to help patients understand their abusive object relational approach. Once the analytic observations make contact with a patient's internal world, other interpretations that speak to unconscious meaning, anxiety, and defense can take place more effectively.

Such therapeutic observations are designed to help patients emerge from their withdrawal into a psychic retreat (Steiner, 1993) in which they feel powerful and in charge of a kingdom of their own making. The analytic observation aims at showing patients the destructive nature of how they treat their objects and ultimately how they have neglected themselves and sent their more vulnerable true selves into exile. However, the transference acting out that is so common with narcissistic and borderline patients must be firmly and directly addressed. As the Kleinian approach advocates, the negative transference is crucial to consider before working with other aspects of the treatment. The analyst must speak to the underlying narcissistic organization and the death instinct (Rosenfeld, 1971) to begin working through such highly resistive, combative, and complicated patterns of relating and non-relating. Part of the benefit of such analytic observations is that they focus on the patient's inability to partake in depressive position functioning, such as concern and care for the self or others in any real, genuine, and vulnerable way. Once the more firm observations are made, more traditional interpretations can follow. In the case of the narcissistic patient, this means that the lack of concern for others and the one-dimensional view of the self must be faced and then followed by interpretations that work with the patient's fear of dependency, difference, and gratitude, as well as the resulting shame, exposure, and sense of failure. By these descriptions, it is clear that analytic observations are targeted at the death instinct and the way the patient is crushing the life out of his objects and refusing to consider his own fragility and helplessness in life. Of course, it is only through the acceptance of not ever knowing everything and realizing our imperfections that we can truly appreciate the world and others, and begin to actually learn and grow.

In conceptualizing how the death instinct is at the core of such narcissistic issues, it is useful to consider Steiner's (1987) ideas about how when narcissistic and borderline patients find an established psychic existence somewhere between the paranoid and depressive position, they do not simply try to kill off their objects and reign supreme. Instead, they try to stun, deaden, or control their objects in a death grip that allows the object to still breathe enough to stay alive but be completely at the mercy of the narcissist's desires. As a result, the thick-skinned narcissist or the thin-skinned narcissist can still remain close to the hated or dreaded object without being isolated, abandoned, or lost to eternal loneliness.

Part of the technical approach of using analytic observations is tied to the belief that the moment-to-moment transference situation and the nature of the patient's object relational phantasies must be consistently addressed in great detail. This is in line with Joseph's (1985) idea of the total transference and Joseph's (1989) important viewpoint about how we must listen to how the patient takes in our comments. Therefore, I have arrived at using analytic observations by noticing how certain narcissistic and borderline, and even some entrenched neurotics, react to standard interpretations of unconscious motivation, anxiety, and defense. Based on carefully listening to how they don't or won't listen, I have tried this different method. When I use Joseph's approach to listen to how the patient hears or takes in the analytic observation, I often notice a shift that indicates a readiness for a more standard interpretation. The case material in this chapter shows how, in many cases, after one or two analytic or therapeutic observations, patients were less combative, restrictive, or closed and were more open to hearing interpretations about the meaning of their acting out and the nature of their anxiety in relationship to their objects or to themselves.

Conclusions

This book is a unique and intimate examination of the day-to-day stress, confusion, and difficulty encountered when practicing psychoanalytically with the more disturbed patient. The reader has been invited into the analyst's office to hear and ponder the taxing and stormy therapeutic process that takes place when working in depth with the more pained, disturbed, and demanding patients that analysts typically see in private practice. Life has not been kind to these individuals, and they have not been kind to themselves or others. But, within a slow and turbulent process, analytic treatment can offer them a hand up and out of their strained, frightening, and depressing emotional prison.

In this book, I have explored the theoretical and technical aspects of modern Kleinian psychoanalytic work with borderline, narcissistic, and psychotic patients who are in great psychological conflict and who struggle to find stable footing in the relational world. These are the patients who are most taxing and troubling for analysts, the individuals who suffer most in life and who tend to leave a great deal of suffering in their wake. Throughout, I have attempted to give the reader a close-up clinical view of what really takes place in psychoanalytic treatment with psychologically disorganized, predatory, or internally terrorized patients who, often, can barely begin or maintain a therapeutic relationship, as they experience it as so emotionally threatening.

With the aid of very extensive case material, I have defined and illustrated a number of issues, including counter-transference, interpretation, pathological defensive organizations, and the establishment of analyst contact. The book is unique in that it presents such a wealth of here-and-now verbatim case reports for the reader to take in and really get a sense of how the modern Kleinian analyst works.

I have shown how the modern Kleinian clinician uses the techniques originally discovered and described by Melanie Klein to help patients find respite from and resolution of their internal torment. In particular, the concept of analytic contact strongly endorses the regular observation and interpretation of transference, projective identification, and phantasy as the cornerstone to psychological transformation. The total transference and the complete counter-transference serve as two important areas for information about the patient's immediate anxieties and phantasies and the best approach for containment, translation, and interpretation of these unconscious issues.

I have described how today's practitioner typically treats a great number of hard-to-reach patients who, while prone to intense acting out and early termination, are still in great need of psychological assistance. Regardless of diagnosis, length of treatment, or frequency of sessions, the modern Kleinian approach creates a clinical climate that offers patients a rich working-through process, regardless of their internal difficulties. Many cases barely get off the ground due to levels of pathological conflict and destructive phantasy that make object relational connection extremely fragile. This is especially true with the more predatory narcissistic patient and even the more libidinal narcissist. However, the modern Kleinian approach makes it possible to potentially establish analytic contact within even the most chaotic clinical situations and create a therapeutic experience that can be significant and meaningful. In doing so, there can be a healing process and the birth of new object relational experiences and interpersonal exchanges.

Many of our hard-to-reach patients exhibit a cruel sense of judgment and expectation that they project and then feel surrounded by. While they crave a loving, soothing object that can rescue them from their internal torment, they also work against the union with a good capable object, unless it is ideal and fully capable of providing all at all times. Therefore, they tend to maintain a degree of separation from the analyst, expecting a great deal, not wanting to give much, and forcing distance and preventing any healthy dependency. These types of more narcissistic and borderline patients find contempt in any possible hint of mutuality or understanding. Because of this aggressive stance against accepting regular, non-ideal attributes of the self or object, patients are unaware of what they do obtain from the analyst or of what they are capable of achieving themselves. In the interpretive realm, this means a consistent following of the transference and patients' phantasies, as colored by excessive projective identification.

The more difficult borderline, narcissistic, and psychotic patients highlighted in this book are living life in a tailspin with their internal world chaotically swirling around them. In order to assist them, we must step into that fast-paced, shadowy peril without much knowledge of who they are and how they will use us, need us, or fight against us. This is where the exploration of the transference and counter-transference is so important, as well as the gradual understanding of the patient's core phantasy conflicts. Over time, the grounding, containing, and translating functions of analytic observations and interpretations can help some patients out of their inner darkness towards the light of change and growth.

These are, however, really the most trying and turbulent cases we have, and it is equally important to balance our faith in the analytic method and our therapeutic perseverance with a fundamental acceptance of failure along the way. It is a fact that many of these patients will leave treatment early or quickly solidify an impasse state that then collapses into a sudden termination. This is the nature of such pathology. Part of the analyst's task is to do his or her best to provide a depressive-position, whole-object acceptance of such matters. In other words, when dealing with such volatile paranoid-schizoid dynamics, the analyst must learn to live in the depressive position as much as possible, for the analyst's own benefit as well as the patient's. We allow ourselves to be pulled into the persecutory realm of our patients' phantasies so that we can better understand their projective efforts. But we keep a firm foot in the more reality-based, mature position of understanding, forgiveness, balance, grief, loss, acceptance, reparation, and other life-affirming ways of thinking.

So, when our patients fail to thrive, terminate suddenly, and even get worse, we stand firm in our conviction that they may be down but not for the count. We stand ready to help them up and to be by their side for another round. Ultimately, we must believe that there is a possibility that one day we can both exit that unconscious zone of combat and find our way into a more peaceful and fulfilling existence.

When working with the most demanding, most damaged, most entitled, and most injured of patients, we must closely examine our clinical conception of success and failure. To meet with a person in great distress, one who wants help yet acts out and fights off any assistance, requires us to be as balanced, firm, and curious as possible. To sit with a person in such an internal and external firestorm for often only a brief period, often with less than optimal frequency, and then to have them turn away and disappear so suddenly can feel like a great wounding failure unless we first define our task as consistently *trying* to establish analytic contact. We may never be able to, but we must remain faithful to the goal.

I define analytic contact as a process in which the analyst slowly collects transference and counter-transference information to understand the nature of a patient's phantasies and object relational conflict state. Once we have some degree of knowledge of how our patients view themselves and others and how they are using their objects, how they are interested in and caring for (or not interested in and not caring for) themselves and others, we try to convey this knowledge. We translate the *how* and *what* of our patients' internal landscapes, describing how they are positioning themselves vis-à-vis their objects and what is taking place in their unconscious phantasy worlds. Our knowledge comes from the total transference situation and the complete counter-transference situation.

If we can convey our knowledge of how our patients are experiencing their objects and themselves, we can begin to work with them to reach the *why* of that inner climate. In other words, we can begin to interpret the unconscious reasoning and motivation that drives the countless patterns of conflict between self and other, internally and externally. This is the operational definition of success in analytic work that I believe lets us be best available to work with these most difficult and often disappointing cases. It is helping patients to gain self-knowledge and reality-based awareness of their objects. If we can help them to tolerate this new knowledge about themselves, to take in all the aspects of their personalities, both good and bad, and consider it as potentially valuable instead of probably toxic, they might use that knowledge to find change, choice, and growth. This is therapeutic success. Failure is simply what happens if we don't try to establish analytic contact with every patient we see.

About the Author

Robert Waska, LPCC, MFT, PhD, is a 1999 graduate of the Institute for Psychoanalytic Studies, an International Psychoanalytical Association affiliate organization. He conducts a full-time, private psychoanalytic practice for individuals and couples in San Francisco and Marin County, California. In addition, he has taught classes, presented papers, and provided consultation internationally.

Waska's clinical work, now thirty years in the making, focuses on contemporary Kleinian topics, including projective identification, loss, borderline and psychotic states, the practical realities of psychoanalytic practice in the modern world, and the establishment of analytic contact with difficult, hard-to-reach patients. He emphasizes the moment-to-moment understanding of transference and phantasy as the vehicle for gradual integration and mastery of unconscious conflict between self and other.

He is the author of eleven published textbooks on Kleinian psychoanalytic theory and technique, is a contributing author for two psychology texts, and has published more than ninety articles in professional journals. He also serves on the review committee for several journals and book publishers.

Finally, Waska is an artist who creates unique combinations of photography, poetry, and digital design. He also writes humorous short stories and reflective essays on the nature of the human condition, some of which can be found at photos2inspire.com.

Bibliography

Bateman, A. (1998). Thick- and thin-skinned organizations and enactment in borderline and narcissistic disorders. *International Journal of Psycho-Analysis, 79*, 13-25.

Bion, W. (1959). Attacks on linking. *International Journal of Psychoanalysis, 40*, 308-315.

Bion, W. (1962). *Learning from Experience*. New York: Basic Books.

Bion, W. (1963). *Elements of Psychoanalysis*. New York: Basic Books.

Britton, R. (2004). Narcissistic disorders in clinical practice. *Journal of Analytical Psychology, 49*, 477-490.

Britton, R. (2008). Narcissism in narcissistic disorders. In *Rosenfeld in Retrospect*, John Steiner (Ed.), 22-34. London: Routledge.

Brown, L. (1987). Borderline personality organization and the transition to the depressive position. In *The Borderline Patient: Emerging Concepts in Diagnosis, Psychodynamics, and Treatment, Volume 1*, James Grotstein, Marion Soloman, and Joan Lang (Eds.). London: Analytic Press.

Bursten, B. (1973). Some narcissistic personality types. *International Journal of Psycho-Analysis, 54*, 287-300.

Cairo-Chiarandini, I. (2001). To have and have not: Clinical uses of envy. *Journal of the American Psychoanalytic Association, 49*, 1391-1404.

Carpy, D. (n.d.). Fantasy versus reality in childhood trauma: who's to blame. Unpublished paper.

Carrese, K. (2010). Psychoanalysis conducted at reduced frequencies. *Psychoanalytic Psychology, 27*, 153-164.

Carstairs, K. (1992). Paranoid-schizoid or symbiotic? *International Journal of Psycho-Analysis, 73*, 71-85.

Cartwright, D. (2010). *Containing States of Mind: Exploring Bion's Container Model in Psychoanalytic Psychotherapy*. London: Routledge.

Charlen, J., Yeoman, F., & Kernberg, O. (1999). *Psychotherapy for Borderlines*. New York: Wiley.

Feldman, M. (2004). Supporting psychic change: Betty Joseph. In *In Pursuit of Psychic Change: The Betty Joseph Workshop*, E. Hargreaves and A. Varchevker (Eds.), 20-37. London: Brunner-Routledge.

Feldman, M. (2009). *Doubt, Conviction, and the Analytic Process*. London: Routledge.

Gabbard, G. (2004). *Long-Term Psychodynamic Psychotherapy: A Basic Text*. London: American Psychiatric Publishing.

Galatariotou, C. (2000). 'Psychoanalysis, Psychoanalytic Psychotherapy and Supportive Psychotherapy: Contemporary Controversies' by Otto F. Kernberg. *International Journal of Psycho-Analysis*, *81*, 385-401.

Gold, S. (1983). Projective identification: The container and reverie as concepts in applied psychoanalysis. *British Journal of Medical Psychology*, *56*, 279.

Grinberg, L. (1962). On a specific aspect of countertransference due to the patient's projective identification. *International Journal of Psycho-Analysis*, *43*, 436-440.

Grinberg, L. (1964). Two kinds of guilt—their relations with normal and pathological aspects of mourning. *International Journal of Psychoanalysis*, *45*, 366-371.

Grinberg, L. (1968). On acting out and its role in the psychoanalytic process. *International Journal of Psycho-Analysis*, 49, 171-178.

Grinberg, L. (1977). An approach to the understanding of borderline disorders. In *Borderline Personality Disorders: The Concept, the Syndrome, the Patient*, Peter Hartocollis (Ed.), 123-141. New York: IUP.

Grotstein, J. (1977). *Splitting and Projective Identification*. New York: Jason Aronson.

Grotstein, J. (1985). A proposed revision of the psychoanalytic concept of the death instinct. In *The Yearbook of Psychoanalysis and Psychotherapy*, *Volume 1*. New York: Jason Aronson.

Grotstein, J. (1994). Projective identification and countertransference: A brief commentary on their relationship. *Contemporary Psychoanalysis*, *30*, 578-592.

Grotstein, J. (2000). *Who is the Dreamer Who Dreams the Dream?* London: Analytic Press.

Grotstein, J. (2009a). *But at the Same Time and On Another Level, Volume 1*. London, Karnac.

Grotstein, J. (2009b). *But at the Same Time and On Another Level, Volume 2*. London, Karnac.

Hinshelwood, R. (1999). Countertransference. *International Journal of Psycho-Analysis*, *80*, 797-818.

Hunter, V. (1993). An interview with Hanna Segal. *Psychoanalytic Review*, *80*, 1-28.

Joseph, B. (1983). On understanding and not understanding: Some technical issues. *International Journal of Psychoanalysis*, *65*, 291-298.

Joseph, B. (1985). Transference: The total situation. *International Journal of Psycho-Analysis*, *66*, 447-454.

Joseph, B. (1987). Projective identification: Clinical aspects. In *Projection, Identification, Projective Identification*, J. Sandler (Ed.). Madison, CT: International Universities Press.

Joseph, B. (1988). Object relations in clinical practice. *Psychoanalytic Quarterly*, *57*, 626-642.

Joseph, B. (1989). *Psychic Equilibrium and Psychic Change: Selected Papers of Betty Joseph.* Edited by Michael Feldman and Elizabeth Bott Spillius. The New Library of Psychoanalysis. London and New York: Tavistock/Routledge.

Kavaler-Adler, S. (1993). The conflict and process theory of Melanie Klein. *American Journal of Psychoanalysis*, *53*, 187-204.

Kernberg, O. (1967). Borderline personality organization. *Journal of the American Psychoanalytic Association*, *15*, 641-685.

Kernberg, O. (1975). *Borderline Conditions and Pathological Narcissism.* New York: Aronson.

Kernberg, O. (1978). Contrasting approaches to the psychotherapy of borderline conditions. In *New Perspectives in Psychotherapy of the Borderline Adult*, James Masterson (Ed.). New York: Brunner/Mazel.

Kernberg, O. (1992). An ego psychology-object relations theory approach to the transference. In *From Inner Sources*, Gregory Hamilton (Ed.), 29-51. New York, Aronson.

Kernberg, O. (1987). Projection and projective identification: Developmental and clinical aspects. In *Projection, Identification, Projective Identification*, J. Sandler (Ed.), 95-96. New York: IUP.

Klein, M. (1935). A contribution to the psychogenesis of manic-depressive states. *International Journal of Psycho-Analysis*, *16*, 145-174.

Klein, M. (1940). Mourning and its relation to manic-depressive states. *International Journal of Psycho-Analysis*, *21*, 125-153.

Klein, M. (1946). Notes on some schizoid mechanisms. *International Journal of Psycho-Analysis*, *27*, 99-110.

Klein, M. (1952). The origins of transference. *International Journal of Psychoanalysis*, *33*, 433-438.

Lopez-Corvo, R. (1999). Self-envy and intrapsychic interpretation. *Psychoanalytic Quarterly*, *68*, 209-219.

Meissner, W. (1979). Narcissistic personalities and borderline conditions: A differential diagnosis. *Annual of Psychoanalysis*, *7*, 171-202.

Millon, T. (1985). *Personality and Its Disorders: A Biosocial Learning Approach*. New York: Wiley.

Palacio Espasa, F. (2002). Considerations on depressive conflict and its different levels of intensity: Implications for technique. *International Journal of Psycho-Analysis*, *83*, 825-836.

Quinodoz, J. (1996). The sense of solitude in the psychoanalytic encounter. *International Journal of Psycho-Analysis*, *77*, 481-496.

Rey, H. (1994). *Universals of Psychoanalysis in the Treatment of Psychotic and Borderline States*. London: Free Association Books.

Rosenfeld, H. (1964). On the psychopathology of narcissism; a clinical approach. *International Journal of Psycho-Analysis*, *45*, 332-337. Reprinted in *Psychotic States*. London: Hogarth Press, 1965.

Rosenfeld, H. (1971a). A clinical approach to the psychoanalytic theory of the life and death instincts: An investigation into the aggressive aspects of narcissism. *International Journal of Psycho-Analysis*, *52*, 169-178.

Rosenfeld, H. (1971b). Contributions to the psychopathology of psychotic patients. In *Problems of Psychosis*, P. Daucet and C. McLaurin (Eds.). Amsterdam: Excerpta Medica.

Rosenfeld, H. (1979). Difficulties in the psychoanalysis of borderline patients. In *Advances in Psychotherapy of the Borderline Patient*. J. LeBoit and A. Capponi (Eds.), 203-204. New York: Jason Aronson.

Rosenfeld, H. (1987). *Impasse and Interpretation: Therapeutic and Anti-therapeutic Factors in the Psychoanalytic Treatment of Psychotic, Borderline, and Neurotic Patients*. New Library of Psychoanalysis, Volume 1. London: Tavistock.

Roth, P. (2004). Discussion of David Taylor's chapter. In *In Pursuit of Psychic Change: The Betty Joseph Workshop*, E. Hargreaves and A. Varchevker (Eds.), 151-152. London: Brunner-Routledge.

Scharff, J., & Scharff, D. (1992). *Scharff Notes: A Primer of Object Relations Therapy*. New York: Jason Aronson.

Searles, H. (1978a). Psychoanalytic therapy with the borderline adult. In *New Perspectives in Psychotherapy of the Borderline Adult*, James Masterson (Ed.). New York: Brunner/Mazel.

Searles, H. (1978b). A dialogue on psychoanalysis. *Modern Psychoanalysis*, *3*, 3-11.

Segal, H. (1962). The curative factors in psychoanalysis. In *The Work of Hanna Segal*, 69-80. New York: Jason Aronson.

Segal, H. (1974). *An Introduction to the Work of Melanie Klein*. New York: Basic Books.

Segal, H. (1975). A psychoanalytic approach to the treatment of schizophrenia. In *Studies in Schizophrenia*, Malcolm Lader (Ed.). London: Headly.

Segal, H. (1977a). Counter-transference. *International Journal of Psychoanalysis, 6*, 31-37.

Segal, H. (1977b). Psychoanalytic dialogue: Kleinian theory today. *Journal of the American Psychoanalytic Association, 25*, 363-370.

Segal, H (1993). On the clinical usefulness of the concept of death instinct. *International Journal of Psychoanalysis, 74*, 55-61.

Segal, H. (1997). *Psychoanalysis, Literature, and War: Papers 1972-95*. Edited by J. Steiner. London: Routledge.

Segal, H., & Britton, R. (1981). Interpretation and primitive psychic processes: A Kleinian view. *Psychoanalytic Inquiry, 1*, 267-277.

Shafer, R. (2005). Caring and coercive aspects of the psychoanalytic situation. *Journal of the American Psychoanalytic Association, 53*, 771-787.

Spillius, E. (1983). Some developments from the work of Melanie Klein. *International Journal of Psycho-Analysis, 64*, 321-332.

Spillius, E.B. (1992). Clinical experiences of projective identification. In *Clinical Lectures on Klein and Bion*, R. Anderson (Ed.), 59-73. London: Routledge.

Spillius, E. (1993). Varieties of envious experience. *International Journal of Psycho-Analysis, 74*, 1199-1212.

Spillius, E. (2007). *Encounters with Melanie Klein: Selected Papers of Elizabeth Spillius*. London: Routledge.

Steiner, J. (1979). The border between the paranoid-schizoid and the depressive positions in the borderline patient. *British Journal of Medical Psychology, 52*, 285-391.

Steiner, J. (1984). Some reflections on the analysis of transference: A Kleinian view. *Psychoanalytic Inquiry, 4*, 443-463.

Steiner, J. (1987). Interplay between pathological organizations and the paranoid-schizoid and depressive positions. *International Journal of Psychoanalysis, 68*, 69-80.

Steiner, J. (1990). Pathological organizations as obstacles to mourning: The role of unbearable guilt. *International Journal of Psychoanalysis, 71*, 87-94.

Steiner, J. (1992). The equilibrium between the paranoid-schizoid and the depressive positions. In *Clinical Lectures on Klein and Bion*, New Library of Psychoanalysis, Volume 14, 46-58. London, Routledge.

Steiner, J. (1993). *Psychic Retreats: Pathological Organizations in Psychotic, Neurotic and Borderline Patients*. London: Routledge.

Steiner, J. (1994). Patient-centered and analyst-centered interpretations: Some implications of containment and countertransference. *Psychoanalytic Inquiry*, *14*, 406-422.

Steiner, J. (1996). The aim of psychoanalysis in theory and in practice. *International Journal of Psychoanalysis*, *77*, 1073-1084.

Steiner, J. (1998). Transference and its impact on education. Inter-regional conference: Vienna. Report in *International Psychoanalytic Newsletter*, 2000.

Steiner, J. (2000). Containment, enactment and communication. *International Journal of Psycho-Analysis*, *81*, 245-255.

Steiner, J. (2004). Gaze, dominance, and humiliation in the Schreber case. *International Journal of Psychoanalysis*, *85*, 269-284.

Steiner, J. (2005). The conflict between mourning and melancholia. *Psychoanalytic Quarterly*, *74*, 83-104.

Steiner, J. (2006). Interpretive enactments and the analytic setting. *International Journal of Psychoanalysis*, *87*, 315-320.

Steiner, J. (2011). *Seeing and Being Seen: Emerging From a Psychic Retreat*. London: Routledge.

Taylor, D. (2004). Beyond learning theory. In *In Pursuit of Psychic Change: The Betty Joseph Workshop*, E. Hargreaves and A. Varchevker (Eds.), 136-150. London: Brunner-Routledge.

Tuckett, D. (1989). A brief view of Herbert Rosenfeld's contribution to the theory of psychoanalytical technique. *International Journal of Psycho-Analysis*, *70*, 619-625.

Vaughan, S., & Roose, S. (1995). The analytic process: Clinical and research definitions. *International Journal of Psycho-Analysis*, *76*, 343-356.

Waska, R. (2002). *Primitive Experiences of Loss: Working with the Paranoid-Schizoid Patient*. London: Karnac.

Waska, R. (2004). *Projective Identification: The Kleinian Interpretation*. London: Brunner-Routledge.

Waska, R. (2005). *Real People, Real Problems, Real Solutions: The Kleinian Approach to Difficult Patients*. London: Brunner-Rutledge.

Waska, R. (2006). *The Danger of Change: The Kleinian Approach with Patients who Experience Progress as Trauma*. London: Brunner-Rutledge.

Waska, R. (2007). *The Concept of Analytic Contact: A Kleinian Approach to Reaching the Hard to Reach Patient*. London: Brunner-Rutledge.

Waska, R. (2010a). *Treating Severe Depressive and Persecutory Anxieties States: Using Analytic Contact to Transform the Unbearable*. London: Karnac.

Waska, R. (2010b). *Love, Hate, and Knowledge: The Kleinian Method of Analytic Contact and the Future of Psychoanalysis*. London: Karnac.

Waska, R. (2010c). *Selected Theoretical and Clinical Issues in Psychoanalytic Psychotherapy: A Modern Kleinian Approach to Analytic Contact*: New York: Novoscience.

Waska, R. (2010d). *The Modern Kleinian Approach to Psychoanalysis: Clinical Illustrations*. New York: Jason Aronson.

Waska, R. (2011a). *Moments of Uncertainty in Psychoanalytic Practice: Interpreting Within the Matrix of Projective Identification, Counter-Transference, and Enactment*. New York: Columbia University Press.

Waska, R. (2011b). *The Total Transference and the Complete Counter-Transference: The Kleinian Psychoanalytic Approach with More Disturbed Patients*. New York: Jason Aronson.

Williams, G. (1997). Reflections on some dynamics of eating disorders: 'No entry' defences and foreign bodies. *International Journal of Psycho-Analysis*, *78*, 927-941.

Index

Lightning Source UK Ltd.
Milton Keynes UK
UKOW040206301012

201364UK00001B/28/P

9 789042 035744